SCIENCE AND THE EVOLUTION OF PUBLIC POLICY

SCIENCE
AND THE EVOLUTION OF
PUBLIC POLICY

JAMES A. SHANNON *Editor*

PUBLISHED BY *The Rockefeller University Press*

 NEW YORK CITY · 1973

CONTENTS

INTRODUCTION

The science enterprises of the nation* are vigorous, diversified, and generally characterized by excellence. But, looking to the future, there are uncertainties which may limit their effectiveness. The recent erosion of federal support for science may be less a factor in this than the lack of suitable mechanisms to guide the further evolution of science programs and adjust their goals to the needs of society. Federal actions are particularly important, because of the dominant role of federal agencies in these regards.

The profound influence of science and its derived technologies on contemporary society is obvious. But the reverse—i.e., the pervasive influence of societal need and its attitude on the magnitude and substantive content of contemporary science—is less evident, even though a mix of domestic and international forces are common determinants in the definition of both the character and the scope of the nation's scientific inquiries. In this view, scientists should have a sensitive and clear understanding of the needs of society and the role science can play in their satisfaction. But also, in these complex interactions, society would do well to understand its own obligations. It must recognize that demands are imposed on scientists by the internal dynamics of their fields, compliance to which directly determines the effectiveness of their enterprises.

THE SOCIAL BACKDROP 1945–1970

The last quarter of a century was a period of dramatic change in the lives of all nations and the relations of many to one another.

1945–1955: The United States was clearly a superpower of great affluence, and there seemed to be few limitations on its domestic or international capabilities. Concurrently, there was a progressive decay in colonialism and many new nations emerged, each with a limited modern capability. In consequence, the world influence of some Western European nations lessened, despite the rapid restoration of their industrial

---

* Science is used here as a general term to encompass research, development, and their associated educational enterprises. The term covers both academic and industrial activities that are supported by official and private agencies alike.

plants, and that of the U.S.S.R. increased as it developed a substantial technological competence. These happenings were accompanied by open conflict in the Far East, continuing unease in the Middle East, and increasing tension between the United States and the U.S.S.R.

The overall influence of these occurrences on U.S. science was mixed, but throughout the decade there was a general expansion in the federal support of academic science, somewhat hampered in the latter years as national resources were expended during the terminal phases of the Korean conflict. Cutbacks in the support of science as a result of the Korean conflict were less evident than a slowing of the anticipated growth.

1955–1960: The United States during this mid-period had many costly international commitments. But by compromising one conflict (Korea) and taking initial steps in another (Vietnam), there was a firming of the polarization between the United States and the Communist nations. Then, there was a progressive disillusionment of many dependent nations in the benevolence of the great powers and the emergence of "third world" nations, poor as well as uncommitted. The U.S.S.R., with nuclear weapons available, put both missiles and man in orbit, thus challenging the technical preeminence of the United States.

This period was particularly important to scientific research and development in the United States. The superiority of U.S. science seemed secure during the early years of the fifties. While early-warning systems (for aircraft) and the propulsion and guidance of rockets were troublesome, the defense agencies selected short-range targets for emphasis, accompanied by a beginning withdrawal of its support for academic science. Although NIH programs burgeoned beginning in 1956, modest increases were given to the newly developed National Science Foundation, and the Atomic Energy Commission embarked on the peaceful use of nuclear energy, some academic programs in the physical sciences were in jeopardy. Academic programs supported by the Air Force were in the process of substantial reduction when the Russian challenge of Sputnik I and II sharply reversed the downward trend and signalized a sharp change in national priorities. Preeminence was given to space and defense-related science and technology, and to associated educational activities. The growth of biomedical programs continued and were not particularly affected.

1960–1970: The past decade has seen the United States disturbed by events surrounding the firm establishment of a Communist nation in the Western Hemisphere, its resources drained by an increasingly unpopular war in Southeast Asia, and other costly international commitments. Then there was a flare-up of open hostility in the Middle East, with the

U.S.S.R. committed to support what it viewed to be its own interests in both Southeast Asia and the Near East. The period also covered the open break between the U.S.S.R. and mainland China. The latter, with great hostility to the western world and a beginning competence in modern weaponry, was viewed as a threat to peace in its own right. Then there was a break in the solid front of the NATO nations, a deterioration in the industrial capability of some member nations, and an increased capability of others. The counterpart took place to a lesser extent within the U.S.S.R. and some of its satellite nations. Political instability became a way of life for a number of nations, but there was increasing disillusion- ment of an increasing number of nations with war as an instrument of national policy. Also, the costly arms race between the United States and the U.S.S.R., and some appreciation of their inability to continue in their present operational modes, led to beginning attempts to find areas of mutual accommodation.

It is not surprising that increasing social unrest was more common during this period than social tranquility and that rational guidelines for the future development of many nations were less than clear. The United States entered the decade an arrogantly affluent nation with the appearance of having unlimited resources. It ends the decade with many uncertain purposes, but with a profound appreciation of unmet social needs.

There are two coupled imperatives, as we now view our national life. First, our priorities do not seem to reflect our national needs, and the extent of the shift that will be required is now only dimly apparent. Second, the nation's ability to satisfy its internal needs has as one essen- tial a continuing healthy economy. Science and technology must find their place within the framework of these coupled imperatives. This will be a complicated undertaking and will impose strains on our national purposes and the vigor with which they are pursued. The undertaking will be made more difficult or more simple, depending on the correctness of our estimates of:

the resources that are expended for defense;

the consensus we reach on the priority given to competing social objectives and on the rate of progress we deem to be reasonable;

the resulting balance that obtains in the allocation of resources for social and all other purposes.

All this is complicated by the increasing development of humanistic life styles of large segments of the population, by public disenchantment with the power of science and technology to solve complex problems, by the impatience of some groups to share in the fruits of affluence, and the unwillingness of others to place their recent economic gains in jeopardy.

THE SCIENCE SCENE

With this pot pourri of domestic and international problems, it is not surprising that fundamental trends relating to science were perturbed by transients. The important trends include a progressive increase in all science and technology and a general increase in the educational level of the nation. These appear to be permanent and seem to reflect the needs and capabilities of an increasingly complex technical base for society. The transients are reflected in increases in the allocation of resources for science, as in the post-Sputnik period of 1955–1965, or in decreases, as in the Korean war, 1953–1955, the Vietnam war, and the domestic crises of the late sixties.

As to the future, it is unlikely that the longer-term benefits of science will be too long deferred for the more immediate benefits of service-oriented social programs. Some balance between the two competing objectives must be reached, it is to be hoped by mechanisms that can be responsive to changing circumstances of national life. But this responsiveness must be accomplished with a full appreciation that the time scale of scientific achievement and technological application is long, as is that of major social change.

A decade ago, it was fashionable to say that the future of our nation would be determined largely by how well we develop and exploit our intellectual resources, the continued exploitation of natural resources being expected to yield progressively diminishing returns. This view, our relative affluence, together with the international tensions and rivalries, found expression in broad R and D programs in defense, space, energy, and health, and led indirectly to the extensive support of the intellectual life of the nation. There was a determined, but incoherent, broadening of the educational base and sharp, but uncoordinated, increases in the support of all research and development. The science base was rapidly expanded and a beginning was made in the support of the humanities. These were occurrences of the late fifties and early sixties, when science was viewed not only for its utility but also for those characteristics that made for high adventure. But changing national circumstances have changed national attitudes, and disillusionment with science is more common than is hope in its high purposes. It is unlikely we will soon again encounter the conjoining of forces that fostered the general expansion of science which occurred in the 1960–1965 period.

These changing national circumstances warrant serious analysis. It is scarcely sufficient to conclude that our social needs are great and our resources limited. Rather, we must define those needs more precisely, and articulate how we propose to sastify them within what time scale. At the same time, we must recast our thinking about science and the needs of science for societal purposes.

For example: What is the essential science base for a valid and lively educational enterprise in our universities and professional schools? What is its size and what should be its character today and a decade hence? Then, what are the areas of science that have special significance to health and well-being, to our industrial needs, and to a better understanding of the world we live in? What are the unmet technical needs of our society—as best we can now project them—in housing, in our cities, in our production and utilization of energy, in transportation, in the reclamation of our environment? And how can these needs be stated in terms of scientific and technical objectives? How can programs so derived be best administered? All these and other considerations, including those that relate to the health and vigor of science itself, are necessary to provide a more rational base for the scientific enterprise. These considerations are well beyond the executive apparatus of the present federal establishment and always will be, unless the planning process is taken more seriously, is accompanied by flexibility in the execution of program, and the resulting program is subject to continuing review. For science begets technical innovation, which frequently begets social change with feedback into the science base.

Social change that reflects the evolution of changing value systems made possible by affluence, which is based in turn on a broad science base that fosters industrial development, is nowhere more clearly portrayed than in the United States during the past quarter of a century.

Initial Emphasis on the Physical Sciences and Engineering

It was prudent to give high priority to the physical defense of the nation, in the nation's research and development, when we perceived our national security to be in jeopardy. It may also have been wise, as we then interpreted our affluence and the Russian challenge to our technological preeminence, to embark on a race to the moon. There can be no doubt about the reasonableness of research and development objectives in the energy field, particularly the changing emphasis of programs in nuclear energy from simple weaponry to the coupled development of power production and water desalination. Each of these general programs was complex and costly, but each could be visualized in terms of concrete objectives and the work scheduled in a way that was amenable to reasonable programing.

The fields that benefited from these endeavors were many and diverse. Some, such as material development, electronics, and new conceptions of engineering were quite close to the point of industrial application. Others, derivative of the same objectives, were more fundamental in nature, e.g., mathematics, experimental and theoretical physics, and advanced chemistry. A second derivative of these two lines of endeavor was an extraordinary series of developments. These vastly influenced communications, instrumental and computational devices, the areospace and other industries, as new information on matter, energy, material, and control systems rapidly emerged from a mixture of fundamental and applied research and were applied to our newly acquired competence in advanced engineering. The broad support of research and development which emphasized the physical sciences and engineering, and which stemmed from needs perceived to be urgent, had profound influences on our industrial, scientific, and educational capability.

Many of the same tensions that spawned competitive activities in defense and space radically changed the broader objectives of the nation. The Office of Education, a small staff agency in the pre-Sputnik period, was precipitously projected into wholly new and broad educational endeavors through the National Defense Education Act programs of the late fifties and their subsequent extensions. The growth rate and the program content of the National Science Foundation were also influenced. Beginning in the early to mid-fifties, the development of the agency was initially retarded by the influence of the Korean War and by the prior preemption of many fields of science by mission-oriented agencies; but later, the NSF was aided by the broad and uncritical post-Sputnik support of science and technology in the physical fields.

Health, Education and the Public Welfare

The nation was less than precise in seeking objectives that related to the health and well-being of its population.

The biomedical sciences fortunately developed early; their rapid expansion began in 1956. These programs had important and explicit social purposes and acquired a life of their own* as the nation sought to solve its disease problems, particularly those of a chronic nature, pri-

---

* Viewing the comparative development of the NIH and the NSF during the 1956–1965 decade, it is clear that the NIH had overt social purposes while the programs of the NSF tended to be perceived by many as self-serving of science and exotic to social concern and need, with no clearly defined and understandable purpose. The NIH flourished and the NSF languished because of these differences in perceived objectives.

marily through research. The impetus for their development was largely domestic. But federal action in the health field was limited by the belief that the education of physicians and the delivery of health services were largely the responsibility of the states and the private sector, whereas support of research was a proper function of the federal establishment. This attitude did not foster balance within the health-related programs in the period of rapid research growth (1956-1965) and was to cause difficulty later.

Direct federal concern for education (including medical education) and many other social services awaited changes in the conventions governing the relationships between state and federal responsibilities. These changes found explicit expression in the social legislation of the Johnson administration, which provided for a variety of programs in general education, health, and welfare. Many of the new programs were particularly directed toward the needs of disadvantaged groups. But there were other programs, some enacted into law, some proposed, which related to the more general needs of society.

General

The programs of science that emerged from this tumultuous period of 1956–1965 were hardly coherent when viewed in the aggregate, and the federal support of higher education emerged largely as a derivative function. A minor portion of the educational expansion was directly financed by the Office of Education and the National Science Foundation, but support of graduate education has yet to become a series of well-articulated programs with visible and rational objectives.

In recent years, it has been quite impossible to provide the needed stability for established programs and, at the same time, to develop others. In the latter group are a number with frankly social purposes, such as those that relate to the delivery of health services and the provision of adequate general education and welfare. Other needs involve the environment, housing, urban affairs, and transportation. Many major principles for federal intervention have been defined by new legislation but without attendant budgetary support and with imprecise methods for their implementation. This mélange of problems is discouraging, but is not overwhelming in its seriousness or its complexity. Solutions are reachable, even within the foreseeable constraints on public spending.

Such an optimistic view stems from the belief that we have been profligate in the expenditure of our resources, must reassess our national priorities, and must introduce more rational processes in the allocation of resources and in program execution. Optimism is also based on the belief that the substitution of clearly enunciated national policies and goals for the present slogans can buy some of the time required for program readjustment. This is not to suggest an absent sense of urgency. Indeed, this is an overriding consideration, and poorly chosen courses of action can be very costly.

Current Problems

Our scientific and educational enterprises are now in serious jeopardy. A progressive curtailment in their support began in 1965. The rate of program increase of an admittedly large R and D activity could not continue indefinitely, but when it was considered seriously in 1965, there was no consensus on reasonable priorities and rates of growth. Then there was an increasing demand to satisfy international commitments and, later, internal social programs. These complex needs and continuing inflation resulted in a general retrenchment in the R and D area. This, in turn, produced technological dislocations in some industrial areas and a reduction in funds for academic science and graduate education that had a devastating influence on institutions of higher education.

The reductions in federal support have not yet become catastrophic to industry or the university. Admittedly, reduced university support has posed particularly difficult problems, since this is accompanied by pressures to extend university activities into new social areas. But importantly, a set of forces has been set in motion that, if unopposed, will have a long-term deleterious effect upon the effectiveness of the university and its professional schools and upon the options available for remedial and effective action.

THE SEMINAR SERIES

From a consideration of this background, it would seem that thoughtful inquiry into the philosophical base of these interrelated problems is desirable. It is to be hoped that sets of imperatives and desiderata can be developed to serve as guides for the continued involvement of the federal establishment in the nation's scientific affairs. But in the future, the federal programs must be concerned with institutions as well as with the science they contain, and the problems of education must be given consideration in their own right. These facets of the problem are already clear.

Program change in these sensitive areas will not be simple, and will benefit from the thoughtful, nonparochial, unselfish participation of industry and the university world. Generally speaking, most executive agencies of government have served the nation well in the evolution of a vigorous science, but it is quite clear that the time has passed when the general role of federal policy formulation in science and its related educational activities can be taken to be the simple sum of the policies of a number of federal agencies, each with its own purposes. It is also apparent that, for the industrial and university worlds to make use of their potential for participation in the formulation of science policy, responsible focal points for the input of information into the federal system must be developed.

The Program

These, then, are some of the concerns that were to be the subject of inquiry in the proposed series of lecture-seminars.

The evolution of *federal support of science and technology* has been dominated by both domestic and international needs during the past quarter of a century, but in the more recent years (i.e., 1950–1965), the substance of science in its performance was dominated by the internal logic of science itself, a situation made possible by the circumstances of unparalleled growth. It is not surprising, then, that such a set of circumstances has produced scientists who are less aware of the interactions of science and society than of the opportunities and the demands of science itself. Also, a developing generation of young scientists and professionals, only recently faced by the brutalities of a less-than-perfect set of national and international conventions, tends toward nihilism. And harried executive and legislative branches of government desperately seek definitive answers to problems that cannot be solved by simplistic approaches and that are worsened when slogans replace thoughtful policies, goals, and derivative programs.

These matters have been explored extensively, but in a fragmented fashion, by a number of executive and congressional groups within the context of the nation's political apparatus. They also have been the subject of periodic consideration by a number of professional societies in relation to the problems of their membership.

The broad forces that have been operational in providing an interaction between science and society are quite apparent in a fairly gross manner. But their translation through political processes into discrete programs, supported at a given level of effort, is normally subject to another set of forces. These relate to the nation's fiscal policy and very general national goals, subject to modulation by partisan and special-interest groups. The interaction of these two sets of forces is less clear. Nonetheless, a more precise understanding of the system must be obtained if the system itself is to be more responsive to the nation's needs.

It is within such a range of considerations that The Rockefeller University proposes to develop a series of working seminars that will examine the evolution and execution of public policy in science and related education.

IN RETROSPECT

The comments above formed the opening sections of the grant application to the National Science Foundation for support of the lecture seminar series on which this volume is based. Two years have elapsed since that application was submitted. Since that time, much has happened in both legislation and appropriations, the long-term effects of which are certain. Two points warrant special note. The downward move of appropriations in support of science programs has been reversed, at least for some programs of some agencies. Then, new legislation established the health and vigor of higher education and its institutions as matters of legitimate concern of the federal establishment. However, one must await the further evolution of these programs before passing judgment on their suitability and adequacy. These new beginnings should be viewed with very cautious optimism and only as points on a curve of continuing program development.

It will be obvious to the reader that the nation's science programs are productive but are not without problems, faults, and deficiencies. Some of these are the result of frank errors in program design or execution, others to a limit in the options available at the time that critical policy and program decisions are made. But then, these are the uncertainties that will always accompany large and complex programs that are important. Fortunately for us, time and circumstances both encourage and permit change, and it will be in rational change that perfection of the nation's science must be sought.

JAMES A. SHANNON
The Rockefeller University

September 15, 1972

ACKNOWLEDGMENTS

THE LECTURE-SEMINAR SERIES on which this volume is based and the production of the volume itself were made possible by The Commonwealth Fund and by the National Science Foundation (Grant #Q-001706).

The Rockefeller University was most generous in providing resources for both the lectures and the book; The Rockefeller University Press and Mrs. Helene J. Jordan prepared the book for the printer. Special thanks are due Dr. and Mrs. William C. Olson of The Rockefeller Foundation's Bellagio Study and Conference Center, Bellagio, Italy, who were gracious hosts while I worked on the manuscripts during the summer of 1972.

The basic work in this volume is, of course, contributed by its 12 authors. Except for a general outline of the topics to be discussed, the book is a reflection of their wholehearted cooperation in presenting their interests and concerns on various aspects of science and its relation to public policy.   J.A.S.

THE PURPOSE AND
UTILITY OF SCIENCE

I · *Science and Social Purpose*

CARYL P. HASKINS

IN HIS INAUGURAL BERNAL LECTURE, delivered at the British Royal Society on March 4, 1971, Sir Eric Ashby, Master of Clare College, Cambridge, invoked a paradox that epitomizes in striking fashion some central concerns which surely lie before us in any discussions of science and public policy. His paradox is that a crisis of disillusionment with science and technology in the affluent societies of the West was reached precisely with the first successful landings on the moon. Until that time, many people were prepared to adopt almost subconsciously assumptions we would hardly think of accepting uncritically today: that the social benefits of science and technology were largely fortuitous; and that the disorders and shortcomings of society were, for the most part, beyond the power of men and women to correct.

But, at the moment of the extraordinary lunar triumph, sharp criticism appeared from many quarters. The deeply significant thing about that criticism, as Ashby points out, was that it was not aimed primarily, if at all, at the achievement itself, nor at the extraordinary means devised to carry it out, nor at the unprecedented skills of research and technology or the organization and the genius required. The criticism was of the goal itself. If this is the power of technology organized on such a scale, why was it mobilized, at such enormous cost, for so exotic a purpose? Why was it not — why should it not be — directed instead toward alleviating the social disorders and problems so critical at home: to issues of the city and the urban poor; to power shortages; to our glaring needs in the field of health care; to vital issues of pollution? Why did we, the questioners, we who have to live with all these potential threats to our fragile earth and ourselves, not have more influence in the choice of the priorities that so absorb our corporate energies and resources? In these questions, one believes, are limned some major issues of our

CARYL P. HASKINS Former President, Carnegie Institution of Washington, Washington, D.C.

time; major indicators of a watershed in social concern of which we at present can discern only the nearer and lower slope.

It is not enough to reply that the challenges of pollution and urban blight or the distribution of health services and of educational opportunities made adequately available are intrinsically far more formidable issues than going to the moon, although the fact is evident. Nor is it enough to remark that science — and even engineering — can, by their very nature, play ony an auxiliary role in many of these areas. The truly central question involved, of course, was one of national priorities. The general perception of the paradox gave explicit articulation, on a wide scale, to something that had lurked uneasily in the back of our minds, becoming ever more insistent, for at least a decade. This was the recognition that, strong as we have always believed ourselves to be in talent, organizing capacity, and wealth, that resource is not infinite. We must make choices in what we elect to do. Our efforts must indeed be governed by recognized priorities; and the determination of overall priorities, especially in science and technology, is one of the most difficult, as well as one of the most unaccustomed, of all tasks.

But the basic social issues of our time — the issues against which all our efforts, including those in science and technology, must be set — go deeper, I think, than priorities, and we must constantly be sensitive to this. As Irving Kristol emphasized in his striking book, *On the Democratic Idea in America*, the current awareness of the need for setting priorities, and the now-insistent popular demand that we do so, may actually blur a more profound, pervasive, and critical element in contemporary national thought and feeling — an element more specifically characterizing that watershed of shifting social attitudes with which we live, the upper profile of which is not yet sighted. Some of the discussions about such matters as consumer protection or pollution, although on the surface addressed to specific priorities and their reordering, may in fact sometimes point to a demand for a much more general reordering of our social and political life. Consumer protection may serve as surrogate for the worth of the free enterprise system; pollution may symbolize materialistic value standards in our society.

What we may be witnessing is a widespread and deeply genuine concern about what we mean, today, when we speak of the promise of American life. George Bernard Shaw wrote and was recently quoted by Daniel Moynihan: "Later on, liberty will not be enough: men will die for human perfection, to which they will sacrifice all their liberty gladly." Because science itself is so closely entwined with both freedom and promise in our culture, these are spring tides of great significance, especially in the context of social purpose.

Controversies over fundamental beliefs and goals touch the very heart of national existence. They cannot occur without risk of grave national damage. Yet it can be argued that they *should* take place occasionally, and that they themselves provide vivid proof of the vitality of the nation and the readiness to confront — and indeed embrace — important change. Surely we can justifiably take pride that the process, with all the hazard it brings, has long been peculiarly characteristic of our nation. De Toqueville noted this during his travels in North America in 1831. More recently, within the last few years, Jean-Jacques Servan-Schreiber remarked on the prominence in American life, and particularly in the best of American industry, of the talent for anticipating, welcoming, and even maneuvering change (*The American Challenge*). With this characteristic of American society, Servan-Schreiber singled out another: the dedication, as principal commitment, to the development of men and women. These are national attitudes, forged through three centuries of American development, and now deeply ingrained. If priorities are determined by goals, so also our predilections in the selection of goals — and above all our penchant for reassessing them, as we are now doing — are themselves rooted in just such national attitudes.

Thus, although there is undoubted danger in this time of profound questioning, there is also great opportunity for science in society. At precisely such a time, the imagination can be liberated to an unusual degree for fresh assessments and new concepts. It is precisely at such a time that stocktaking becomes most important. This is the larger perspective against which, perhaps for only a very brief time, we may view the vast issue of science and social purpose.

The subject demands that we take account of the intrinsic qualities and inherent capability of science to assess and to realize appropriate goals during the next decades. How is science likely to be cultivated and employed by the society and how socially regarded in the years ahead? The future of American science itself will be conditioned by these considerations, for it is as true today as it has always been that a nation will be great in those areas in which it desires greatness, perceives greatness, and rewards and esteems greatness — and nowhere else. Greatness in a nation does not come by accident; and nowhere will it long survive neglect. Our general confidence in scientists is a very recent development. It is well to remember that some other great episodes of western culture, such as that of classic Renaissance art, did not persist in fullest creative vigor so very much longer than this. We cannot take endurance and greatness for granted in any facet of our society.

Therefore, a prominent part in such inquiry should be assigned to the nature of the support of science by society and to the further vital question of the social deployment of science. How much, for instance, should the conduct of science, and its very goals, be subjected to public control? How should the inner autonomy of science be protected? Should process and product be socially monitored, or should the former, but not the latter, continue to be given the kind of freedom that from long experience we feel to be so important?

At the outset of such a discussion, it is well to contrast two kinds of purposes of science itself, a contrast, of course, well known to us all and yet basic and important enough to bear repeated emphasis. The purposes internal to science's own disciplinary structure reflect the drive of scientists to perfect and balance, and to extend and enrich, the very fabric of scientific knowledge and thus to enhance a major element of human culture, and, in no small measure, to fulfill the joy of individual discovery. Equally important are the purposes that society as a whole sees for science. A way of underlining these distinctions, perhaps, is to think of science as a way of life and also as a way of getting things done. Both purposes aim at social service, but in very different ways and through very different means, and their optimal fulfillment may require very different kinds of social integration. For the first is still, in our day, as in the past, essentially an esthetic undertaking, governed by esthetic values. Its service to society, over any short range of time and in any particular context, is almost certain to be far from generally obvious, and so to go widely unperceived. Over longer spans of time, the social service that it embodies involves something far more profound than the mere expansion and further perfection of a culture on which much of western society has been built. The principles that govern its operation, the nature of its code, and the joy of discovery that it generates compare fully with the best of art in any age. In our time, perhaps no better or more conspicuous paradigm is available of that antimaterialistic cast of life to which we aspire.

"External" scientific purposes, looking toward immediate service to the society, of course dominate the ethos of so-called "applied" science. The formal methodology of applied science and technology is characteristically difficult to distinguish from that of "pure" research. Its principal operational distinction is the more direct service-coupling of its purposes with those of society. Indeed, so visible has that coupling become that, in recent years, a remarkable assumption is not infrequently encountered. According to this extreme notion, science not only produces knowledge: it can formulate and determine social goals and even determine the policies of governments.

This picture of the relationships of political purpose and scientific knowledge is, of course, an all-too-obvious caricature. Yet it is not without practical social significance. It has surely generated a great deal of fear and dislike of science among those who are convinced of it. By indirection it brings home forcibly the responsibility of "externally" directed science — which, over the past decades, has played an extraordinarily important and visible role in facilitating political goals and purposes and, on occasion, in substantially enriching their content — to so gear itself, and especially to so train those who labor in its vineyard, that the sensitivity, the effectiveness, and the scope of that facilitation can be maximized in coming years. I shall return to this point.

There are important things to be said, I think, about each mode of science in the context of social purpose. Of the first, it may be no overstatement to describe one of those contexts in terms, quite literally, of social survival. As we evolve more complex, direct, and specific roles for science in the matrix of our social purposes, as we certainly will be doing over the next years, we had better be assured that our elemental bases remain secure. For nothing can be more fundamentally and consistently true in human affairs than Alfred North Whitehead's dictum, expressed many decades ago: "In the conditions of modern life the rule is absolute; the race which does not value trained intelligence is doomed. . . . Today we maintain ourselves. Tomorrow science will have moved forward yet one more step; and there will be no appeal from the judgment which will then be pronounced . . . (on the uneducated)."

Lately, this home truth seems to have been honored in some countries outside the United States more presciently than at home. It is interesting to note here that, according to a report recently issued from the British Centre for Russian and East European Studies in Birmingham, although the percentage of growth in the financing of science in the Soviet Union had declined from 12 per cent in 1963 to approximately 9 per cent in 1968, there was a sharp reversal of policy in 1970, bringing a 20 per cent growth in expenditure on science — a record rise for any comparable period in the last decade.

A central point to be borne in mind about pure research is that achievement has only been possible in the past, and can only be possible in the future, by virtue of the freedom granted by the society on which it depends to disregard all specific purpose or control save that imposed by the inner logic of the discipline. It is, in the truest sense, "internally related." The directions of research are chosen according to their capacity to illumine the subject and for their estimated tractability, and it is the skill and prescience of the investigator in sensing these qualities, as he lays his scientific bets, that his own productivity — and ultimately his stature — must depend. Thus the effectiveness of the investigator's work absolutely demands that he and his working colleagues set the goals — no one else can, outside his operating program.

The obverse is just as clear. It is extremely difficult for any working scientist qua working scientist, deeply immersed in a particular corner of his discipline, to make effective choices among wider priorities, even within the context of science itself, as we have sometimes learned to our cost. Dedicated to the arduous task of hewing out further special knowledge, the organization of his thought modes must be quite different from that required for more general surveys. If the scientist focuses instead on "externally oriented" science, and even more if he works at the interfaces between science and social goals, he must shift radically the nature and parameters of his thought. That is a difficult thing to do. Yet it will clearly be an increasingly important requirement in the service of science to the nation. One of the vital tasks in science education for the future surely will be to train an adequate cadre of those who can work along these frontiers, with sensitive understanding of the parameters on either side. This brings me specifically to applied science.

In applied or mission-oriented science, the pattern of actual work is still much as in basic research. The subject matter and the standards in general are the same. But the primary purpose here, of course, is to assist directly in fulfilling social goals and aspirations. The primary tasks are more like those in the fields of engineering and of administration and politics.

On one front, education for applied science must deal with such issues, for example, as the development of types of skills badly needed in our society and still far too rare — the competences to deal intelligently with, and work intelligently within, those extraordinarily complex social-technical systems at the base of so many of the large-scale social issues confronting us. These are the skills of multiple-purpose planning and operation. Far too many of us today, as engineers, industrialists, government officials, or developers, are by training and temperament single-purpose planners. We are far too little conditioned to estimate (or even to try to visualize) collateral consequences of what we do: of the dams we build or the road networks we plan or the computer systems we install. In many cases, these consequences can be designed to take account of individual choice and so to foster a sense of personal integrity among those affected by them, but too often are pointed toward efficiency alone. At a yet higher level of complexity and difficulty, it is widely recognized that effective technology assessment, if achieved in any field, might supply a powerful instrument in our attempt to link applied science and technology to social goals and purposes over the years ahead. Yet how few men and women there are with the comprehensive knowledge and skills for this unusually difficult task!

Thus far, in speaking about internally and externally oriented science, but particularly the former, I have been dealing with relatively invariant characteristics and requirements: with fundamental elements of structure, need, and imperative that have endured in the radically changing social environment against which we view them and that, concomitantly, may be vital to preserve. Now I would turn to some of the changes the evolving sociology of science has brought to the nature, the tasks, the capacities, and the appropriate demands upon pure and applied science in more recent years.

Undoubtedly, issues and challenge confront inwardly directed science today that relate particularly to its own structuring and function and to its intellectual "gearing" to the natural world. Not new in principle, these problems are felt in our time with unusual force. They relate directly to the vigor and health of pure science itself and must ultimately reflect the estimate of society. Hence they are significant.

One of these factors concerns that subtle, elusive, hard-to-estimate parameter that might be defined as the limits of knowledge in a given field. It is a commonplace that as a dynamic branch of science evolves, the winning of novel, and therefore significant and, above all, interesting, results frequently becomes more and more arduous, demanding ever more powerful and ingenious instrumentation and often posing increasingly formidable challenge to investigative talent. I say often because the exceptions, of course, sometimes amount to the great breakthroughs of insight, opening or creating entirely new fields. But the general problem was vividly characterized for solid-state physics a few years ago by Professor A. B. Pippard of Cambridge University when he said (I cannot, at this distance, quote him with assurance of perfect accuracy): "We who entered this field found it a green and fertile intellectual valley; we shall leave it a dust bowl." Perhaps it would be fairer to say not a dust bowl, but a field where novel insights will indeed continue to be achieved, as they are being achieved today, but with ever greater subtlety and difficulty.

A factor probably far more significant than this local information poverty is that of more general information richness. Much broader in its impact has been the phenomenal growth in both the massiveness and complexity of accumulated scientific knowledge and the increasing importance of integration if that store is to remain socially meaningful. This issue has several aspects. One is the burgeoning intrinsic complexity of many of the most significant fields of inquiry today, which demands closely integrated teams of investigators for resolution. Nowhere is this more true than in many fields of biology and health.

A second aspect is even more significant. The task of sorting out and integrating and interpreting the findings of many investigators working even in a single complex field for no more than a year is more challenging and more essential than it has ever been. This is vividly attested by the evident increasing importance, in recent years, of the review paper, of the serial reviews, and of the man who can, from a firm and insightful scientific background, guide and formulate such undertakings. Here, again, is a primary challenge to the linking of scientific knowledge with society itself, and most of all to the kind of training to fit men and women in the science of tomorrow to meet that imperative.

Many of the fields that pure science is likely to be most deeply concerned with in the future deal with universes of highly organized, closely interlocked, and exquisitely coordinated elements. They include biological development in all its aspects, from the modes of transcription of genetic information to chronic diseases of an organic nature, and from reproduction to neural function. These are systems of extraordinary variability, which for the most part must be investigated empirically. Even though we now have won general concepts in, say, the field of inheritance, it is extremely unlikely that, at least for a long time to come, comparably comprehensive theories can be evolved to guide research in those higher biological systems that are so important to us.

Moreover, these areas of research comprehend subjects that are of wide public interest, such as physiology, neurophysiology, health, and disease. It is vitally important that scientific progress in them be reported publicly and interpreted appropriately. That necessity imposes a demand for yet another dimension of scientific training in the future, to which I shall return.

These elements unite what may well be the most crucial challenges to the winning and dissemination of new knowledge of the natural world that we have faced since the time of Newton. The demands upon the capacities and the preparation of the young investigator contemplating entry to a field, and the order of commitment required when he makes that crucial career decision, are perhaps more critical today than they have ever been. It is precisely for this reason that we must try to see to it, over the years ahead, that those, more highly selected than ever for talent and motivation, who choose this difficult road, are protected and encouraged at least as much as their colleagues, equally talented and motivated, who choose the alternate paths of applied science, with all their present and future importance.

Applied, no less than pure, science, in company with technology, has its own challenges today in public service and public attitudes. Sometimes public attitudes are not related as directly to deeper questions of purpose and goal and social control as to more elementary estimates of continuing social use and pertinence. There is a whole generation today, and indeed it is the generation that before the end of this decade will assume control in national affairs, who must conclude that from the time they were born there has been no advance of design in the automobile more basic than an altering of windshield or fender. The only really visible change has been the decay in its overall social effectiveness — the growing congestion of traffic; the slowing of practicable urban speed until, it is said, the average time per mile by automobile across New York City is approximately what it was across Athens by chariot. (Not even to mention, of course, the problems of pollution).

The same basically static picture in another important area of technology must strike the members of that critical generation who are young enough (and it isn't so very young) not to have witnessed the last striking technical advance in commercial aircraft: the advent of the jet. Rates of change and growth in innumerable other areas of technology have slowed or disappeared as the maturity of a particular development approached. Such pictures of apparently diminishing returns with respect to the fruits of applied science, and even more of the technology with which it is associated, are likely to be considered by a part of the society which supports them as evidences of failure. Unless challenged, such a view can seriously erode public confidence and esteem.

Related to this, and exacerbating it greatly, is the exorbitance of the demands widely made on applied science and technology to deal comprehensively and swiftly with the central social problems that are the foci of our deepest concerns: those issues, as we repeat over and over again, of population and urban blight and the social complexity, diffuseness, and *anomie* that are so characteristic of a technological and service-oriented society. If the complexities of the natural systems that research deals with today surpass all our earlier imagining, how much more is this true of the plight of applied science in the vast social issues that beset us! And in the case of applied science particularly, there is no escaping the challenge. Unless we make the attempt directly as best we may, using the still-inadequate tools that we have, we shall be turning aside from our duty, and will be indeed defeatist. As we do try to meet this challenge, the achievement will inevitably fall far short of public expectation for many years. But lists must be entered and battles fought without, if possible, diminishing public confidence and public support.

Again, mission-oriented science suffers from that other popular misconception that science (pure and applied) and technology alike can make and execute public policy, can choose public goals as well as aid in fulfilling them, and that, in fact, they do precisely this, without the consent, or even the knowledge, of those who will be deeply affected until the results are in. This may be the most powerful catalyst of popular pressure to maintain close social control of applied and, to some degree, of pure science.

One of the most pervasive factors may well be the widespread, vague, but often intense general mistrust of our time in the intellect itself. A progressively orthodox reliance on the sufficiency of reason to solve all man's relationships with the world (a reliance that increasingly characterized the latter half of the nineteenth century and the first half of the twentieth) may be responsible for the considerable loss of faith in reason itself, which is conspicuous in our time. But the very fact that our problems are so complex and that we are only at the very earliest empirical phases of pondering how to tackle them (consider the problems of health delivery as one example) has greatly augmented such loss of faith, a loss that might readily evolve to an attitude not only anti-scientific but anti-intellectual, as well.

Finally, of course, all these negative factors have impinged together just at the time when the aftermath of the Vietnam War, the stringent fiscal and social situations at home with all their repercussions, and simple social weariness after the great stress of the last years, have left us in a mood of retrenchment on every front.

All these factors bring into focus questions about both the level and mode of social *support*, as well as the social *use* of science in the future. What level of federal support should obtain for science in the years ahead? How can we try, officially, to recognize and deal with those substantive and operational differences between pure and applied science that are real — the differences in requirements, in the outlook and goals of those engaged in them and, above all, the differences in usefulness to the society and in the link to the social fabric? Shall we support minimal public control on goal and on mode for pure science and on mode for applied? What proportioning of federal support should we fashion for the two areas of science, insofar as we can overtly distinguish them — a feat itself often difficult enough? And what should be overall strategy in such a general framework? How, for example, can we improve our procedure to give greater assurance, at any level, of that continuity of federal support which science so desperately needs if it is to flourish? Should we maintain our current plurality of agencies in government for the financing of science or is consolidation better? Should we constitute a single National Institute of Advanced Study and Research, combining federal programs of basic research with those of higher education, and combining programs in the natural sciences with those in the social sciences and humanities — that challenging and thought-provoking proposal advanced in 1970 by the Daddario Subcommittee? Should we support a single Department of Science at the Cabinet or sub-Cabinet level, as has been proposed repeatedly over the years? What of the new cancer agency? Is it to be contained within the framework of the National Institutes of Health?

What can be done about estimating priorities in pure science — an area where we deal professionally with unknowns rather than knowns and where, moreover, opportunities far outrun resources of money and of gifted and suitably trained men and women? Or do we, at this point, have *too many* men and women trained to the doctoral level? What can, and should, we do about technology assessment — that subject in which immense quantities of paper and ink have already been invested, and where real work is only now in its earliest stage?

Questions crowd upon us. Many would hardly have been raised a decade ago. They are the tips of the iceberg, hinting at the enormous dimensions and varieties of the issues and the opportunities that a time of transition lays before us.

The result of these and other factors, and of the uncertainties that have clearly resulted in the public image of and confidence in science, were sharply reflected in, and to some extent exacerbated by, declining levels in federal dollar support over the last few years, as we know only too well. That, of course, stimulated more steeply declining levels of actual support, not only because of dollar inflation, but also because of "scientific inflation." The latter can be defined as the need, in many fields, for ever-more sophisticated, and therefore more expensive, equipment, as well as the need for ever-higher levels of training for those who would man the advancing frontiers.

According to data prepared by the National Science Foundation, federal obligations for basic research in the nation grew from about $200 million in 1956 to about $2 billion by 1967, an astonishing rate of 21 per cent a year. But from 1965 to 1970, the average rate of growth dropped sharply to approximately 7 per cent, and then remained for several years almost level, in the sense of formal dollar commitments. In 1969, the National Science Foundation was allotted $435 million, including some carry-over from the previous year; for the fiscal year 1970, the corresponding total was about $438 million. For fiscal 1971, the figure was $506 million. The overall effect was to constrict expected programs of federally supported research by 20 to 25 per cent in some 550 institutions in the country.

These developments were, and continue to be, highly unsettling to the scientific structure of the nation as a whole. Yet their social significance, seen in later perspective, may prove to be somewhat different from its appearance at the time. For most recently there seems to have been some turnabout in rate. Total obligations for research and development on the part of the federal government requested by the President for 1972 were $16.7 billion, almost 8 per cent higher than the $15.5 billion of the previous year. This increase may exceed the conventional estimate for the annual increase in the cost of research activities (the "scientific inflation" that I mentioned), which is commonly reckoned at 5 or 6 per cent, and so, for the first time in a long period, may provide some margin for absolute growth. Most interesting to note, however, has been the change in priorities reflected in that budget. The total 1972 budget for the National Science Foundation, including the funds for education, reached $622 million — a striking increase of more than 20 per cent.

At the same time, the support of research by industry, which held up remarkably well during the severe depression in federal support, has also increased, and some added attention to support of basic research is evident. But a most interesting — and, over the long run, perhaps a very significant — shift in emphasis is becoming increasingly apparent.

At the beginning of this paper, I referred to the role of the moon landings in stimulating a skeptical questioning of national goals, pointed out by Sir Eric Ashby. I think that we shall look back on another aspect of the same adventure as of equal social significance. At its beginning, although the moon had been under searching observation by modern astronomers for more than a half century and we thought we knew a great deal about it, we had little idea of the depth and range of the psychological impact that direct contact, even though vicarious, could bring. Throughout the critical decade before the first actual landing, there was widespread speculation that the moon might harbor life in some form. But after that landing it suddenly became evident that, from indications so far, life may be a unique property of our planet, at least within our own solar system. That was a disappointing development for many men and women not trained or particularly sophisticated in the life sciences, but for a variety of reasons greatly interested in them, and it may have been more deeply disappointing than we realized at the time.

But disappointment, I suggest, was not the truly significant social consequence. The most important impact may well have been an abrupt and seismic shift in our view of our own world and of ourselves in it — a shift perhaps fully comparable to that epitomized by Copernicus and the publication of *De Revolutionibus Orbium Coelestium*. As the certainty of the lifelessness of the moon struck home, as the image of its inhospitality was affirmed by the amazing views transmitted by the astronauts and communicated so widely through television and print, men and women generally gained a new order of appreciation of their own celestial island. Perhaps, too, they gained an intensified sense of isolation and insecurity in this new vision. The crowning impact may well have been provided by the pictures of planet earth taken from the moon. Those views of the variegated, beautifully colored, lonely globe must have had a powerful, perhaps a decisive, influence in impressing upon men and women everywhere an enhanced respect for the planet so completely in their keeping and a greatly deepened sense of their total dependence upon it.

Now, as the federal support of science shows some signs of renewed, if modest, expansion, the effects of these and other influences are becoming visible in new emphases across the board. Industry is committing added research potential and dollars to ends that coincide with general views of social need — to attacks, for example, on problems of pollution. At the National Science Foundation, lively discussion and widespread controversy within the Congress and without have been stimulated by the plans for project RANN (Research Applied to National Needs), aimed at giving increased proportional support to specifically goal-directed research and implying the added and immensely difficult challenge of trying to identify those national needs. Technology assessment, that elusive concept which I have referred to so often and which was first made conspicuous in the deliberations of the Daddario Subcommittee, commands renewed attention and has elicited some action, even though the term is still groping for clear definition. Thus, the Mitre Corporation recently completed five assessments for the Office of Science and Technology, and some three dozen projects of this general kind are being supported by the National Science Foundation. Legislation to institutionalize an assessment function within government is pending before both the Senate and the House. And in industry, programs of research-on-research are beginning to appear. These involve such questions as the modes of selection of research and development projects, the evaluation of the effectiveness of such programs, the proportional sums to be spent, and ways in which the sharing of goals between research and development and corporate management can be improved.

All these trends are signatory of the times. All suggest that the depression in the federal and other public support of science probably did mark a significant transformation in American attitudes toward science — a transition that may be of much significance for the future.

Now as in all transitions of this magnitude, it is extraordinarily important to manage change effectively (that art in which Servan-Schreiber credited us so much) and to be quite sure that, in our enthusiasm for the sweep of novel emphasis, we do not unwittingly sacrifice part of an indispensible base both of science and of the support of science, which, once lost, cannot be rebuilt for many years. That reflection emphasizes once again the unique strengths of the triangle of research support for science and its prosecution — government, industry, the academic environment — upon whose interactions our national capacities have so much depended. That tripartite partnership has been the envy of the world. One of the great challenges ahead will be to make it work better; to achieve greater permeability and greater playback among the three sectors. But I would repeat that, above all, we must be very careful that, in the turbulent rush of our new imperatives, we also remember older areas of concern that continue to be vital to us, protecting the structures that implement them from being seriously eroded or even dismantled, something that almost unintentionally could easily happen.

One damaging road that could be taken all too easily would be to allow the equilibrium of support among the federal government, industry, and the academic world to become critically disturbed, and with that distortion to stimulate another that could be equally hazardous — to modify unduly the ratios of support between pure and applied science. This brings us to the future course of the academic member of this triangle.

We are all keenly aware of the extent to which the impacts of changing patterns of perceived goals in the nation, of the changing patterns of priorities that have accompanied them, and of the combined effect of the various depressing factors that we have discussed have been directly and often well-nigh disastrously felt within the universities and within academic science itself. The precipitous wave of federal support of academic research in the sixties broke suddenly upon the universities and strained heavily at their foundations. The succeeding and equally abrupt waves of parsimony then brought utter disaster. It may not be hyperbole to say that the priceless infrastructure of advanced training capability that was assembled and promoted at such extraordinary cost during the decade of the sixties has been seriously eroded and, in some quarters, actually dismantled. If that trend were to persist well into the seventies, it could indeed be disastrous. For even if the tide were then finally turned, recovery of strength would be slow indeed. And as I mentioned earlier, this is just the era when there is evidence that some other developed or developing nations are making precisely the opposite decisions about supporting training for and prosecution of basic research in their societies.

As Professor Don K. Price of Harvard has recently emphasized, a part of our current dilemma is broader. We are surely in need of a basically new pattern of federal support for graduate education as a whole in

America. Indeed, we are desperately in need of a coherent pattern. For, as Price has presciently noted, our policies of federal support for science in the nation right up to this day have been least satisfactory in their relation to the general system of higher education. As he has underlined, one may exaggerate little in observing that a dangerous feature of the system of research grants which marked our last era of support was that it became a palliative, postponing the painful process — or indeed any widespread feeling of the critical need for the painful process — of developing a consistent federal program for higher education as a whole.

Today the issue is further sharpened by a circumstance to which I referred earlier. In sharp contrast with the situation a decade ago, we seem, in pragmatic terms, to be confronted with a current overproduction of trained Ph.D.'s in science emerging from the universities and a current oversupply of those so trained in our society. In the short run, of course, this is true. The current unemployment figures for graduate Ph.D.'s are well known. They make a grim prospect, reviving memories for all concerned older people of an earlier and grim time. So why, the logical question can run, give strong attention to increasing our resources of men and women in a class already overpopulated, postponing more immediate use of their talents by society, and inflicting greatly added costs in money, time, and effort?

During the final year of the last decade, the number of both bachelor and doctoral degrees awarded in physics and chemistry in the nation was the greatest in our history. During the past 15 years, the number of chemists and chemical engineers who graduated annually had doubled. At some point between 1968 and 1970, we apparently moved from a deficiency to a surplus of highly trained scientists and engineers to man the positions currently available in the nation. This situation, although not extraordinary in a statistical sense, will almost certainly be with us until about 1983. Twelve years of a surplus of this kind is a long time in the perspective of a contemporary college graduate trying to decide whether to remain in science and, if he does remain, whether to invest another three to five years in striving for a doctorate. These facts are bound to depress our immediate future resources of the scientifically trained. They may also fuel the indifference and even the hostility, which, it must be said, have been substantial impediments in attacking the vital questions of a truly novel and adaptive policy of both undergraduate and graduate education in science and of university structuring and support as a whole.

Twelve years is not long in terms of the generation that even now is entering college. And for youngsters currently entering high school, it represents the approximate time that they will need to commit to higher training in any case if they seek to complete the doctoral level. An extremely interesting point that has been made in several quarters is that, from the demographic data available, it looks very much at present as though our surplus of doctorates in relation to our needs might peak and then reverse just about in 1983. Thereafter, the excess may decay rapidly. From about 1987 to the close of the century, we may be confronted with a real shortage of scientists and engineers to supply the needs of the nation. It is a deficit, moreover, that is likely to be exacerbated by new kinds of service that the nation will surely need to an ever-increasing degree — roles outside the conventional realms of practicing science and engineering as we normally think of them, and yet which will require sound and thorough training in precisely those areas.

Ahead only a little more than a decade, we will almost surely see, in greater clarity and with far greater urgency than we do today, two pressing needs in the nation: first, a need for *more*, not fewer, Ph.D. graduates in the sciences, some of whom will certainly have aspirations different from most of their elders and will be called to new kinds of services; and, second, a comparable need for many more men and women thoroughly trained at a postdoctoral level. This is a challenge to our system of general education and its support that we had better think about now more concretely than we have done so far. It is a challenge of a different kind, already visible in outline, that will not diminish through the years ahead.

More and more, as the years pass and the frontiers of research in basic science are pushed ever further, the need increases for a corps of men and women trained in their fields far beyond the level of the doctorate. This must be a highly selected group indeed, in terms of both intellect and dedication. It will never be large; it will never form more than a minuscule proportion of the society as a whole or even of its scientific population. Yet it is precious far beyond its numbers, for upon these men and women, in large measure, must depend our progress in the next century in the new areas of understanding upon which so much of our future must depend. For these reasons, and because of the nature of science itself, the education of this group is of vital importance and must be of a special kind that has seldom been (and perhaps seldom can be) best served by the more conventional educational environments in the nation. Indeed, we hardly know today what the most promising patterns for education of this sort really are, except that they must be highly individual, that the ratio of teacher to taught must be very high, and that the training must be of a "working" kind, approaching that of apprentice and master.

Are other patterns of postgraduate education conceivable, others that might be more practicable in the future and could bear promise of being at least as effective? I know no question in the whole field of science education for which it is more difficult to find an answer. Moreover, it is hard to know precisely where to turn for the experience with and understanding of the basic elements of the problem so crucial to new thinking in this arena.

But it seems to me that there is one class of institution in our society that is especially qualified for this difficult and vital task. I refer, of course, to the "research" universities of the kind represented, among others, by The Rockefeller University and the Carnegie Institution of Washington. There are not many of these in the nation: perhaps they could be counted on the fingers of two hands, if not of one. But their assets for the task are enormous. There are, of course, their experience and sophistication in the field and their great dedication to it, extending, in the case of Carnegie and Rockefeller, over nearly seventy years. Even more important are other priceless assets that they alone possess: freedom and flexibility in operation and, to a greater degree than any conventional university, some independence of financial support. Commitment to creative thinking and action — and to education — in this crucial arena must be, I think, one of their leading obligations for the future. If indeed it is a significant social function of science to influence the determination of extrinsic social goals, are not these institutions particularly fitted to sow the seeds in this field, and to pioneer the way?

In conclusion, I want to return to an issue that I have alluded to repeatedly. I refer to two rather new kinds of scientific function, which, stimulated by the evolving relationships between science and society, are certain to grow in importance over the years ahead. One is the public interpretation of science. Its challenge and its critical significance demand that some of the best and best-trained young people in science devote their energies to it over the years ahead. This, in turn, will demand a fundamental change in attitude — even something of a revolution — in the criteria for esteem in the scientific world. In the arts, there is a special niche of esteem and encouragement for the brilliant interpreter. Such a niche is largely lacking in science. It will be vital, in the coming years, that one be created, and with it a profession adequately populated and appropriately trained.

The second function is that of thinking and operating creatively at the frontiers that are, and will become, the interfaces between science — pure, but especially applied — and social policy: social goals and purpose. That is not itself a new interface, as I have already emphasized. Indeed, it was manned crucially and especially effectively in the crisis situation during World War II. But that was the most stringent emergency, and the nation called upon its leaders of scientific background not only to operate, but essentially to invent, the interfaces themselves. Now we are in another era. The interface frontiers are quite different in content and they are immensely more varied and complex than they were thirty years ago. Aims and imperatives, too, are far differetnt. Many, many more people will be required to implement them and their qualifications will differ. Where will those men and women come from, when so rarely in our educational system do we find the appropriate environment to train those who must be knowledgeable in the formulation of both ends and means in the areas where science and society meet? Should we not, in our planning, link this need with the "surplus" of Ph.D.'s that we seem likely to have over the next few years, and begin to think very hard indeed about ways in which some of them, qualified by temperament, background, and desire, could best be prepared to assume such roles? Should we not look critically at such schemes as that suggested recently for England by Professor Pippard? He proposed that undergraduates enrolling in science faculties should be given a two-year general education in science leading to a bachelor's degree and presented primarily as an art and only secondarily as a technical skill. Afterwards, those who wish to go on to more professionalized work and are suited for it should pursue intense courses of specialization for another two years.

These ideas provide only a beginning for our thinking, but it is a significant line of thought. It is an imperative that returns us to that typically American challenge of which Servan-Schreiber spoke so explicitly — the commitment, once again and on a new frontier, to the development of men and women. Of all the multifarious and complex facets of the relations of science and the social purpose, none, over the coming years, can be more significant than this.

II · *The Utility of Science*

W. D. McELROY

"The utility of science" is a phrase that has come into wide general usage primarily since that utility has been subjected to serious questioning by the public. Of course, in the past, "the utility of science" has had a specific meaning to most of its practitioners. The standard definition of the phrase might be somewhat as follows: "The process whereby scientists build a stockpile of fundamental knowledge that may then be employed in applied research and development to create technological innovations."

That definition once functioned as an effective rationale in seeking public support of fundamental science. Today, however, the definition can place spokesmen for the utility of science very much on the defensive. Because technology in the United States has come to be regarded as a mixed blessing, so has science — through guilt by association. In the minds of many, especially large numbers of young people, technology — and, by extension, science — is equated with weapons of war, with industrial pollution and the deterioration of our environment, with what they feel, rightly or wrongly, is a wasteful expenditure of vast sums in areas remote from pressing human problems, and the depersonalization of our society. In this view, the disutility of science outweighs its contributions to mankind as a whole.

Many basic scientists are equally uncomfortable with the term utility of science, but for different reasons. They are quick to point out that the achievement of technological change through the application of new discoveries does not, in fact, motivate fundamental research. They say that they are pushed by curiosity, or by the desire to add significantly to the body of knowledge in their respective fields.

If anyone doubts that this science-for-the-sake-of-science attitude merits public support, scientists are also quick to point out that ultimately the

WILLIAM D. MCELROY Chancellor, University of California at San Diego, La Jolla, California.

most seemingly irrelevant field may find application to meet the needs of society, often in unexpected ways. But for any field of science to maintain that potentiality, it must be allowed to proceed by its own internal guidance system, whereby support goes to research which meets the test of being good science.

Of course, what we mean by good science is a point one can debate. However, the best system we have devised to date is that involving peer judgment; we should use it until we find a better one. Even in this system, however, there should be room for some venture capital to support "way-out" ideas that do not always fit in the bureaucratic system. "Safe" applications to a granting agency do have a way, in some cases, of replacing creative and imaginative approaches to a problem.

Still, I think the question of utility may not be as absent from the deliberations of fundamental scientists as their rhetoric seems to suggest. Most such research scientists, both the gifted and the ambitious, do not seek trivial answers — that is, useless results. Rather, they devote their time to the pursuit of solutions to important unanswered questions in their field. More often than not, these questions are also important to the people concerned with technological advancement or with society's benefit.

All of the preceding describes, loosely, one classical route whereby basic science interacts with technology: the process by which fundamental scientists stockpile a body of knowledge that the engineers and the technologists can draw on for socially useful purposes — today, tomorrow, or in some distant future. There are other routes. Sometimes the problem is technological at the outset — as is true in industrial research — but it, in turn, leads to the formulation of questions that require the expertise of fundamental research.

In 1968, Melvin Kranzberg, in an article entitled "The Disunity of Science-Technology," published in *American Scientist*,[1] pointed out that the interactions of science and technology have been complex, historically. For instance, an observation of a technological phenomenon — the inability of suction pumps to lift water more than 32 feet — led Galileo to formulate some theories about vacuums and pneumatics. His disciple Torricelli gave firmer expression to the scientific principles, which led to the development of the barometer — a piece of technology built for science. The barometer led to the speculations of Pascal, Hooke, Boyle, and others, which, in turn, made possible Savery's construction of a working steam and atmosphere engine — for the purpose of pumping water. When James Watt perfected the steam engine, he was building on previous technology, such as Newcomen's engine, not upon hitherto unknown or unused scientific knowledge. The perfection of the steam engine, of course, kindled new scientific interest in the subject of thermodynamics.

Kranzberg described the contemporary dialectic between technology and science as a spectrum. "At one end is still the lone inventor working in his basement or garage; at the other is the 'little' scientist working with a graduate student or two on a small problem at some frontier of his own choosing." As one moves from the realm of pure technology toward the center of the spectrum, one encounters first "the technological activities constructed upon scientific work so long established that it is generally known to most of the intellectual community; then the technologies which rely specifically upon known scientific work and actually do the scientific work needed to fill certain gaps before the technological purpose at hand can become feasible; and finally the scientific technologies which actually enlist scientists for the applied scientific work necessary to technological purpose."

I hope it will not be inferred from the Kranzberg model that the only effective articulation between science and technology takes place when representatives of both ends of the spectrum are placed under the same roof and assigned a common mission. Although the scientific community has been urged to adopt a Manhattan Project approach to all the great social and environmental problems facing our nation and the world, it is obvious that such an approach might work for some problems (energy distribution and utilization, major air and water pollution, mass transportation, etc.) but certainly not for other problems, such as cancer prevention, heart disease, atmospheric circulation, weather control, etc. The wisdom of what Vannevar Bush wrote 25 years ago *(Science, The Endless Frontier)*[2] still pertains. The Manhattan Project approach was, of course, a massive, strongly disciplined team approach; Bush was talking about support of individual scientists. An alternative to the "great laboratory" approach, he said, "is to select scientific men of great power — men who are thus regarded by their colleagues — and see to it that they get every bit of support which they can utilize effectively, in their own undertakings, and in accordance with their own plans. Such an effort should cover every contributory field. . . ." This alternative is to be preferred, Bush contended, whenever a practical goal requires that a sizeable amount of fundamental research first be conducted.

In other words, practical progress depends deeply on fundamental research, as was demonstrated dramatically in a study by the Westheimer Committee of the National Academy of Sciences, published in 1966.[3] The committee examined the citations and acknowledgements found in patent applications and announcements of a selected set of important practical discoveries in chemistry. It broke these acknowledgements into three categories: those that included references to journals of fundamental research; those that referred to journals of applied research; and those that referred to patents or disclosures published elsewhere. References to journals of fundamental research exceeded other references by a factor of three for industrial inventions and by a factor of 10 for pharmaceutical discoveries.

This kind of mutual reliance between fundamental research and technology has been well documented. The history of science is full of examples of usefulness contributed to a problem by a seemingly remote field of scientific inquiry. Discoveries in solid-state physics and electrochemistry, for example, made possible Xerography, the basis for the spectacular developments in dry-state duplicating and reproduction techniques. Number theory, once considered to be primarily a pleasant pastime of mathematicians, was integral to the development of the digital computer, which led to simulation technology, which made possible the launching of space vehicles. One can trace another line from number theory through digital computers to recent developments in game theory. Surprisingly, game theory has been the basis for sophisticated analysis of numerous problems associated with population and urban dynamics.

The history of the development of the video-tape recorder for high-quality recording and reproduction of television pictures is another interesting and informative example. This development brought great change to the television industry along with a concurrent economic impact. It is noteworthy that the early motivation was not to develop the video-tape recorder, but rather to develop the audio-tape recorder. Studies conducted for the NSF by the Illinois Institute of Technology Research Institute and entitled "Technology in Retrospect and Critical Events in Science" (TRACES) [4] identified a number of fundamental studies that led to this mission-oriented research. Basic studies in magnetic and recording materials, magnetic theory, frequency modulation, and electronics were essential for these developments.

The development of the oral contraceptive pill is another interesting example from the NSF TRACES studies. Most of the basic information came from scientists who were motivated primarily by their desire to understand the physiology of reproduction. The motivation to find cheap sex steroids was originally due to the successful application of these chemicals in alleviating ovulatory and menstrual disorders.

Some of the early observations on physiology of reproduction include the work of Evans and Longs, University of California, Berkeley (1922), which indicated the influence of the gonad-stimulating hormones on the induction of ovulation; the identification of progesterone by Corner and

Allen (1929), at the University of Rochester, as the corpus luteum hormone; Levins' observation in 1930-31 at St. Louis University that ovarian hormones prevent conception in animals; and many other fundamental studies, leading finally to clinical trials of synthetic steroids by Pincus and Chang (Worcester Foundation) in 1953. A similar historical account can be made for the fundamental research in hormone and steroid chemistry. All of these studies eventually led to the application to the Food and Drug Administration in 1957 for approval to treat menstrual disorders with ENOVID®, the final development of the oral contraceptive.

This brings us sharply into the present and, more importantly, face to face with a future in which science will be called upon to deal with ever more subtle and complex issues. Therefore, the autonomous enterprise of fundamental science must continue to receive generous public support and public tolerance of its independent direction. A body of basic knowledge must be ready when we come to deal with social and technological changes now beyond our foresight. What is called for is an *addition* to this fundamental enterprise, a selective emphasis in new directions to help our nation solve complex social and environmental problems.

All branches of fundamental science must be kept in health because their potential utility can never be ruled out. Nonetheless, in some instances it can be perceived that an added push at the level of basic research, or at the level of development, or at both levels, will likely lead to significant breakthroughs. In such cases, consideration of societal problems may make that added push imperative. Some appropriate steps in this direction have already been taken by the National Science Foundation through its program called RANN — Research Applied to National Needs. As examples, here are some of the projects currently receiving support through that program.

First is added research emphasis on superconducting power transmission, on energy conversion techniques, on technology for new power systems, and on ways to utilize and conserve energy effectively. A related area is analysis of the total biological cost associated with power production.

Second, the time is ripe for developing a high-energy electron accelerator that can produce intense beams of negative pimesons, or pions. Here the social mandate is clear, for negative pions have important potential advantages over methods of radiation therapy now being used in the treatment of cancer. This is due in part to the large amounts of destructive radiation energy that can be delivered to a localized spot without great damage to surrounding tissue.

In the past few years, chemical reactions involving enzymes have begun to be worked out in detail. Now we are beginning to appreciate that enzymes may have considerable potential as catalysts in industrial processes. Current research has shown that enzymes are able to carry out processes such as selective oxidation, which are very difficult to achieve by normal methods. It is now possible to attach enzymes to inert material and still retain catalytic activity. This permits the preparation of large, inert columns that have specific enzymatic characteristics. Thus, the enzyme can be used over and over again by passing the material to be degraded through the column. Starch solutions have been completely converted into glucose solutions by this technique. Such techniques might be used eventually in certain sewage treatment processes, as well as for preparing specific catalysts for insertion in the human body. Thus, studies in the new field of enzyme technology are being supported by the Foundation.

Given the continuing urbanization of America, and the continuing need to install transmission lines, water and sewerage pipes, and subway systems underground, RANN believes the time is propitious to advance the art of excavation technology. Major advances in the field require much fuller understanding of rock mechanics, the introduction of new cutting techniques, and the development of new superhard materials.

One last example. The social sciences are sufficiently advanced to attempt to provide us with a "social report" to assess the quality of life for American citizens, much as our economic data now give us a picture of the well-being of citizens in the area of goods and services. Here, too, projects are receiving Foundation support.

One interesting program supported by the RANN program concerns refuse disposal in New York City. Working with an interdisciplinary team at the State University of New York at Stony Brook, the City of New York was able to program garbage collection in a way that saved the city approximately $10 million. Sanitation costs in the United States run well over $2 billion, so it is clear that much can be done to relieve this financial burden. Other studies are concerned with socioeconomic characteristics of population groups, national trends in social and occupational mobility, and attitudes of blue-collar workers toward their work situations.

This brings us to another and all-pervasive aspect of science in the contemporary world. A recent report of the Ad Hoc Group on New Concepts of Science Policy of the Organisation for Economic Co-operation and Development [5] acknowledges that "the realization of the aspirations of society still depends to a major extent on additional economic resources that can be provided only by growth, and that growth demands further improvements in the level of efficiency and productivity. . . ."

But the report goes on to state "we must also recognize that, increasingly, man cannot live by bread alone and that the use of the economic system to contribute to human happiness rather than merely material satisfaction presents a challenge to the imagination that the developed countries must begin to take up seriously during the coming decade."

Certainly the economic and social priorities of the advanced nations will undergo major shifts in the 1970s, and the science and technology policies of those countries must be shifted as well. Increasingly, for example, national policies will be concerned with the relations between man and nature — seeking to block the deterioration of the natural environment and alleviating the social problems that arise from growing populations and the concentration of people in large urban agglomerations. Increasingly, economic output is likely to shift from the production of private goods for the market to the production of "public goods," such as education, health care, public safety, and public recreation facilities. Increasingly, nations will have to deal with problems of saturation: of population, of pollutants, of traffic, of information inputs to individuals.

One result of these imminent shifts is that the need for ecological understanding has become critical. A second result is that science is now being called upon to deal with subtle, complex problems in which the human components are prominent. For example, in addition to its contributions to the understanding of the biology of individual diseases, the scientific community is being asked to contribute to understanding of such sociomedical pathologies as drug addiction, alcoholism, and environmentally induced diseases or stresses. To deal with these problems effectively, stronger linkages than have existed in the past must be established between the natural and the social sciences.

A third result will be to thrust new importance on technology assessment, a field that must also deal with problems of great subtlety and complexity. The OECD report, mentioned above, describes the obligation of the scientific community:

Science will be important not only for generating specific technologies to prevent or reverse the deterioration of the environment, but also for assuring better use of society's resources through better decisions about technology. The emphasis will shift from establishing feasibility to choosing the most desirable developments out of the rich menu of alternatives provided by science, and it will fall partly to science to develop the criteria of selection and to illuminate the implications for various social values of alternative technological choices.

A possible fourth result, also identified by the OECD report, may be a challenge to science to find new goals for technological, social, and institutional innovation that relate to the adaptation of work-styles to the psychological needs of individuals rather than, as in the past, the adaptation of man to work-styles set by technology and demanded by economic efficiency. This will obviously demand close cooperation between the social and engineering sciences, because knowledge of the true origins of work dissatisfaction is very limited. The debilitating effect of mass production upon individuals, for instance, is now being recognized by unions and management. Although this is clearly a difficult problem, new methods and techniques are being developed (flexibility of time schedules, goal-oriented assignments, participation in decisions, etc.) that promise to grapple with this type of problem.

An adequate assessment of the utility of science for our nation, in addition to noting specific societal problems on which fundamental research has some bearing, must also take into account the relationship between science and the health of the economy of the United States. More properly speaking, the whole science-technology spectrum bears on the well-being of our economy — or, in the customary shorthand, "research and development."

The productivity growth rate in the United States has been falling off and now stands at about 2 per cent a year, as against 3 per cent between 1960 and 1970. In contrast, the nations of Europe, which twenty years ago averaged slightly more than 1 per cent in annual productivity growth, now have an average productivity growth rate of close to 5 per cent a year. Japan, which had an even lower rate twenty years ago, now has a productivity growth rate that exceeds 10 per cent a year.

Particularly significant for this discussion is that the United States' balance of trade is negative, relative to other advanced nations, for raw materials and manufactured items in which technology is not an important component. The balance is favorable in products related to agriculture and technology, and only in these two areas is hope for an overall favorable balance realistic for the future. But foreign competition in highly technological industries is growing. Already there has been considerable foreign penetration of our market in such items as automotive products, textile machinery, machine tools, and communications and electronics equipment. Since 1957, the value of industrial machinery produced in the United States — chiefly boring, drilling, and milling machines and lathes — has dropped from $1.87 billion to $1.1 billion in 1971. And last year, only 10 per cent of the radios sold in this country were manufactured and assembled here.

Comparisons have been made between industries that invest heavily in research and development and those that have a low R and D investment. On the average, the former tend to show large productivity increases, fast growth, and a trade surplus. Examples are the commercial aircraft industry, computer manufacturers, the electronics industry, instrument manufacturers, and chemical industries. In contrast, industries with a low R and D investment tend to show low productivity, slow growth, and tax deficits.

If technological superiority through continuing innovation is the key to our economic health, then we can look only with dismay at current trends in expenditures for research and development. The total United States' investment in R and D has fallen by 10 to 15 per cent in real terms since 1968. The federal investment in R and D, largely because of cutbacks in Department of Defense and NASA programs, has fallen 20 per cent in real terms since that year. Employment growth in research and development has also leveled off, mostly as a result of declines in industries tied to military and aerospace programs.

I know that in some circles it is regarded as unseemly to speak favorably of economic growth. We are told that we should stop that growth, end our preoccupation with the dollar, cease being fascinated with technological change. We should, instead, get on with the business of redistributing our assets and resources to enhance the quality of life for all our citizens. But it is well to bear in mind that the multitude of goals to be achieved under the rubric "quality of life," from eradicating poverty to cleaning up the environment, can be financed only partially by shifting our present national priorities. Solutions to these problems will be heavily dependent on a healthy annual increment of economic growth. Solutions will also be heavily dependent on the marshaling of new knowledge through fundamental research and the achievement of new technologies.

Regrettably, the present situation has constructed a block to both economic and technological progress. Technological innovations supported by a sizeable increase in R and D could not only help solve major problems of our own society. They could become profitable export items to other countries facing the same problems. For example, we could be doing much more than we are to develop technologies to improve recycling and lower its costs, to develop new materials that use natural resources more intelligently, and to develop improved ways of putting marine environments to work for us. We could also, to cite another area, be taking the leadership in the technology of mass-produced housing.

Thus, in attempts to come to grips with the tremendous and unsettling changes of our time, science as a whole offers a utility quite as important as the sum total of individual research projects dealing with those changes. It is not unlikely that the infusion of science into our general culture has accounted, more than have most other factors, for our tolerance of new and unorthodox ideas and our ability to adjust to the shifting demands of a rapidly changing society. Despite the suspicion with which science is regarded in many quarters today, our citizens have a tendency to approach many problems scientifically. This has been an effective counterforce to the familiar historical process whereby major social changes tend to rip a people from their moorings and often render them insecure, reactionary, and defeatist.

Some may prefer to call this quality "reason" or "reasonableness," and some may argue that my assessment of its prominence in our culture is too optimistic. I believe that the loftier term "scientific thinking" is appropriate because of a distinctive quality of our culture: our belief in experimentation. Foreign observers, from as long ago as de Toqueville to as recent as Servan-Schreiber, have noted that we are a pragmatic people. For us, in almost every realm, the proof of the pudding is in the eating. We tend to adopt whatever works. And restlessly, like every practicing scientist, we are always attracted — and sometimes dazzled — with anything new. Something of this quality has been with us since the very beginning of the American experience, because we had the privilege and obligation of building many aspects of our culture from the ground up, unbeholden to tradition.

I know it is unfashionable these days to praise our educational system, but I believe credit must be given the schools for strengthening and shaping the scientific outlook of our citizens — both in and out of formal science courses. As the median level of education in this country has risen and as the educational system itself has improved, our tolerance of diversity and our adaptability to change have, I believe, improved markedly. Our younger generation demonstrates these qualities to an abundant degree, and certainly they did not create these qualities all by themselves.

The roots of our American tradition of open-mindedness lie in eighteenth-century England, when the political principles that came to govern our constitutional democracy were first being enunciated. It is no accident that those liberal principles were born in the same climate in which experimental science was beginning to flourish. Science had secularized truth by establishing the tests of observation and experiment, and it had demonstrated to the world that it could only progress in an atmosphere of freedom, unfettered by doctrine.

One who explored the ramifications of these developments for politics was that giant of a philosopher, John Locke. Because he believed fervently in the scientific approach to truth, Locke rejected the notion of the divine right of kings, as he rejected all notions that anyone has the right to force an opinion — or obeisance to an opinion — upon another. Because Locke shared with later scientists an optimistic belief in the ultimate ascendancy of reason, he advocated putting decision-making power in the hands of representatives of the people, and that is a system which, on the whole, has worked very well for us. A direct line runs from an essential tradition of scientific inquiry to the freedoms embodied in the First Amendment.

Events of subsequent centuries have somewhat eroded our optimism about the ascendancy of reason but, if I am right, not so seriously that we will be unable to cope with the great social changes facing us. It would be folly to argue that science is irrelevant to those social changes. After all, science is not apart from but is a part of society, and as such has an important contribution to make. Some day in the future, when the factors we subsume under "quality of life" are imparted to every individual, when mankind is living in harmony with the resources of nature, men will look back and wonder how the utility of science could ever have been questioned.

REFERENCES

1. Kranzberg, Melvin. The disunity of science-technology. *Amer. Sci.* 56: 30 (1968).
2. Bush, Vannevar. Science, The Endless Frontier. (A Report to the President on a Program for Post-War Scientific Research.) U.S. Government Printing Office, July, 1945.
3. Westheimer Committee. Chemistry: A New Look. W. A. Benjamin, Reading, Mass., 1966 (paperback).
4. Illinois Institute of Technology Research Institute. Technology in Retrospect and Critical Events in Science (TRACES), Volume 1. National Science Foundation, 1968.
5. Secretary-General's Ad Hoc Group on New Concepts of Science Policy. Science Growth and Society. Organisation for Economic Co-operation and Development (OECD), Paris, 1971.

DEVELOPMENT AND GOALS

III · *Organization and the Growth of Scientific Knowledge*

HAROLD HIMSWORTH

WHEN FUTURE HISTORIANS look back at the period in which we are now living, they are likely to see it as that time in which scientific knowledge emerged from its adolescence to become a major factor in the affairs of human societies. They will notice the problem that this posed for scientists and society alike and, with the benefit of hindsight, will pass judgment on the extent to which we took the measure of its significance. In this connection, they will pay particular attention to the grasp we showed in dealing with a new element in the situation — that of relating scientific knowledge to public policy — and, actions speaking louder than words, to the way we shaped our arrangements to this end. For this reason, I have taken as my topic that of the relation between the growth of knowledge and the evolution of organization. But I do not believe that it is possible to appreciate the significance of organization at any particular point in time, save in the context of what has gone before. Still less do I believe that, conditioned as we are to interpret the present in terms of the past, we can easily distinguish changes in our situation apart from this historical background. I propose, therefore, to approach my subject from the historical point of view.

II

A condition of survival for any species of living organism is that it adapt itself to the hazards of its natural environment. To this we can attribute that inherent trait in man which, whether it derives directly from a conscious sense of need or from the sublimation of that sense which we call curiosity, impels him to inquire into natural phenomena.

HAROLD HIMSWORTH   Former Professor of Medicine, University of London, and Secretary, Medical Research Council, U.K.

In the nature of things, however, it was not until men came to live together in organized communities that this could lead beyond the limits of individual experience. Then, with the opportunities for men to specialize in their interests, specialized occupations developed and, on the basis of these, collective bodies of particular knowledge came into existence. In this way, specialized organizations arose within human societies with the dual purpose of putting their expert knowledge into practice and developing it still further.

But, with the further growth of specialized knowledge, a new requirement inevitably came into the situation: the need to provide training to fit a man to engage in a specialized activity. Such training led to the apprenticeship system in occupations such as the practical arts. In occupations with a greater intellectual content, more sophisticated measures were required and special schools began to arise. In Western civilization, the first of these was the medical school at Salerno; the next the predominantly legal school at Bologna. More general in their interests were the cathedral schools, which prepared men not only for the church and the rudimentary administrative duties then required but, law and medicine not having yet separated from the church, also gave instruction in these subjects. From these bases, some 800 years ago, the universities emerged as identifiable centers for higher education and the cultivation of learning. Thus, in the second stage of this evolutionary process, the further growth of knowledge brought into existence a further type of organization.

This was a notable event. In relation to natural experience, however, its scope was only partial. Universities arose out of the needs of the three learned professions of the church, the law, and medicine. To these they remained oriented, and so had little concern with man's material environment. For centuries, this was of little moment. Then, with the advent of oceanic voyages and the discovery, in the form of gunpowder, of a source of energy that could be liberated at will, a revolution occurred in men's attitude to natural phenomena. Whole new worlds were opened to inquiry, and problems of physical forces, structure, and the diversity of materials became proper matters for intellectual curiosity. But these developments took place in a world that was foreign to academic thought as it then existed. As a result, men were driven to seek for another means to develop the new knowledge. This they found in the device of the scientific academy or society. At the outset, such societies were concerned with natural experience in general and were strongly oriented to practical achievement. With the further growth of knowledge, however, specialization was increasingly forced upon them. In consequence, this, the third device, came to take on the form of a body with specialized interests. As a result, its most typical expression today is the society that is confined to a particular subject, such as chemistry, physics, physiology, and so on.

We thus come to the opening of the last century. Scientific knowledge was now beginning to attract increasing attention, and coming to find its place in academic institutions. As a consequence, universities moved increasingly into the forefront of scientific progress until, by the end of the century, they were providing the acknowledged leadership in scientific thought.

This brief outline of the different kinds of organization that have successively come into existence in response to the growth of knowledge is obviously grossly over-simplified. Nevertheless, I hope it is sufficient to bring out the essential feature of the process. In regard to expert activities, organization arises as a result of the growth of knowledge. It is this, not considerations of the social need to which the activity in question ministers, which determines the form that any change in organization will take and, further, the time when it will make its appearance. Growth of expert knowledge and growth of organization for its development and deployment stand in the same relation to each other as do cause and effect. If, at any particular point in time, the requirements of a situation fail to be appreciated, progress will be retarded until that failure is remedied. If, on the other hand, the requirements are appraised correctly, and organization is devised accordingly, then, over long periods of subsequent time, growth can continue within the framework thus provided.

From time to time, however, as knowledge grows, situations arise that pose requirements which exceed the unaided capabilities of existing arrangements. That happened in the twelfth century, when the growth of knowledge impelled men to devise a special kind of organization, the university, to provide for education and the further promotion of learning. It happened again in the seventeenth century, when the extension of scientific inquiry into new territories of natural experience led to the emergence of yet another kind of organization, the scientific academy, complementary to those already existing. Now we in the twentieth century are again in a situation in which men are exercised by problems of organization. We might well ask ourselves, therefore, whether we, like our predecessors in the twelfth and seventeenth centuries, are living at a time when scientific knowledge is evolving into a still further stage that is impelling us to reconsider the arrangements that have previously sufficed for its development.

III

If one compares the ideas men held about scientific research at the beginning of the century with those they hold at the present day, one cannot but notice how their attitude has changed. In our fathers' time, research, other than that immediately incidental to practice, was generally regarded as a scholarly occupation that might mysteriously, but unpredictably, yield knowledge of public relevance. As such, it was largely supported as an act of faith, and the benefits that accrued from it were regarded as essentially gratuitous. Today this has changed completely. Now scientific investigations are supported in the substantial expectation that by their means progress will be made toward the realization of some intended intellectual or practical objective. The result has been, both in the private and the public sectors, the emergence of organizations for the promotion of research, characterized, not by a general spirit of philanthropy, but by a purpose-directed approach toward scientific achievement.

In the private sector, this changed attitude has found its expression in the private research foundation that bases its policy on its own selection of individuals and projects to be supported, rather than on bequests to institutions to be disbursed at their discretion. To this end, such foundations have adopted a form of organization which is significantly different from that of the charitably motivated bodies that preceded them. Not only have they included distinguished scientists among their trustees, but they have engaged their own secretariat of scientific experts to assess the progress of knowledge in their field of interest and to keep an informed watch on projects to which they have given support.

Developments of comparable significance have emerged in the public sector. These have taken the form of centralized national research organizations that derive their support from the public funds. At the outset, these were conceived to be merely a means of dealing with certain public needs that existing organizations either could not, or would not, meet. It was invariably found, however, that such ad hoc requirements could not always be met on the basis of existing knowledge, nor could reliance be placed on the chance that the interests of others would, incidentally, produce that which was required. As a result, these centralized organizations have been driven to sponsor their own inquiries to fill the gaps in knowledge that they had identified. To this end, they have evolved a policy of selective support for research in the universities, professions, and industries, supplemented, in most cases by the direct employment of their own staffs. As a result, under pressure from the realities of scientific investigation, central research organizations have come to operate in depth on a national scale and so have become the main support of research in their particular spheres of interest, quite irrespective of the specific purposes of the agency concerned.

Thus, in both the private and the public sector, this century has seen the emergence of research organizations distinguished by a purposive approach to the development of scientific knowledge. Naturally, of course, research foundations based on private wealth can appear only in rich countries. But central research organizations can be set up anywhere. It is in relation to these, therefore, that I suggest we consider the significance of purpose-directed research organizations.

It is never easy to appreciate the full significance of a change when one is part of the circumstances in which the change arises. As Francis Bacon himself remarked at what may have been a comparable time in scientific evolution: ". . . things in themselves new will yet be apprehended with reference to what is old."[1] It is not surprising, therefore, that the tendency has been to interpret the significance of this new kind of scientific organization in terms of previously established interests. Thus, among scientists, the tendency has been to see the new structure as essentially a means for meeting the increased cost of research in existing organizations, rather than as a development in its own right. Because central research organizations operate largely through the agency of other bodies, such as universities, that impression is not unnatural. But in most countries, other channels already exist for financing universities, and it would have been a simple matter to augment the flow of funds through these. Similarly, the administrator has tended to see the new organizations in terms of his own particular interests. To him they are essentially a means to enable him to realize the social policies he wishes to bring about. Clearly, however, unless it has become scientifically possible to develop research purposefully, it would be merely self-deception to believe one could create an organization for this purpose.

Of course, neither of these views is entirely without justification. Today, research *is* more costly. Today, national governments *are* more dependent on scientific knowledge. But is not the increased cost of research the result of scientific knowledge having evolved to a stage at which it requires more sophisticated methods for its cultivation and, further, by its promise, attracts more workers to its service? And is not the public recognition of the increased dependence of governments on scientific knowledge caused by the increasing effect with which that knowledge can now be developed? In other words, are we not in danger of mistaking cause for effect if we try to explain the emergence of purpose-directed research organizations as essentially a response to economic or social pressures?

Throughout the ages, men have been striving to increase their understanding of happenings in the world of natural phenomena. Traditionally, in doing so, they were satisfied to pin their faith on the hope that if they blindly and scrupulously followed their investigations wherever they might lead, truth would eventually emerge. But now, rightly or wrongly, the belief has grown up that scientific knowledge can be developed purposefully. This view accounts for the widespread appearance during the current period of some form of purpose-directed research organization in so many different countries with such widely different social structures and needs. If, therefore, we are to take the measure of our times, it is clearly of vital importance for us to know the extent to which this new-found belief is justified. Is it a total delusion? Are we merely seeing an increased number of fortuitously relevant achievements as a consequence of doing more research? Or is it that scientific knowledge is now passing into a stage in its evolution that is disclosing a new order of potentialities for its purposive development? We can only answer these questions by seeing how scientific knowledge developed in the past and how it is developing in the present.

IV

If we ask ourselves what we actually are doing when we undertake a piece of scientific research, the answer is obvious. We are inquiring more deeply into some natural phenomenon. Thereby we hope to find out what underlies it and other phenomena of its type and so to understand them more fully. As a broad generalization one could say, therefore, that the path of scientific research is always from the more particular toward the more general. Historically, this is evident. It was man's attempts to understand the mariner's compass that launched him on the path that led by successively less-particular steps to his knowledge of electricity. It was his attempts to account for the fact that a "suction" pump would not raise water beyond a certain height that led him to appreciate the nature of a vacuum. On this basis he came to invent the steam engine and, later, to elaborate the subject of thermodynamics to explain the engine's action. His investigations into the properties of materials led him to see the relations underlying their differences and so to construct that body of generalizations we call chemistry. By seeking to explain the prevalence of certain species in relation to particular environments, he was led to the ideas of evolution and natural selection.

In each case, inquiry started in an endeavor to find out what underlay particular phenomena. Each, as it proceeded more deeply, uncovered successively less-particular phenomena, which became of progressively common concern to neighboring trains of inquiry. Thus, we can picture the process of scientific development as depending essentially on the interaction of knowledge coming down from the level of particular phenomena and that dredged up from the level of the less particular. Herbert Spencer put this succinctly more than a hundred years ago: "A more general science as much owes its progress to the presentation of new problems by a more special science, as a more special science owes its progress to the solutions that a more general science is thus led to attempt."[2]

This, obvious as it may be, is a far cry from the traditional idea, to which we are all so deeply conditioned, of how scientific knowledge has developed. There is little support here for the Baconian concept that finds its analogy in the growing tree through the trunk of which the sap of basic knowledge rises up to promote the growth of the branches of applied science and development. Yet, although we may have come to discard this picturesque analogy, the attitude of mind engendered by it is still an effective, if unacknowledged, influence in our thinking. To see this, we have only to ask ourselves how often we refer to science as an entity and how unquestioningly we accept the concepts of basic, applied, and developmental science. We might, therefore, look a little more closely at how the development of scientific understanding actually does take place.

Consider, for example, the well-known story of how we came to recognize the existence of vitamins and to appreciate their role in the economy of the body. The particular instance I have chosen starts with the identification of the disease beri-beri and its further definition by means of pathology. There the matter rested until an explosive epidemic of the condition broke out among the sailors in the Japanese navy. Upon inquiry, Takaki found that it appeared after a change was made in the dietary ration, in which milled rice was substituted for unmilled. Following up this clue, he then established by epidemiological trials that the association was valid. The way was thus opened to the experimental pathologist, and it was not long before Eijkman showed that a diet of milled rice would produce beri-beri in animals and that millings from whole rice would prevent or cure the disease. Now the biochemist and chemist could come into the picture, and I need not recapitulate the subsequent story of how the active principle in the millings was isolated and eventually synthesized, nor how the investigations were carried through into the cell to show that this accessory food factor — or vitamin, as it was now called — was an essential component of certain enzyme systems. But let us look at what actually happened.

The process by which understanding developed in this case was one in which a series of subjects came successively into play as knowledge advanced. In this succession there was a logical order. Epidemiology could make no contribution until clinical medicine had first defined beri-beri. Experimental pathology could not start until epidemiology had revealed the association of the condition with a particular dietary deficiency. Biochemistry and chemistry could not enter in until experimental pathology had shown that there was something in the millings of rice that prevented beri-beri. Cellular biology could not start until that substance was isolated. All these different subjects were necessary to the final result. If any one had been missing from its place in the sequence, or insufficiently developed to take up the unfolding story, the progress of understanding would have been halted until the omission was rectified.

Had I the time at my disposal, I could go on multiplying such sequences indefinitely and extend the examination, as I have done elsewhere,[3] beyond the biomedical into other fields of scientific endeavor. I could, for instance, trace the development of our understanding of heredity from the primitive lore of the stockbreeder or agriculturist through Mendel to Garrod, with his identification of genes with enzymes, to Avery, with his recognition that DNA was the stuff of which genes are made, and to Crick, with his elucidation of the genetic code. We could follow the trains of inquiry that led to the emergence of fluid dynamics or aerodynamics. But I think that I have said enough for my present purpose.

Scientific subjects do not exist in isolation, nor is their development entirely generated by the particular aspect of natural experience in which they specialize. Each develops in the context of other subjects with interests contiguous to its own. To these each contributes its own particular knowledge and experience, and from these each draws information and ideas relevant to its own interests. It thus comes about that, in relation to any field of natural experience, subjects order themselves in a logical sequence within which knowledge is continuous. And indeed this must be so, for the particular aspects of natural experience with which individual subjects concern themselves are all part of some interrelated train of events in the happenings of the real world. In regard to the understanding of any natural phenomenon in its entirety, therefore, it appears that we must think in terms of the sequence of subjects, not the individual subject.

But sequences, like subjects, cannot exist in isolation. They fall into natural groupings. Thus, the sequences in biomedicine, in bioagriculture, in the study of materials, in the field of energy, and so on, have natural affinities with each other that draw them together. To such groupings I would give the term "provinces of knowledge." Each province corresponds to a coherent body of experience in the natural world. All at their external frontier, where they abut on advanced practice, are engaged with mission-oriented inquiries. All as they travel back from here, become engaged in progressively less-specialized inquiries of increasingly common interest to many of their component sequences or even to developments in adjoining provinces. If I were asked to suggest a model for this concept of the situation, I should, as I have done,[3] propose that of a vast globe of primitive ignorance, from different places on the surface of which inquiries are being driven in toward a distant common center where knowledge, if we ever get there, will be entirely unspecialized. The places on the surface from which these penetrations of inquiry start correspond to the enduring search of man for health, for food, for materials, for sources of energy, and so on; the converging penetrations of inquiry from each of these to the different provinces of scientific knowledge.

It seems to me, therefore, that the unit of thought now needed when considering the development of scientific knowledge is not the subject, but the province. It is, in consequence, from this point of view that we should approach the question we asked previously; namely, has scientific knowledge now entered on a new stage in its evolution and given rise to new requirements of which we now must take account?

V

Clearly, if it is possible to identify a sequence, like those we have been considering, within a province of knowledge such as the biomedical, we have the basis on which to formulate a policy for its further development. The broad line of advance is evident. The requisite subjects are there to be seen. The relative state of development and the potentialities of each can be assessed individually and effort can be deployed accordingly. Even if the situation is less definite and there is, as yet, only an indication that a sequence is emerging, it can still serve as a provisional basis for a purposive approach. Consider, for instance, those sequences that relate to cancer research. Here, at their mission-oriented extreme, we see the various forms of cancer being differentiated clinically and defined by pathology. By means of epidemiology, clues are being uncovered that point to an association between particular cancers and exposure to such agents as chemicals, ionizing radiations, viruses, and so on. Ways are thus being opened for the experimental pathologist and, with the experimental production of various cancers, to the biochemist, pharmacologist, and geneticist. In no time, inquiries are probing into events within the cell and stretching down to the level of the molecular biologist. To date, none of these particular sequences has crystallized out in its entirety. But the indications are beginning to appear and to provide us with a rational framework for an intelligent development of our inquiries.

Of course, I am far from suggesting that, at the present time, scientific knowledge has developed to the stage of covering all provinces of natural experience with such sequences. Over vast tracts of any province, progress is represented by only isolated points of activity or fragments of possible future sequences. Here we have no basis for purposive development. In consequence, we have no option but to support such investigations on trust and to content ourselves with that laisser faire policy toward the situation, which is all that is possible for scientific development in the earlier stages of its evolution.

But in each of the several provinces of scientific knowledge, sequences such as I have been describing are crystallizing out with increasing frequency. Within these, the subjects concerned with the different fragments of natural experience are beginning to establish increasingly meaningful relations with each other and to provide the basis for those syntheses of understanding upon which the comprehension of a natural phenomenon as a whole depends.

If this be a correct appraisal of the present position, scientific knowledge has indeed entered upon a new situation. Hitherto, our whole approach to natural phenomena has been to break them down into simpler fragments and to investigate each individually. Of course, analysis must precede synthesis. But, when analysis has laid the basis, synthesis becomes not only possible but intellectually necessary for the further development of understanding. This, in my opinion, is the stage that scientific development is now reaching in regard to a growing number of its problems. The increasing need to synthesize the knowledge gained by studying those fragments of natural experience we have distinguished as separate subjects is the new requirement in the scientific situation. It is from this point of view, therefore, that we should now be looking at the capabilities of the different kinds of organizations at our disposal for the promotion of scientific development.

VI

By the turn of this century, as we have seen, three such organizations had come into existence; the specialized occupations, the universities, and the scientific societies. These, however, are each oriented to different tasks. In consequence, the emphasis in their research is also different. Let us look at each in turn.

The professions and specialized industries (with which today we might group government departments) are oriented to practice and hence to inquiries at the external frontier of the province of knowledge with which they are concerned. Necessarily, therefore, their contributions to the stock of scientific knowledge will be slanted toward the mission-oriented. The universities are oriented toward higher education, with its purpose of providing men with the basis of general understanding that is required if they are to adapt themselves to the varieties of future experience in their particular fields. In consequence, the contributions from universities will, in general, tend to be weighted toward the more generalized, or basic, aspects of knowledge. The specialized scientific societies are concerned with the intensive promotion of knowledge of particular subjects. Taken together, the contributions from these three different sources collectively cover the range of knowledge necessary for the syntheses of understanding that are now necessary. But none of these three instruments is directed to the promotion of scientific development, comprehensively and in perspective, over the whole range. Indeed, aimed as each is to tasks that impose a particular orientation on their researches, it is difficult to see how any one of them could do so without impairing its ability to meet the particular need that constitutes its raison d'etre. We may well look, therefore, at the fourth and new type of instrument that has come into existence in recent years.

As we have seen, central research organizations were set up ostensibly for the purpose of meeting certain scientifically based public needs. Thus, from the outset, they were oriented to the purposive development of scientific knowledge. And, as we have also seen, it has proved to be impossible to develop mission-oriented knowledge apart from the long sequence of progressively less-specialized subjects that lie behind it. Thus, it was inevitable that, as they evolved, the purpose-oriented organizations came to identify themselves not with subjects, but with provinces of knowledge, and assume comprehensive responsibility for their development. Can we really dismiss this happening as fortuitous? Is it not that, just as in the seventeenth century when the needs of evolving scientific knowledge led to the emergence of a new kind of instrument — the scientific society or academy — so now, in the twentieth century, the further evolution of scientific knowledge has called into existence yet another kind of organization to meet the further needs that are now emerging?

As I see it, therefore, just as in the past scientific knowledge progressed from the mere recording of natural events to their analysis, so now it is entering a stage in which its further progress will depend increasingly upon the ability to synthesize knowledge gained at the level of individual subjects into comprehensive understanding of phenomena as a whole. This is the new requirement in the scientific situation that has brought purpose-directed research organizations into being.

Whether the purpose of such an organization is intellectual or practical is immaterial. In either case, the requirement is for a comprehensive approach to the development of related subjects. In consequence, whether the ostensible purpose is to promote the intellectual development of scientific knowledge or to integrate it into public policy, the specifications that any such purpose-directed organization must meet are essentially the same. We should do well, therefore, to spell out what these specifications are.

VII

James Bryce once said, in an otherwise unpromising context, that for any organization to be a success, it must satisfy both of two fundamental requirements. First, it must be in conformity with the deeply held sentiments of those who have to make it work. Second, it must be equally in conformity with the natural realities of that which it seeks to organize.[5] Translating this dictum into the terms of our particular problem, it is not difficult to see the specifications that have to be met.

There can be no question that only insofar as an organization for scientific development is able to command the confidence of scientists can it be made to work. To this end, two things are necessary. First, the organization must be under the autonomous direction of men whom scientists recognize as their professional peers and who collectively cover the whole span of knowledge required. Second, it must operate on a sufficiently large scale to enable it to realize its policy by selecting individual interests to be supported rather than to embark on the futility of seeking to impose direction on creative workers.

The natural reality to which such an organization must conform is clearly the province of natural experience to which its scientific knowledge is the intellectual counterpart. But we must be quite clear on this matter. It is the whole length and breadth of such a province. Nothing less will suffice. To believe, as some still do, that one can divide a province of knowledge horizontally, as it were, and assign its more basic moiety to one organization and its more mission-oriented to another, may have been possible in the earlier, analytical stage of scientific evolution. To do this today, however, would be to perpetuate an anachronism. The new organizations must be concerned with a province in its entirety, for only then can individual subjects be seen in their intellectual context and rational policies identified for a purposive approach to scientific development.

Equally, the province of scientific knowledge is the key to integrating scientific development into the machinery of public policy. If one asks oneself what it is that governments need in the way of scientific information, the answer is self-evident. It is information and assessments that bear on purposes in the sphere of public affairs, or, more explicitly, mission-oriented scientific knowledge. This, and only this, locks directly into governmental concerns. Yet the fact remains that mission-oriented knowledge can be promoted and, in its developing stage, its significance assessed, only in the context of the great mass of unspecialized knowledge that lies behind it. Because of their identification with the whole of a province of knowledge, central research organizations are in the position to do not only this, but also, through their mission-oriented extreme, to link their particular province of scientific knowledge into the machinery of social organization. In this way, the communications gap between political and scientific considerations can be bridged and subjects like molecular biology and nuclear physics, which stand at several removes from the mission-oriented, can be brought into a meaningful relation with national purposes. As I see it, therefore, the professions and specialized industries are responsible for meeting the needs of human societies through the application of their expert knowledge in practice, and the universities for meeting the need for men with the intellectual education to act as experts; so central research organizations have as their public role that of meeting the needs of modern societies for integrating scientific knowledge into public policy.

Of course, it is no matter for surprise that changes in the possibilities for developing scientific knowledge should be reflected in changes in the aspirations of public policy. After all, scientific knowledge is concerned with increasing man's understanding of his natural circumstances and, hence, his ability to master them. Of necessity, human societies are impelled to exploit all the knowledge that is available in these respects. Inevitably, therefore, advances in the potentialities of scientific knowledge immediately raise problems in the field of social organization. But we must not mistake such an effect for a cause. This is particularly important when expert knowledge, in this case, scientific, becomes such a compelling factor in the generation of public policy that it cannot be neglected by a national government. In such circumstances, the danger is that society will seek to impose on scientists systems of organization that are ill-suited either for achieving the political ends that it has in mind or for promoting the further development of the scientific knowledge upon which those ends depend for their realization. The scientific community would, therefore, be defaulting on its responsibilities, in regard both to society and to the promotion of its own knowledge, if it failed to appreciate the real significance of these new developments in organization and to make it its business to see that they are used effectively. Just as, in the past, men of expert knowledge have taken the responsibility for the proper functioning of the scientifically based professions, the universities, and the scientific societies, so now also, in the age into which we are entering, scientists must take responsibility for new purpose-directed research organizations. However, they can do so only if the scientific community is prepared to recognize that the promotion of scientific development today and the integration of its results into public policy are as much a part of its duty as to teach and make known the results of scientific investigations. That, I take it, is what the Academician Kapitsa had in mind when he said that the pressing need of scientists today is to breed a specialty of "actor-managers" who speak both the language of science and that of public policy. [6]

VIII

This, then, is the situation as I see it. Scientific knowledge is now evolving to a stage at which it can be more than fortuitously effective. Now it is becoming possible to bring together specialized findings derived from the intensive study of fragments of natural phenomena and to effect syntheses of whole ranges of understanding that will enable us increasingly to comprehend phenomena in their entirety. This change in the status of our knowledge has brought with it a new organizational requirement for its further development and, at the same time, disclosed a new order of possibilities for introducing scientific considerations into the formation of public policy. As a result, we are now being faced with the need so to order our affairs as to promote the development of knowledge both analytically and comprehensively and, at the same time, to provide for integrating the understanding thus gained into the machinery of social organization.

In principle, as I have sought to show, this problem is not unprecedented. Any expert activity that becomes socially important is, ipso facto, driven to come to terms with the society in which it operates. To this end, it is compelled to organize its activities in such a way that they meet both its professional needs and the human expectations that its achievements have aroused. In the past, as scientific knowledge has developed, the complementary instruments of the professions and specialized occupations, the universities and the scientific societies have successively come into existence. Today, we, in our turn, are faced with a situation that calls for yet a further kind of instrument to meet the new requirements and thus to realize the new possibilities that the further evolution of scientific knowledge has now disclosed. The purpose-oriented research organizations, each identified with a particular province of scientific knowledge, appear to be the natural response to this situation. Such organizations are normally in contact with the extremes of scientific activity, that which is mission-oriented and has direct social relevance and that which is quite fundamental. The stimulus to a productive program in such a situation will usually be provided by a variety of studies that bridge the gap between the two extremes. And so the well-organized mission-oriented agency is in a well-prepared position to comprehend the range of considerations required to promote the necessary synthesis of scientific knowledge and its integration into the machinery of public policy.

If this indeed be so (as I, for one, am satisfied that it is) then we as scientists not only must recognize the significance of such organizations, but also identify ourselves with their development, just as, in the past, we have identified ourselves with the development of the professions, the universities, and the scientific societies or academies. These are all professional organizations. As such, their effectiveness depends essentially upon the extent to which they are recognized, both by scientists and society, to be a professional responsibility.

REFERENCES

1. Bacon, F. Novum Organon. New Organon and Related Writings, Aphorisms, Bk. 1. Liberal Arts Press, New York, 1900, p. 34 (reprint).
2. Spencer, H. Essays Scientific, Political, and Speculative, Vol. 2. Williams and Norgate, London, 1891, p. 71 (reprint).
3. Himsworth, H. The Development and Organisation of Scientific Knowledge. Heinemann, London, 1970.
4. Bacon, F. Of the Advancement of Learning. The World's Classics, Oxford, 1951, p. 100 (reprint).
5. Bryce, J. The Holy Roman Empire. Macmillan, London (Papermac 1968), Chapter 24, p. 488 (reprint).
6. Kapitsa, P. The Future Problems of Science. *In* The Science of Science. Penguin Books, 1966, p. 126.

IV · *Problems of Science, Goals and Priorities*

ROBERT S. MORISON

ALL OF THE CONTRIBUTORS to this book are part of the same scientific subculture or establishment, which makes a certain amount of redundancy inevitable. However, I shall try to take the previous discussions one step further into the clouded, turbulent, and sometimes bloody world of decision-making. We first ask how scientists ordinarily decide what to do next or, in the stilted language of bureaucracy, how they set their priorities. We then look at some of the reasons why scientists can no longer be left entirely alone in making such decisions, and conclude, to paraphrase Clemenceau, that science is too important to be left to the scientists. Finally, the greater part of the chapter is concerned with ways in which the nation as a whole can grapple more effectively with the problem of setting priorities, especially in the areas of research and development applied to national needs.

As do at least two out of the three preceding authors, I recognize a distinction between basic and applied science, but I won't try to define the distinction, because it is a mistake to become too clear in words about what is not at all clear in practice. Nevertheless, I will emphasize that, in spite of the vagueness of definition, applied research and development require a rather different administrative framework than does the most general sort of basic science. Until recently, scientific commentators and policy makers have felt it necessary to give special attention to the problems of basic, or pure, science. It was rather generally felt that applied science grew naturally out of clearly envisioned needs and attracted the necessary financing almost automatically through the enlightened self-interest of intelligent entrepreneurs. Pure science was

ROBERT S. MORISON Program on Science, Technology and Society, Cornell University, Ithaca, N.Y.

felt to be so remote from ordinary human concerns as to require constant explanation and defense. The result of this distribution of philosophical interest may be that we now understand the problems of basic science more clearly and explicitly than we do those of applied research and development. The recent shift of public interest from problems of national defense and space to the improvement of the quality of civil life has revealed many inadequacies in the machinery for applying technology to novel problems.

Before becoming too entangled in the complexity of the present, let me begin by reviewing briefly how individual scientists or small research groups have historically gone about deciding what to do next. The criteria they ordinarily have used are not the same as those most easily understood by the general public; in any case, they are arrayed in quite a different order.

1. The first, and in some ways the purest, of the motives driving an individual scientist in a given direction is frequently spoken of as simple curiosity, or the impulse to understand. Perhaps the professional psychologists can help us to decide whether this is simply the elaboration at the human level of the natural tendency of many organisms to engage in "exploratory behavior." In any event, scientific curiosity is frequently, although not always, closely coupled to an assessment of the importance of the proposed work in relation to the advancing front of knowledge. In such cases, the "importance" of a given finding is judged primarily by criteria internal to science, by the way it fits with other findings and interpretations to help complete the conceptual framework within which a given set of phenomena can be better understood. It thus may be spoken of as internal, or *intrinsic,* importance, in contrast to the *extrinsic* importance of a new idea or device as judged by its ability to advance human welfare by solving a recognized practical problem. In what Kuhn has called "normal science" with a well-developed paradigm,[1] there is a high degree of agreement as to where to look for the next piece to add to the developing picture. The prospect of satisfying this group expectation before someone else does is a strong motivating force for the majority of scientists.

2. A second factor that may prompt the individual scientist to develop his work in a given direction is the awareness that he has in hand a method or an instrument which will help him find an answer to the question he has in mind. For example, by developing a new way of classifying plants, Linnaeus produced a handle to the unknown world of nature that legions of biologists after him have grasped to open many doors. Similarly, the invention of the electron microscope made certain discoveries of the function of cellular organelles almost automatic for

those who trained themselves in the technique. Two sorts of errors must be guarded against in using this criterion. On the one hand, an investigator may be tempted to rely on the new instrument, rather than on his own imagination, to turn up something new. At the other extreme is the stubborn enthusiast who insists on struggling with an obviously important problem even though a suitable technique is not yet available.

3. In choosing what to do next, scientists often reveal themselves as much like other humans in being influenced by how other qualified people will regard success and what this, in turn, will do for their careers. Closely allied to this kind of motivation is the competitive desire to show conclusively that somebody else's views are wrong. This, in fact, is not at all an irrelevant or unfortunate goal. Some very prominent philosophers of science maintain that the progressive disproving of inadequate hypotheses is the very essence of the scientific method. [2]

4. Scientists are also human in that they need help and support of various kinds. As we shall see, the availability of such help is an increasingly important element in the determination of scientific priorities.

5. Finally, the scientist and, perhaps more commonly, a research group, will be influenced by the extrinsic importance of the topic or its importance to the solution of practical problems that the average man will also consider important.

As noted earlier, the lay public takes a very different view of these criteria than does the individual scientist, and in most cases they want to array them in a different order, paying much more attention to the extrinsic importance of a topic than to its intrinsic importance, and worrying relatively little about the availability of an effective method of investigation. Furthermore, increased public awareness of science and its mounting cost work together to raise doubts about the validity of many of the traditional criteria just outlined. The greatest doubt of all concerns whether any method that relies primarily on summing individual choices is adequate for producing the amount and kind of science and technology the nation needs. There is less faith than there used to be in an invisible hand guiding the thoughts, tastes, and impulses of individual scientists so that the total enterprise emerges as an ideal national plan for the advancement of knowledge.

Let us turn, then, to a reconsideration of what might be called the classical criteria of scientific choice in the light of current conditions.

Curiosity, for example, is often regarded by men of affairs as an uncertain guide to policy. At worst it is denounced as mere self-indulgence, unworthy of anything but the contempt of the taxpayer.

The existence of a good lead into the unknown — either a bright new idea or a shiny new instrument — used to be the most certain guide to the supporters of science. Now it, too, can be called into question, and from two quite different directions. Somewhat surprising to the orthodox is the uncomfortable fact that sophisticated technological progress and even basic scientific advances can, to a certain extent, be *forced* by pouring money into a given field. When Basil O'Connor, a self-confident layman, undeterred by scientific doubts and scruples, began his celebrated attack on poliomyelitis, there were no clear leads and few visible handles. Nevertheless, there is no doubt that the effort succeeded in preventing the disease much sooner than would otherwise have happened. Not only that, but it very probably hastened the discovery of how to grow animal viruses in tissue culture, a matter of such general importance that it must be ranked with basic science rather than with technology.

Looking at the same criterion from the opposite direction, one is less sure than he once was that the mere existence of a good lead is not only a necessary but a sufficient reason for enthusiastic pursuit of an idea. Those who lack faith in man's ability to control his own impulses point out, for example, that one must consider the possibility that "dangerous knowledge" may result from any new research. There is even an extreme wing of opinion which holds that the financing of basic research should be held up until all possible future developments from it have been explored and declared innocuous.

The fourth criterion of choice, the availability of money and other forms of support, is one of the factors that is forcing science to consider ever more carefully the social context in which it operates. It is worth remembering that, until recent times, scientific research was carried on mainly for the fun of it, with the investigator deriving his support as a landed proprietor, a physician, a teacher, a clergyman, or a wizard. In the nineteenth century, a few full-time professorships became available in Europe and, by the middle of the century, in the United States. The really new thing in our time is that very large numbers of people are paid primarily to do research. This has led some of them to believe that jobs in which one can do almost exactly what one pleases are part of the nature of things, rather than a novel and possibly transient happening. The recent budgetary stringency has revealed the uncomfortable truth. Legislatures are now suggesting that faculty members should really be spending more hours in contact with students. Others are asking embarrassing questions about the relationship of a given piece of research to the practical object for which the original appropriation was made. Thus, it appears that the availability of money is becoming an increasingly important determinant of what scientists choose to do.

Our fifth criterion, the importance of a given piece of research for the solution of practical problems, is, of course, an immensely important criterion from the point of view of the public, and we will have much more to say about it in a moment. For the individual investigator, however, it still operates in a spotty, haphazard, and unreliable manner. Certainly, many plasma physicists have in the back of their minds a possible solution to the world's need for electric power. Others are simply captivated by studying atoms in unconventional relationships to each other.

So much, then, for the way the scientific community in and of itself decides what to do next. In theory, and still to a large extent in practice, the focus is on the individual scientist who has a question, thinks he has a way of answering it, and knows how to raise the necessary money. As his questions become more and more specialized and esoteric and his needs for money more insistent, and as society becomes more and more aware of the power of technology to produce both good and evil results, this idyllic, laissez-faire, invisible guidance system to the best of all possible worlds is, as we have noted, beginning to come apart. Science is, of necessity, becoming aware of the context in which it operates.

In other words, scientists are now acutely aware that the limiting step in the series of reactions which determine what they do is the availability of resources, and the latter is more often than not determined by agencies outside of science itself. These agencies, in turn, are likely to be principally concerned, as we have seen, with our fifth criterion of choice — the importance of scientific and technological advance as a means for solving practical problems. Thus, perhaps, the principal problem for science today is to develop machinery for priority setting and research allocation that will combine a sophisticated concern for the needs and possibilities of science and technology with an equally alert sensitivity to the needs of society. What we are groping for is often spoken of as a national policy for science. It is not the intention of this chapter to describe what such a policy might be in all its completeness. Science policy has been evolving over a considerable period of time and it will doubtless continue to evolve in the future. At the moment, the principal concern is with the development of more effective ways of producing technology as needed for a healthy civilian society. The remainder of this chapter reviews briefly the major steps that brought us where we are today in science policy and suggests what the next step might be.

As long as most experiments could be done with sealing wax and string and as long as most scientists derived their daily bread from astrology, alchemy, teaching, and doctoring, they felt little need for a national science policy. On the other side of the fence, the general public felt almost nothing at all. The relationships between science on the one hand and industry and public health on the other were vague, at best. If one thought about industrial technology, attention was focused on the ingenious inventor rather than the natural philosophers — the Isaac Watts and Thomas Edisons rather than the Sadi Carnots or Clerk Maxwells. A national patent policy to reward inventors and promoters was all that was felt by the general public to be needed in the way of a science policy.

In the still largely laissez-faire society of the nineteenth century, development of basic research and the training of scientific manpower were left mostly to the private sector. The architects of science policy between 1870 and 1940, although they would scarcely have thought of themselves in those terms, were university presidents like Eliot, Gilman, and Harper, and a handful of foundation officers and trustees, of whom perhaps Abraham Flexner and Frederick T. Gates were the most illustrious.[3] It was during this period that most of our present apparatus for encouraging science was worked out — the university science department with full-time salaries for professors who were expected to devote substantial time to research, the research institute, the general research-support grant, the project grant, and the pre- and postdoctoral fellowship. At this stage, there was nothing like an explicit national policy for science and little in the way of a conscious effort to select objectives or order priorities. There was simply a general feeling that science and scholarship were good things, appropriate to a great nation, and that we were, in fact, lagging rather far behind other great nations in their development.[4]

Perhaps the earliest substantial example of a conscious policy decision to concentrate financial support for science on the development of a specific disciplinary area was made by The Rockefeller Foundation, which about 1930 decided to concentrate its support for the natural sciences on the application of physical and chemical techniques to biology.[5] Looking back on this decision 40 years later, it is easy to trace its effects toward the creation of what we now call molecular biology. Based as it was on a careful assessment of the state of the relevant sciences (incidentally by two mathematicians), we can class this as an early example of priority selection on the basis of *leads*.

At the same time, the same Foundation decided to concentrate its medical support on the development of psychiatry and the basic sciences related to it. This decision appears to have been based not so much on the existence of promising *leads* as on an awareness of the suffering caused by mental illness. It is thus an early example of priority setting on the basis of *needs*. Ever since then, scientific priority setting can be thought of as a continuing effort to keep these two rather poorly matched horses, "needs and leads," pulling in the same direction on the same road.

Having been closely associated with both of these programs in their later days, after all the important decisions had been made by others, I should perhaps confess to having emerged with a considerable prejudice toward determining priorities on the basis of leads rather than needs. Perhaps the best procedure of all, however, is to achieve a perfect marriage between the two. Again, The Rockefeller Foundation may have shown us how to do this with its yellow fever and other health programs and, most recently, when it established an International Rice Research Institute.

As everyone knows, great changes in the public appreciation of science came immediately after the close of World War II. The stage was then set for the advancement of science as a national policy. The most explicit statement of policy at the time can be found in the document *Science, The Endless Frontier*, published over the signature of Vannevar Bush. The policy was at first almost automatically implemented, however, not by carrying out the carefully prepared suggestions for a national foundation for science, but by an almost spontaneous outpouring of congressional enthusiasm for the scientific activities in the Department of Defense, the Atomic Energy Commission, and the United States Public Health Service. By the end of the 1940s, there seemed no doubt of the national commitment to the enlistment of science in battles against disease and foreign enemies. In 1961, the concept of international competition was broadened to include the race to the moon.

It was not noted at the time, but the rapid growth in the funds made available by these decisions made it unnecessary to give much conscious thought to the setting of scientific priorities as such. The President and the Congress could set national goals in terms of national defense, disease control, and putting a man on the moon, but within these very large allocations scientists were able to find funds for almost everything they wanted to do if it met certain intrinsic standards of scientific merit. Indeed, the decision to fund or not to fund a given scientific project turned in those wonderful days (approximately 1945-65) almost entirely on the question of merit. Far less attention was paid to elaborating the overall strategy of science or determining the appropriate distribution of funds among the various fields.

About five years ago, this happy state of innocence began to change rapidly. The rate of increase in funding for all fields slowed down sharply and, in some areas, gave way to a decrease.[6] Actually, it felt like a decrease in all fields, because the costs of doing research and the number of people trained and wanting to do it continued to increase everywhere. Jolted by these abrupt changes, everyone concerned with the scientific establishment now realizes that painful decisions must be made about how to allocate scarce resources to the most promising, most deserving, or most needed programs.

It is worth pausing a moment to review the factors that may have led to a slowing of support for our current pattern of science and technology, if only to keep the scientific community from making similar mistakes (if they were mistakes) in the future. Perhaps more important is to identify modes of operation that proved successful, so that they may be applied with suitable modification to meet the problems of the future.

The following reasons can be put forth to explain the slowdown in the rate of growth of support for science:

1. The law of nature that nothing goes on growing faster and faster forever.[7]

2. The budget for research and development became so large as to be highly visible to the public, to the Office of Management and Budget, and to the Congress. To these groups it began to look more and more like any other money — on the one hand a burden on the taxpayer, but on the other a source of support for jobs in local areas. In other words, the science budget became a legitimate subject for political debate.

3. The public became increasingly aware of the importance of science, especially to health and to the economy, not only nationally, but in particular regions. Regional inequities in distribution were resented, not only because of an immediate loss of jobs, as described in 2, above, but because of longer-term effects on productive capacity and cultural level.

4. In spite of the large amounts of money spent on R and D, the quality of American life seemed not to improve proportionally, as it was supposed to.

   a. Particularly trying, perhaps, was the growing inadequacy of the medical care system, as judged both by every man's experience with increasingly inconvenient and costly services, and by the vital statistics which revealed a widening gap between this and other civilized countries.[9]

   b. Hitherto overlooked, dangerous side-effects of technology began to become painfully visible — with solid, liquid, and gaseous wastes accumulating everywhere.[10]

   c. Most recently — only in 1972 for most of us — has come the realization, as Dr. McElroy has documented in Chapter II, that other countries are increasing man-hour productivity in certain areas faster than we are.

5. The high concentration of talent and money in defense and space, to the neglect of other areas of more immediate importance to the average human being, convinced some people that the scientific community had conspired with an impersonal government to make the United States

an oppressive imperialist power. Even more moderate people cannot help wondering if the national obsession with the military aspects of international communism has not seriously distorted the deployment of our scientific and technological resources.[11]

It is important not to overinterpret the slowdown in support for science and technology as an index of widespread disillusionment with science per se, or even with the life of reason, as some of the more pessimistic would have it. Most of the criticism has been directed only at certain aspects of science and technology, not at the institution as a whole. In more pragmatic terms, budgets for R and D have not been cut "across the board," but have principally affected activities related to the military and to space. It is perhaps an unhappy accident that the Department of Defense and the Atomic Energy Commission supported so much basic research in the physical sciences that a change in national priorities has the effect of reducing basic research in these areas. But it cannot be construed as a sign of public hostility to high-energy physics.

Indeed, even as budgets for military R and D have been restricted, both Congress and the Office of Management and Budget have shown a more venturesome interest in exploring ways of applying science and technology to newly emerging national problems than have many elements in the scientific community itself. Thus, the Congress has recently broadened the mission of the National Science Foundation to include a greater concern for applied research, and the Office of Management and Budget has actively encouraged the new programs known as IRRPOS and RANN. (The former acronym stands for Interdisciplinary Research Relevant to Problems of Our Society, the latter for Research Applied to National Needs.) It is further important to note that these changes have not been made at the expense of basic research, provision for which, in the National Science Foundation budget, at least, has actually been increased substantially in the last three years.

Rather than continuing to discuss these matters in abstract terms, let us turn to what is actually happening in response to the various kinds of public unease we have just described. Most of what I will say is concerned primarily with what is known as applied research and development and which Sir Harold Himsworth discussed in the preceding chapter under the perhaps more useful heading of purpose-directed research. This emphasis is no accident, for I believe that most of our troubles are concerned with research of this kind. It is also the kind of research that costs the most and has the most obvious immediate effects on society both for good and for ill.

The first, and still the most obvious, response to the changed attitudes toward science has been the pressure put on the major government agencies to reduce or eliminate support for research that cannot be clearly related to their stated missions. The declines have been particularly noticeable, as we have seen, in the military services, the Atomic Energy Commission, and the National Aeronautic and Space Administration, but the National Institutes of Health also has suffered.

So far so good, perhaps. At least it can be persuasively argued that defense and space have, in the past, absorbed too high a share of the nation's total research expenditures and with them an equally disproportionate share of the scientific and engineering brains. Furthermore, reasonably effective efforts have been made to enable the National Science Foundation to pick up most of the meritorious basic research formerly supported by these mission agencies. There may have been varying degrees of awkwardness and inconvenience as these transitions were made but, so far as one knows, no real disasters.

How are we proceeding in transferring the emphasis of purpose-directed research from defense and space to the survival of our civilian economy? It is worth raising the question at this time, for it seems to be true that, as the government dismantles the research apparatus that took our men to the moon and puts the military and the AEC increasingly under wraps, it is not rapidly finding ways to employ this excess research capacity in solving more mundane and civilian problems. Furthermore, the most visible expansion in research on the pressing social problems of the day has, so far, occurred not so much in such relevant, mission-oriented agencies as Commerce, Agriculture, Interior, or Health, Education, and Welfare, but rather in the National Science Foundation, which historically has had a far more general mission. In the Fall of 1971, still another possibility was opened up by the appointment of a special assistant to the President for applying technology to national needs, but it is somewhat too early to say just how this will operate.[12]

The total sums available for applied research through the National Science Foundation still are not very large in relation to total federal outlays for R and D, but the rate of the rise has been spectacular — from a few millions of dollars a couple of years ago to $81 million in the President's budget for 1972 (cut by Congress to $54 million). There are many good reasons for encouraging this new role for the NSF and perhaps for a certain reluctance to rely on the established mission-oriented agencies. One may guess that the following kinds of considerations were in the minds of those responsible for this new trend.

1. The legislation sponsored a few years ago by that sensitive and enlightened Congressman from Connecticut, Emilio Daddario.[13]

2. The generally excellent record of the NSF as a supporter of basic research.

3. The fact that many of the relevant mission-oriented agencies have not yet developed research arms in any way comparable to those formerly enjoyed by the military, the AEC, or NASA.

All of these arguments are entirely plausible in themselves, and they doubtless made the NSF the obvious choice at a time when it was necessary to get going as rapidly as possible in new directions. Among other things, the NSF is almost certainly the most appropriate Washington agency for persuading the universities to take a greater interest in practical civilian affairs.

As experience accumulates and there is time for reflection on long-term implications, it may be useful to review the original arguments and consider the situation in the light of a broader range of experience, both here and in other countries. Two quite different questions present themselves. How far can any single agency, whose primary mission is a broadly general one, be expected to solve specific practical problems of great variety and complexity? And, on the other hand, how much will the effort to do so impair its original generic mission?

Most students and practitioners of purpose-directed or target-oriented research are impressed by the need to maintain an almost continuous feedback between the target and the research. This seems easiest to accomplish when the organization responsible for reaching the target also has control of the relevant research. It has frequently been observed, for example, that the outstanding success of medical research in the United States during the last few decades can in large part be attributed to the close assocation of clinicians, clinical investigators, and basic-research personnel in the university-medical school-teaching hospital complex, the plan for which was originally laid down by Flexner in 1910.[14] Similar successes are found in industry, the most outstanding being those in which there is a wide range of research reaching down to basic levels, as in the Bell Laboratories. In government, the National Institutes of Health have compiled an extraordinary record in fostering both extra- and intramural research, related not only to the needs of the United States Public Health Service but to those of the entire medical community. On a somewhat more restricted scale, the Office of Naval Research made a remarkable record in developing research relevant to the Navy's needs[15]; and there are other examples in the military services and, to a lesser extent, in a few other government departments. Perhaps the most outstanding record of all in focusing a very large research effort on a single, relatively narrow range of objectives, has been made by NASA.

It is much less easy to think of cases in which a new technology or device has been developed in some generalized or neutral agency and then rapidly put into practice by some other group. It is common knowledge that the label "not invented here" is too often equivalent to a kiss of death, as General Armstrong found when he tried to get the radio industry to adopt frequency modulation, and Semmelweiss discovered when he tried to get the Viennese obstetricians to wash their hands.

The NSF and the Office of Science and Technology are, of course, well aware of these problems. Indeed, from the very start of the new programs, the responsible officers have made extraordinary efforts to familiarize the other government agencies with what was going on, so that they might be prepared to take over eventual responsibility for projects relevant to their programs. A special committee of the Federal Council of Science and Technology, chaired by the President's Science Adviser himself, has assumed overall responsibility for interagency liaison in the applied research area. History, however, does not encourage the belief that even the most dedicated and skillful administrators can do much to "coordinate" the research efforts of separate and competing agencies.

In order to avoid any possible misunderstanding, it may be important to emphasize that, in directing attention to the advantages that might come from decentralizing and distributing responsibility for applied research related to national needs among the agencies with a statutory responsibility for meeting the needs themselves, we are not derogating or belittling the vigor, intelligence, and dedication with which the National Science Foundation has set about the task that has been thrust upon it. Indeed, we have already agreed that this was probably the most appropriate agency for leading a reorientation of the nation's research effort through its early stages. Our concern is with the long-term possibility that the very success of the short-term NSF effort may lead to less favorable long-term effects. One of these is the danger already discussed — that it will take the pressure away from attempts to develop more satisfactory research arms in the mission-oriented agencies. The other is the effect on the National Science Foundation itself.

It should never be forgotten that the NSF has a mission of its own: the promotion of basic, or general, knowledge. Closely coupled with this is a concern for the health of the establishment in which scientific research and scientific education is carried out. A preoccupation with a wide range of practical problems has time and again been shown to be incompatible with the fostering of more general studies. The simple fact that applied research costs so much more often causes it to overshadow the tender shoots growing at the base of the tree of knowledge. Perhaps equally important is the difference in styles of operation required by the two different enterprises. A certain degree of executive authority, if not outright intervention, may from time to time be necessary to keep an applied-research program firmly focused on its chosen objective. Such supervision from above is widely acknowledged to be completely out of place in the furthering of basic research.

It is perhaps too early to say whether such a change of style in operation is already in progress. It appears to some, however, that the needles on the sensitive recording instruments in many of our university laboratories have begun to quiver at the prospect of monthly reports and almost as frequent supervisory visits to and from Washington.

A shift in responsibility for applied research has important implications, of course, for the setting of scientific priorities. It seems clear that if all the relevant mission-oriented agencies and private industrial establishments were to be provided with the necessary research capability, the setting of priorities for applied science would essentially come about as an integral part of the process by which the nation apportions its entire productive efforts. In the past, for example, research in the areas of medicine, space, and national defense prospered because in each case the entire enterprise, of which research was a crucially important part, was given a high priority by the executive branch of government and by the Congress. In the future, as the government decides to spend a larger proportion of the national budget on the maintenance and improvement of the quality of the environment, on better transport and housing, on making life in cities safer and more interesting, larger sums should automatically be made available for relevant research in these areas. This statement assumes, of course, that ways can be found to persuade the appropriate bureaucrats and industrial executives that science is just as important to their missions as it has been amply demonstrated to be in the military, space, and health areas. This may take a little doing, but there is no reason to suppose that it should be any harder than it was for Vannevar Bush to persuade Admiral King of the importance of the proximity fuse in 1942.[16]

If this course is followed, decision-making in regard to applied research would clearly become part of the political process by which the nation decides whether transportation is more important than housing, or prison reform is more important than going to the moon. It would be foolish not to recognize that the decision to undertake a program of applied, problem-oriented research is based primarily on *needs*, rather than *leads*. It is thus necessarily political, and it should finally be made by those whose primary responsibility it is to assess and respond to the needs felt by the public.

Scientists would necessarily also be involved with the decisions — to make estimates of feasibility, probable cost, and possible side effects. Perhaps their most important function, however, would be to call attention to what science has to offer and, in a sense, to force responsible officialdom to consider all the possibilities. This means that some scientists and engineers must occupy positions of real authority within each agency. This point cannot be emphasized too often. Indeed, virtually all the experienced science administrators whom I have consulted about placing more research responsibility in the mission-oriented agencies have expressed fear, sometimes mounting to outright terror, over the danger that research will be neglected or even actively inhibited by indifferent or hostile administrators at the top. The only way of avoiding this contingency, and at the same time avoiding the undesirable consequences of isolating research in ivory towers, would seem to be to place the scientific administrator at the highest possible level within the agency.

The nation has so far been most successful in integrating politics and technology in those areas in which the public has clearly grasped the fundamental technological character of the problems to be solved. Thus the NIH has prospered because medicine and public health are seen primarily as scientific and technological in character. NASA profited from the scientific image cast by the moon ever since the Babylonians first plotted eclipses. Interrelationships between science and the military have been more complicated and uneven, but engineers and scientists have been key figures in military operations since before Archimedes, and the first engineering school in the United States was not in Cambridge, or in Troy, New York, but at West Point. Finally, no one doubts that the scientists invented the whole field of atomic energy.

Unfortunately, the technological character of many of our most pressing current problems is more obscure, and the agencies responsible for them are not so easily perceived as scientific and technological in character. The Department of the Interior was founded to preside over and distribute the public lands and is still seen as a patron of sheepherders, lumbermen, and oil prospectors. Its excellent scientific activities, such as map-making and resource estimates, are largely hidden from public view. Commerce is thought of in terms of businessmen, economics, and tariffs, not as the protector of the Bureau of Standards or the agency responsible for developing technological solutions for declining productivity. Housing is thought of in terms of subsidies, segregation, and slums, not as a field for technological innovation. Even the Department of Agriculture, representing a field in which spectacular technological changes have been made in this century, is identified in the public mind with price supports, low interest rates, and the survival of populism, rather than as the home of scientists like Sterling Hendricks or E. F. Knipling.

Actually, the technological character of the newer problems is increasingly being grasped at even the very highest level. So far this recognition has not led, as it might have, to a more-or-less massive upgrading of the extra- and intramural research capability of the agencies traditionally responsible for solving the problems themselves. Instead, the tendency has been toward developing ad hoc mechanisms quite separate from existing departments and bureaus. Such, as we have seen, was the origin of the IRRPOS and RANN programs in the NSF, and the more recent appointment of a special adviser to the President for technological solutions to a wide range of problems that are not yet precisely defined.

What is needed now is a further recognition that the technological aspects are integral parts of the problem. The relationship should further be institutionalized by bringing responsibility for solving a limited set of problems together with an increased responsibility for devising the appropriate technological solutions in the same agency.

It is hard, at this stage, to lay down general rules for the direction of great enterprises by administrators, political statesmen, and scientists of approximately equal status. The best past examples all have something odd, almost fabulous, about them. J. Robert Oppenheimer and General Groves; James A. Shannon, Congressman John E. Fogerty, and Senator Lister Hill; James Webb, Hugh Dryden, and Werner Von Braun. If the legendary achievements of such men leave us without a clear or easily replicated organizational chart, they can at least inspire us to hope that even the hardest problems can be solved by the right combination of scientist and administrator. Another possibility is to combine the scientist and the man of affairs in one individual, as Peter Kapitza has suggested.[17] This may be possible in a country more guided by dialectical materialism than we are and where a far higher percentage of men of affairs receive rigorous technical training, but it probably will not happen here very often.

Many people are so concerned about the danger of smothering science in bureaucratic inertia that they prefer an organizational design that separates research entirely from the agencies which must apply the results to practical problems. Sir Harold Himsworth has expressed his misgivings on that score, and the danger is certainly very real, but it may not be so great as the danger that bureaucracies will not utilize research findings produced elsewhere.

In passing, it is worth mentioning that Mr. Nixon has recommended a sweeping reorganization of the executive branch of government. One of its purposes is to group similar functions together in order to clarify the lines of responsibility for effecting desirable changes. No doubt it will be altered a good deal before it is put into practice, if indeed it ever is. Without going into detail, therefore, it may be observed that the proposed plan would make it somewhat easier than it is now to integrate applied research with the functions it is designed to serve. The proposal for a new Department of Natural Resources is especially worthy of study in this regard.

Even if we should succeed in establishing capable research organizations in the individual government agencies, we should still be left with the problem of dividing the R and D budget among them. At the present, such decisions are made by a complicated interaction between the Office of Management and Budget, the Office of Science and Technology, and the Congress. This is not the place to go into this problem in detail, but it may be observed that the scheme has at least two possible defects. In the first place, almost everyone recognizes that the Congress is inadequately provided with scientific and technological advice. On the other hand, the executive has plenty of advice, but it is given on a confidential basis and may be disregarded all too easily. The economists and accountants in the Office of Management and Budget not only have the last word; they have the power of making it appear that the scientists in government agree with them.

In considering possible alternatives, it may be worth studying some recent developments in France — a country that has long had the reputation of doing logically and explicitly what English-speaking countries do by intuition and rule of thumb. France was forced some years ago to develop new arrangements for support of science and technology because of critical lags in productivity and other symptoms of decline. We Americans may therefore find her experience useful as we begin to wake up to the fact that our economy is also losing its former place in the world.

For some years now, although still a private-enterprise, capitalistic country, France has had a national plan or series of four- or five-year plans for economic and social development. Planning for essentially all basic and applied research and a considerable proportion of industrial development is closely integrated with the overall plan through an agency known as the Délégation Générale à la Recherche Scientifique et Technologique (DGRST).[18] This board of 12 distinguished citizens, mostly scientists and engineers, is currently presided over by the eminent physicist Pierre Aigrain. It appears that a succession of governments has essentially delegated to this body the responsibility for dividing the national research budget among the various action agencies of the government, excluding the military. Thus, not only the French analogues of the NIH and the NSF, but also — and very importantly — the applied-research organizations within the ministries for agriculture, industry, commerce, and housing get their budgets on the recommendations of DGRST. It thus appears to combine the functions discharged in this country by the Office of Science and Technology and the sections of the Office of Management and Budget responsible for the science and technology budget. Incidentally — but again, very importantly — DGRST retains approximately 180 million, from its overall allocations of six billion, francs for grants and contracts made directly to research laboratories in the public and private sector. These relatively modest funds are said to have disproportionately large effects in overcoming the inertia and traditionalism so likely to overtake any entrenched bureaucracy, and they provide additional protection against the smothering of research by a particular agency.

This mechanism would seem worthy of extensive study by Americans, who should be gravely concerned by the increasing tendency to centralize decisions regarding even the minute details of the national budget for R and D in the invisible hands of the Office of Management and Budget.

Having emphasized, perhaps overemphasized, the importance of political responsibility in the allocation of the national budget for applied R and D, it is necessary to return for a moment to research that leads to general knowledge that is unconcerned, in the first instance, with specific ends. It has already been emphasized that at least some such research should properly be supported even by action-oriented agencies, because of the probability that it will ultimately be helpful to their missions.[19] But general knowledge should also be supported for more general reasons. All of these have been spelled out on many other occasions and I will not rehearse them here. The nation committed itself to these high objectives when it established the National Science Foundation.

As we have seen, the current tightening of the overall budget for R and D and a sharp reduction in training funds has led some observers to fear that this commitment is weakening. It is important, therefore, to reiterate that the NSF allocations for basic-research projects have increased steadily in the last few years. Approximately $180 million was spent for this purpose in fiscal 1971, $246 million is estimated for 1972, and the President's recommendation is for $275 million for fiscal 1973. In addition, the budget provides for the first installment on what is expected to be a multimillion-dollar investment in the long-awaited, very large array for study of the most fundamental aspects of cosmology.

It also seems to be recognized that the budget allocation for the most general basic research should not be tied to the solution of currently identifiable problems or to external criteria of any kind. Ideally, perhaps, the nation should, as many others have suggested, make up its mind that a certain percentage of the national budget for R and D should be devoted to long-range basic research and the institutions necessary to maintain it. Thinking only of that part of the basic-science budget to be distributed by the NSF as the nation's chosen instrument, 4 per cent of the current R and D budget of approximately $18 billion a year would not be a bad figure (and one that the nation could easily bear). The exact amount of money is less important than the freedom with which it can be used. Its allocation should be determined largely, if not exclusively, on criteria *internal* to science as outlined in the very beginning of this Chapter — the existence of promising leads and effective techniques, the glimmer caught by a few perceptive minds that something of great importance is to be found in the rhythm of the pulsar or the song of the chaffinch.

Everyone recognizes, of course, that it is hard to compare oranges with apples, chaffinches with pulsars, very large arrays with International Biological Programs, or linear accelerators with double helices. But in practice it is not impossible for men of good will to read each other's reports to the Committee on Science and Public Policy of the National Academy of Sciences and, after much talk, persuade each other that the time has come for this or that outlay to help radio astronomy or molecular biology make its great leap forward. It is not entirely easy to describe the process but, generally speaking, it works, unless the total sum of money is so restricted as to keep the whole establishment indefinitely in second gear. In any case, it is not the kind of decision-making that profits by being tied to practical objectives or political considerations, as priority setting at more applied levels might be.

In my opinion, the most difficult problem is how to weigh an undeveloped field of potentially great importance against a well-developed one of demonstrated consequence. Much environmental research, for example, is in the first category. We are not yet clear about the most important kinds of data to collect; we lack, to a large extent, the machinery to collect it; the methods to put it all together in a conceptual model are still primitive. But our very lives may depend on finding out how to do all of these things. How far should we go in supporting reasonably competent people in such enterprises, when other people of proved creativity are increasingly handicapped by lack of instruments that might give us new concepts of the red shift? I, for one, find that very hard to say, and I know of no solution except a compromise that gives something, but not all, to each. Another possibility is to take some basic research in these undeveloped fields of potentially great practical consequence out of direct competition with more general basic research and support it rather as a necessary part of applied research and development.[20]

REFERENCES AND NOTES

1. Kuhn, Thomas S. The Structure of Scientific Revolutions. University of Chicago Press, 1964.
2. Popper, Karl R. The Logic of Scientific Discovery. Hutchinson, London, 1959.
3. Fosdick, Raymond B. Adventure in Giving. Harper and Row, New York, 1962.
4. Wolfle, Dael. The Home of Science. McGraw-Hill, New York, 1972. This gives an excellent, brief account of the beginnings of science in this country, the way some science was bootlegged into government agencies almost in despite of a contrary national policy, and especially of the role of universities in developing a decentralized policy for science.
5. Fosdick, Raymond B. The Story of the Rockefeller Foundation. Chapter XIII. Harper and Row, New York, 1952; Warren Weaver, Scene of Change. Charles Scribners Sons, New York, 1970.
6. National Science Foundation. National Patterns of R & D Resources: Funds and Manpower in the U.S. 1953-1972. NSF 72-300.
7. Martino, J. R. Science and society in equilibrium. *Science* 165: 769 (1969); Bentley Glass, The Timely and the Timeless: The Interrelationships of Science, Education and Society. Basic Books Inc., New York, 1970, p. 67, et seq.
8. The Research and Technology Programs Subcommittee of the Committee on Government Operations. Conflicts Between the Federal Research Programs and the Nation's Goals for Higher Education. House of Representatives, 89th Congress, U.S.G.P.O., June 1965.
9. Ehrenreich, Barbara and John. The American Health Empire: Power, Profits and Politics. Random House, New York, 1971, pp. 18-19.
10. Commoner, Barry. The Closing Circle: Nature, Man, and Technology. Knopf, New York, 1971.
11. Nelkin, Dorothy. The University and Military Research: Moral Politics at M.I.T. Cornell University Press, Ithaca, 1972. Provides a case study of how one university dealt with the problem and an introduction to the growing literature.
12. It now (June 1972) appears that the mission of this office was confined to preparing background materials for the 1973 budget presentation.
13. Daddario, Emilio Q. A revised charter for the Science Foundation. *Science* 152: 42 (April 1, 1966).
14. Flexner, Abraham. Medical Education in the United States and Canada. The Carnegie Foundation for the Advancement of Teaching, Bulletin Number 4, 1910.
15. Carter, Luther J. Office of Naval Research: 20 years bring change. *Science* 152: 397 (July 22, 1966).
16. Bush, Vannevar. Pieces of the Action. William Morrow, New York, 1970, p. 110.
17. Parry, Albert (Translator and Editor). Peter Kapitsa on Life and Science:

Addresses and Essays. Macmillan, New York, 1968. Several essays in this collection will be useful for the purposes of this paper.

18. a) Quinn, James B. National planning of science and technology in France, *Science* 150: 993 (November 19, 1965); b) Report of the Delegate General, Scientific and technological research, fourth plan, *Minerva* 1: 470c (Summer 1963); Pierre Aigrain, personal communication, 1971.

19. Since this paper was written, several developments, especially the President's message on Science and Technology, affirms that it is now national policy to recognize and develop a close linkage between science and technology, and that individual mission-oriented agencies will be encouraged to support basic research; see especially the editorials by Edward E. David, Jr. *Science* 175:13 (January 7, 1972); and 176:357 (April 28, 1972).

20. There is now, in fact, a good deal of emphasis on basic environmental research in the program of Research Applied to National Needs (RANN) of the National Science Foundation.

THE UNIVERSITY

V · *Science, Technology, and the University*

WALTER A. ROSENBLITH

EACH OF THE THREE NOUNS in the title of this paper refers to a singularly complex institution with its own substantive, historical, and societal context.* All three exist in a variety of forms, and each evokes a broad spectrum of societal expectations that range from a futuristic Utopia to the foreboding of an ecological Götterdämmerung brought about by man's hubris in the use of his limited rationality. It is not surprising, then, that numerous books and even more numerous essays have dealt with one or another aspect of this complicated topic from the vantage point of a particular perspective.

I shall not attempt to present a reasonably complete, much less a balanced, scholarly inventory of the views, analyses, and prescriptions that have moved out of the faculty club and the faculty meeting onto the printed page. Instead, I shall deal with each of the three component nouns in a highly subscripted form: the subscripts correspond to my limited personal experience. The dominating features of that experience have been: two decades at the Massachusetts Institute of Technology, participation in numerous professional committees and councils, Washington panels, and advisory bodies, and in quite a few conferences held under the auspices of the American Academy of Arts and Sciences and organized by the editor of *Daedalus* or by the Assembly on University Goals and Governance. These, together with the rest of my background, must thus account for these personal subscripts, that is, for my attitudinal biases, selective perceptions, and parochial perspectives.

---

* In this sense, the components Science and Technology are institutionalized, each with its own hierarchical structure but in an interactive fashion which amounts to an "institution" rather than to a set of individual activities.

WALTER A. ROSENBLITH Provost, Massachusetts Institute of Technology, Cambridge, Mass.

The topic of this chapter belongs to a field in which there is neither theoretical structure nor controlled experimentation and in which there exists not even a meaningful taxonomy invariant across historical periods, societies, or intellectual market places.

SOME HISTORICAL OVERSIMPLIFICATIONS

Universities had their beginnings in the scholastic guilds of more than seven centuries ago. Although many were coupled to society in general through faculties of law and medicine, their relation to the religious establishment and its controversies was a factor that dominated their growth and development until the period of the first industrial revolution and of the French Revolution.

It was the philosophers of the Enlightenment who provided the ideology for a new approach and who were to provide the beginnings of a strong secular base for the developing universities. They argued for the extension of the methods of empirical scientific inquiry from the physical into the biological, psychological, social, and even moral realms. The discovery of the relevant universal laws in these several domains would thus be the true basis of progress toward a society in which both man and the developing man-made technologies would be in harmony with nature. The ideas of the Enlightenment had their greatest impact in France and — largely because of Jefferson and Franklin — in the United States. Early in the nineteenth century, Napoleon reformed the system of French education and focused higher education upon a type of professional education the French state had found by then to be indispensable. Not long thereafter, Thomas Jefferson established the University of Virginia as a secular and nonsectarian institution. During that same period, Wilhelm von Humboldt took the leadership in academic reform in Germany, a reform that brought the German universities into contact with both politics and the generation of new knowledge in the form of science.* (The development of the German chemical industry prior to World War I was strongly university-related.)

The concept that scientific and technical knowledge was useful in the industrialization process spread rapidly. During the first half of the nineteenth century, countries including the Netherlands, Sweden, and Switzerland established their first technological, university-like institutions. In the United States, the land-grant college became the prototype of the socially useful, intellectually based institution after Lincoln signed

---

* The role of students in relation to German nationalism and during the revolutionary period of 1848 is particularly noteworthy.

the Morrill Act in 1862. At that same time, William Barton Rogers — who had come from the University of Virginia — worked on the organization of the Massachusetts Institute of Technology (which, for its first half-century, was better known as "Boston Tech"). Throughout the next century, the concept of the dignity and worth of useful knowledge was to clash with the rhetoric of those who, like Flexner, derided the "cow colleges" as places where "men learned to throw manure about and act as wet nurses to steam engines." Almost 100 years after the Morrill Act, J. Robert Oppenheimer, in a symposium on basic research,[1] tried to resolve this conflict between those who can see only mission-orientation and those who try to generalize the slogan of "l'art pour l'art." Oppenheimer's double leitmotif takes account of both process and product: "new knowledge is useful" and "the getting of it is ennobling."

The past century has thus seen a development in which the universal character of natural science (scientific findings remain invariant under national transformations) has become intertwined via industrial technology with society and via education with the university. This complex set of interrelations has given rise to some of the dilemmas which science, technology, and the university encounter.

All societies exhibit some kind of intellectual metabolism that allows them to transmit their own culture. In the modern world, there has been increasing emphasis on the discovery of new knowledge, a process that has been institutionalized as research; in order to flourish, this process demands the uncommitted neurons of the best young brains. Although the university is only one of the possible forms of organization for the acquisition and transmission of knowledge, in the United States and Russia, at least, it has been approaching a monopolistic position with respect to the young. It also, in modern times, succeeded in combining professional, sometimes almost vocational, training with research and innovation. The broadening spectrum of analytical skills that the university teaches proved increasingly important, not only for intramural research but also for extramural applications of the new knowledge. Given the cumulative character of scientific knowledge and the fast-growing tree (or should we say jungle?) of technological options to which it gives rise, the implications of new technical knowledge for economic and societal change seem as enormous as they are poorly understood.

A decade ago, when faith in science, technology, and progress was still our society's dominant mood, a White House panel on scientific and technical manpower gave us an impressive inventory of the vital national commitments that we could fulfill if we could overcome impending shortages of talented, highly trained engineers, mathematicians, and physical scientists (EMP). This panel, which Professor E. R. Gilliland chaired,[2] listed eleven areas for which an accelerated EMP graduate-training program was critically important. The panel affirmed that

. . . the Nation depends upon scientific and technical manpower for meeting major challenges in —

Economic progress. Growing competition in world trade, an expanding population, stepped-up urbanization, higher living standards, and requirements for an increasingly complex industrial base require fresh innovation in the conversion of new scientific knowledge to technology.

Military security. Extensive and sophisticated research and development serve as critical elements of a modern national defense effort, which increasingly depends upon highly complex systems and diversified military capabilities. In disarmament programs also, science and technology offer important possibilities for new techniques and policies.

Space exploration. Achievement of national goals in space creates an extraordinary new demand for scientific and technological manpower. The highly complex nature of space projects, compressed time scales, and need for high reliability require especially perceptive and able technical management, the best in engineering, and, for the future, new advances in science.

Medical advancement. Problems in chronic disease, disability, mental health, aging, and environmental health, require continuing major efforts, ranging broadly from basic research to medical practice.

Assistance to developing nations. Effectively assisting newer nations to expand their economies and raise their living standards will require more and more persons specially trained to introduce change to traditional, pre-technical societies, and to help adapt appropriate technology to local needs.

Response to technological change. Our Nation's transition to a more technologically dependent and urban society intensifies social problems in conservation of natural resources, pollution of the environment, transportation, and urban planning. Scientists and engineers are needed to develop solutions to these problems, and technically trained persons will be needed in local, State, and Federal Governments to apply the solutions intelligently.

Scientific and technological readiness. Training persons to solve today's problems is not enough. The Nation has responded to unforeseen challenges in atomic power and space exploration; similarly, we must be prepared to capitalize on unforeseen opportunities in the future. Flexibility to solve wholly new technological problems by wholly new methods demands the best in science education and an increased cadre of highly trained persons engaged in research and development, adaptable to a swiftly changing scientific environment.

Education in science and engineering. Educational institutions need more scientists and engineers as teachers to educate the growing numbers of students enrolling in the colleges of the Nation. The need is particularly acute in this decade, as the postwar population bulge enters college.

Education for a better informed citizenry. With science and technology having an increasingly large impact on society, citizens must be better educated in science if they are to conduct their own affairs and perform public duties intelligently. This means, at the least, more and better instruction in science (and other subjects, too) in elementary and secondary schools and in college, which means more and better trained teachers, which means, ultimately, more professors of science and engineering.

Management. It was not so long ago that management in industry and government relied wholly on people trained, or with experience, in business, law, finance, and so on. Today, with developments in science and technology changing the shape of industry and government, and with the policies of industry and government affecting the course of science and technology, management must have its share of people trained in science and engineering.

Intellectual growth. Science, through its efforts to understand the world around us, offers one of the major challenges to man's mind and spirit.

In these many ways, then, science and technology serve society and the Nation. And the role is a dynamic one: Advances in education and research and development compound to yield even greater advances and demands, and combine to push scientific and technological manpower needs to ever higher levels.

This program needs to be put into the context of President J. F. Kennedy's address celebrating the centenary of the National Academy of Sciences,[3] in which he made two (for our purposes) highly relevant statements: (1) he expressed the belief that a great change in the American attitude toward science had taken place . . . a change that had led our citizens to know that progress in technology depended on progress in theory; and (2) he acknowledged that "every time you Scientists make a major invention, we politicians have to invent a new institution to cope with it . . ."; he added, no doubt reflecting preoccupations with space and the atom, " . . . and almost invariably these days and, happily, it must be an international institution."

There is still one other aspect of the university whose historical roots are worth evoking. Members of the university community enjoyed certain privileges and immunities, different in different countries and epochs and yet all related to the privileges Frederick I (Barbarossa), Emperor of the Holy Roman Empire, originally granted in 1158: protection against unjust arrest; trial by peers; and a right to "dwell in security." These rights and privileges were subsequently extended and came, in some instances, to include a right to strike and, more generally, a degree of autonomy and self-government. In Paris, this meant governance by the masters; at Bologna, it meant governance of the university by students, of whom many were, it is true, decades beyond adolescence.

In the United States, this concept of the university as a quasi-autonomous sanctuary has survived at least partially in the guise of academic freedom and tax exemption. But R and D together with the vastly increased population of institutions of higher education, have produced new tensions. Their population growth has made many universities "the biggest payroll in town." It has created many constraints on such municipal services as schooling, transportation (more often just parking), water, etc. In many instances, this general impact has been accentuated by contrasts between the university community and the surrounding area. Contrasts in socioeconomic level, in racial composition, and in political views have provided a perceptual framework in which the invading high-technology industry or the awe-inspiring nuclear facility or even the level of medical service that members of the university community enjoy are being viewed with suspicion.

Inside the university, the autonomy of individual professors and, a fortiori, of departments and laboratories have been challenged. Unpopular radical views of certain colleagues, as well as grants and contracts that certain other faculty members hold from different agencies of the federal government, have become targets of debate — and sometimes more than that. The sanctuary-like nature of scholarly papers and scholarly machines has not always been respected, and the limits of academic freedom have been questioned by those who require guarantees that only that knowledge will be sought after for which there are exclusively beneficial applications.

SOME DISTINCTIVE FEATURES OF THE CONTEMPORARY SITUATION

The first fact we need to consider is that the set of activities we call higher education requires roughly $25 billion per year. That is a modest fraction of the gross national product, because it involves roughly 4 per cent of the total population and an overwhelming share of the nation's best young brains. Within the past century we have gone from about 50,000 students around 1870 to roughly eight million, or half the age cohort, today. During the last century, the number of college students has doubled roughly every 15 years. Between 1950 and 1965 we went from 2.7 million to 5.5 million, and by the end of the seventies we should approach 12 million, if the trend continues. With this figure we would start to approach "higher education for all." Degrees in the natural sciences represent 22 per cent among bachelor's degrees (roughly 200,000 out of 900,000), 20 per cent among master's degrees (45,000 out of 225,000), and a bit more than 45 per cent of all doctoral degrees (about 15,000 out of 32,000).*

In fiscal year 1970,[4] federal academic science obligations amounted

* The figure for doctorates does not include medical degrees or Ph.D.'s in Psychology or in the Social Sciences.

to $2.2 billion,* of which roughly ⅔ were federal R and D obligations toward academic institutions.** In other words (and especially if sources other than federal are also taken into account), funding for science and technology represents roughly 1/10 of the total funding for all of higher education. In fiscal year 1970, federal obligations for academic science to the 100 universities and colleges that received the largest amounts represented 88 per cent of the $2.2 billion. This simply underlines the fact that in these institutions, which are most active in science and technology, support for those fields undoubtedly represents a good deal more than 10 per cent of the institutional budget.

How does the public feel about science which its taxes support via federal grants? In late 1971, Louis Harris surveyed a cross-section of households in order to ascertain public attitudes toward science† and scientists.†

Without attributing an exaggerated importance to the results of this survey, a few sample findings illustrate the ambivalence with which the public views science and scientists.

By a margin of 78 per cent to 9 per cent, the sample population held that "most scientific discoveries have done more personal good than harm" and by 89 per cent to 6 per cent that "America could never have achieved its high standard of living without scientific progress." There was also ample confidence in science being able to come up with substitutes for depleted natural resources and with saving us from being a second-rate power. But by 76 per cent to 13 per cent (with 11 per cent not sure), the respondents supported the view that: "Our scientific progress has gone far beyond our progress in managing our human problems and it's time we concentrated on the human side." Seventy-two per cent against 22 per cent held that science is making people too dependent on gadgets and machines and 62 per cent against 27 per cent opined that scientists have thought too much about what will work and not enough about how scientific discoveries will affect the lives of people. Finally, the percentage of people who said they have a "great deal of

---

* The seven major fields were represented by the following approximate percentages: Life Sciences (including clinical medicine), 38 per cent; Physical Sciences, 15 per cent; Psychology and Social Sciences, 9 per cent; Engineering, 8 per cent; Environmental Sciences, 6 per cent; Mathematics, 3 per cent; 23 per cent for so-called "other sciences," under which heading there were multi- and interdisciplinary projects that could not be classified within one of the above broad fields of science.

** The remaining third is made up of such categories as manpower development, facilities, and other related science support activities.

† Nowhere in the survey are the words technology or engineering used, nor are the words science or scientists defined or explained.

respect for the people running the scientific community" had declined since 1966 from 56 per cent to 32 per cent!

When the public was asked to list benefits derived from science, 34 per cent* listed medical research and another 11 per cent drugs such as penicillin. Other popular responses were major appliances (22 per cent), easier living (19 per cent), utilities (18 per cent), better transportation (14 per cent), longer life-span (8 per cent); only 5 per cent listed space and the moon, and only 1 per cent birth-control pills. When the respondents were asked "What are the two or three biggest problems you feel science has created as far as you personally are concerned?" pollution (45 per cent) topped the list. Next came health problems created by space research (9 per cent) and threat of atomic bombs (7 per cent).

There is a good deal that could be criticized in the foregoing survey.** The intellectual framework in which the alternatives were worded leaves much to be desired. The methodology of this type of applied social science research is by no means impeccable. Yet, we would be foolish not to acknowledge that public attitudes toward "science" (including technology) are shifting. Only medicine seems to be exempt from this shift. We need reliable instruments to measure such shifts and, above all, we need to develop appropriate educational programs to make our society more literate in these areas.

It is not possible here to examine in the necessary depth the so-called "manpower situation" in science and technology. There are several sources of projected "data" or trends of the doctoral supply. When these are examined by several authors in the light of different assumptions, they yield varying forecasts.[5] Whether we are training too few Ph.D.'s or too many depends obviously on how our society will find ways of integrating the many kinds of professionals in the sciences and engineering into activities that range from the advancement of pure knowledge to the fulfillment of the needs of our society. Though market forces clearly affect career choices of the young,[6] one must keep in mind the lag between career decisions and entry into the labor market and the overwhelming influence that federal programs exert in determining just how many scientists and engineers will be needed where. Even the most prestigious universities must prepare their graduate students to look forward to employment in the nonacademic sector. Our entire university system must find ways of dealing responsibly with setting up new Ph.D. programs in both established and emerging institutions.

* Respondents were permitted to cite more than one benefit or problem.

** For our purpose, it is unfortunate that no question was included relating science, technology, and the university (for instance, in the area of professional education).

The past several years have shown that we lack reliable data on how many and who were the unemployed or underemployed scientists and engineers. We also lack adequate mechanisms for self-renewal of this highly trained manpower group. Few professional organizations have exercised the requisite leadership in this area by providing their members with opportunities for dynamic technical and, thus, true social security.

Before concluding this section, it seems important to attempt at least a brief overview of how a nonrandom sample of academics view the contemporary university.

The various publics (including the academics) are, as Roger Heyns pointed out in 1968,[7] without a common view about the nature of the university. Heyns distinguished five commonly held misperceptions: (1) the university is simply part of a larger body politic; (2) the university is divided into three power blocs involving confrontation, collective bargaining, and coalition-making; (3) the university is an instrument of direct, social action; (4) the university is a public utility that should serve the taxpayers' needs (a generalization of Robert Hutchins' formula of the university as an academic service station); and (5) the university is simply an extension of the family. Heyns's own view of the university as a center of learning is not that different from the view put forth by Paul A. Weiss[8] in the more pastoral early 1960s.

Other authors have made their own inventory of misperceptions of the university. Few among them have been as severe as Robert Nisbet,[9] who states that the degradation of what he calls the academic dogma — namely that "knowledge is good" — has been characteristic of the last quarter-century in the American university. To Nisbet, the academic dogma does not mean knowledge for survival or in the service of power or for the sake of affluence or religious piety. To him, knowledge is to be sought in its own service, born in curiosity to obtain an objective knowledge of nature, society, and man. In Nisbet's view, the highest priority for the rehabilitation of the university as the setting for ideas, as the scene of teaching and scholarship, is the "abandonment of the present limitless, boundless, Faustian conception of the university and its relation to man and society." This "Faustian conception" was examined earlier by Nisbet under the headings of the university as the capstone of the research establishment, as the microcosm of culture, as adjunct to Establishment, as radical critic of society, as humanitarian-in-chief, or as a therapeutic community.

Without quoting here some of the more radical critics[10,11,12] of either science or the university, it is difficult to find a more striking contrast than the following quote from James Perkins[13] who said in the year of turmoil 1969: "The university that wrestles with real issues, that accepts the risk of applying its knowledge to them, that concerns itself with what is and should be as much as with what was — such an institution will not be a safe and sheltered refuge. For the rest of this century, the university will either share in the life and the turmoil of our revolutionary world, or it will be a morgue. And if it is a morgue, the bright minds and the lively imaginations will go elsewhere, taking not only the ferment but the hope of the modern university with them."

It is perhaps instructive to compare these views with those developed in a recent publication of the Organisation for Economic Co-operation and Development on the organization of research in France, Germany, and the United Kingdom.[14] In a chapter by Gilbert Caty, we find an attempt to compare "the idea of a university" with its recent evolution. The author concludes that "the university of the elite . . . has yielded place to a mass university at the service of the society." Admitting that many, even in Europe, believe that the university is now merely a center for applied studies or, at most, didactic research, the author mentions that new types of selective universities are being set up with the hope that they may turn out to be institutions ("research universities") in which fundamental academic pursuits will be carried out. Such "research universities should be regarded as the expression of functional specialization in a differentiated network, and not as the translation of a statutory or academic isolation."

DILEMMAS AND DIFFICULTIES

The foregoing sections provide a rough outline of the setting in which science, technology, and the university interact in our society. The society itself is in a period of trouble in which most institutions are subject to critical scrutiny. The earlier lengthy quote from the Gilliland report and the spirit in which President Kennedy ordered its implementation can serve as a bench-mark (maybe better as a high-water mark) that allows us to appreciate how much today's mood and priorities for R and D and the requisite manpower are at variance with those extant 10 years ago.

In this period, our nation* has shifted from a perhaps naive belief in

---

* Other highly industrialized countries have also begun to examine critically the social costs of growth; for the Western countries, the so-called Brooks Report[15] is perhaps the most representative document in this respect. This report attempts to draw the lessons of the last decade; it accepts the fact that even basic science (i.e., university science) will have to respond to needs for selective emphasis as determined by the social, political, and industrial environment.

I feel unable to weigh the extent to which ideological shifts — like the Chinese the unquestioned benefits of the trinity of progress — scientific research, technical innovation, and higher education — to a more questioning attitude regarding the whole process of knowledge acquisition. Only in the area of health do the lay public's expectations still seem to be fairly unchanged and to look toward crash programs in research and more manpower as the solution. The extent to which a given set of diseases is ripe for such a program and the way in which increased manpower* would be used in what is widely called our "health nonsystem" is not yet being widely questioned.

To society at large, science, technology, and the university are all élite institutions whose power is derived from the kinds of expert knowledge held by those who belong to them. Hence, those elements of our society who feel powerless and discriminated against have raised the issue of access to activities that are supported by taxes from all citizens. The institutions of higher education have been faced with demands — mainly from minority and both culturally and economically deprived groups — for "open admission" for students who have graduated from high school. The federal government, on the other hand, has begun to press for affirmative action in all areas of employment, including faculty appointments. Although many admit that a quota system (whether based on population, work force, or even proportion of graduate students) is no satisfactory solution, we cannot help realizing that, in the long run, a rigidly meritocratic approach in mass higher education runs the risk of being neither stable nor socially just. University administrators and more and more faculty members are only too aware that, in many fields of science or engineering, search for competent faculty among women or minorities is highly frustrating. It is often hard to persuade even students from these groups that real opportunities exist for those who are willing to make the extraordinary efforts necessary to obtain effective access to a field in which they have no minority (or women) peers.

The most recent years have seen a perceptible decrease in the number

---

* Let us acknowledge here that in recent years almost 30 per cent of the licensed physicians have graduated from non-U.S. medical schools and that without them many of our inner-city hospitals would be without house officers. This is not the place to discuss this particular form of "brain drain."

---

cultural revolution — reflect similar concerns in a different ideological context. I also feel unable to examine how the developing countries, with their enormous basic human needs, are likely to be influenced by the ongoing debate. What seems clear is that knowledge-affluent societies will hardly ever again take a benign, laissez faire attitude toward scientific-technical research and toward higher education. Both relate in today's world much too directly to the power of responding to a society's needs. And societies expect their investment in science, technology, and the university to be commensurable with the derived benefits.

of students in the physical sciences and engineering, but it is an irreversible fact that the "specific gravity" of science and technology in the university has increased substantially. It little matters what measure we choose, what pie chart or bar graph we draw in terms of faculty members, graduate students, and "postdocs" (those professionals in the acquisition of new knowledge). The fact remains that scientists and, less often, engineers come out "ahead" in resources and facilities, in opportunities for educational innovation and, until recently, in excitement, optimism, and even visibility.

The role of science in both the university and society challenged the prior preponderance of humanistic studies. The humanistic university tradition seemed unable to compete with scientific progress, with its increased influence upon education in the post-Sputnik period, and with its grip upon people's imagination. In a sense, even the controversial — mainly among scientists — mission to the moon led many to reevaluate their view of how man could control nature and his own fate. In the decade since that resolve of going to the moon was announced, many programs — not always well thought through — have started off either from the view that the proposed program was a better use of national resources or with "If we can go to the moon, we can certainly. . . . " The humanities seemed to have little to contribute to these debates.

But these two-culture tensions are by no means the only ones that the growing role of science and technology has introduced into the university. The departmental structure seems optimal for rapid progress in the basic-sciences disciplines and for training graduate students who are destined to become academics themselves. It seems perhaps less appropriate in areas of technology, in which the engineering professions need to draw upon the "applied competences" of nonengineering disciplines.[16] However, the "nonapplied" colleagues from the relevant departments find that the very formulation by an engineering group of a sociotechnical problem (such as in the area of energy policy or transportation) often condemns the project to being of interest to a very limited subset of the social scientists who might have something to contribute. Here is a class of examples in which the intrinsic forces of a discipline-oriented department and the external demands made upon it by their academic colleagues often clash.

Problem-oriented research or research at the interface of various disciplines has, of course, been institutionalized in a variety of ways during the past quarter-century. The influence of such World War II projects as the Manhattan Project or M.I.T.'s Radiation Laboratory[17] constituted powerful examples of how first-rate scientists and engineers from different departments could cooperate when motivated by a technically definable mission. Thus, the period since World War II has seen the emergence of many variably successful interdepartmental or interdisciplinary ventures. When an area was ripe for such an effort — an essential complementarity of skills, a real need for jointly operable facilities, powerful motivation by an external client, *and* coupling of the venture to educational programs — universities have found such "inter"-units desirable and successful (at least for a time!). That is because the natural monitoring of quality in a discipline-oriented department — via visiting committees, professional organizations, etc. — is easier over the long run. Sometimes an external client who considers the interunit the appropriate structure to "resonate" to his own complex needs can assist a university in assuring the continued vigor of such a research *and* educational program.

The structure of knowledge has become so complex that it can no longer be assumed that the structure is a pie which can be divided up easily into sections that are departments. Neither can we expect that curriculum requirements alone will make cohesive in our student's brains what they have learned in courses in the sciences, social sciences, and humanities. Universities are searching for principles of organization, principles that will be valid (both inside and in relation to the outside world), which will allow for both continuity and change in the acquisition and use of knowledge. The late philosopher of science Philipp Frank used to say, "Problems in nature do not come with departmental labels"; and today, when the university's coupling to society has become so much tighter, we might be allowed to add: and in society even less so!

How the various disciplines ("components") of the university can best collaborate is important from several points of view: (1) educationally; (2) socially, as it influences how society thinks about the university, science, and technology in relation to itself; (3) humanistically, such cooperation is undoubtedly a necessary, although not a sufficient, condition for the solution of many human problems.

This topic of interdisciplinary relationships is one that deserves a good deal of study; it is also one to which the great Swiss psychologist Piaget has contributed recently. Interdisciplinarity apparently demands a kind of social cohesion that seems to be the by-product of successful "summer studies" and intensive study programs, such as the ones which the Neurosciences Research Program (NRP) has organized during the last decade.

As we accumulate more and more specialized knowledge, society expects the university to use its talents not only in narrow disciplinary confines. Many in the nonacademic world have difficulty imagining (as students sometimes also do) that academic colleagues who work on related problems in different departments fail to keep up with each other's progress. Society is eager to have "impact statements" of new knowledge, if we may borrow this metaphor from the environmental area. Should society conclude that the university is too unconcerned about the consequences of the new knowledge it generates, new institutions of knowledge assessment might come to attract much of the support universities now enjoy.

Today's university occupies a unique place among our society's institutions. For a certain number of years it has had the custody of the best young brains. Findings of its science and technology faculty — although often inadequately and distortedly reported — influence our fellow citizens' views of themselves and of the universe, shape their expectations of what our society could be like, and modify the education of the professions. In addition, the university exerts influence of a different sort upon its immediate physical neighborhood, and, in the case of private institutions, as an investor whose ethical standards will be scrutinized.

This is indeed a formidable set of expectations to live up to. It makes us appreciate how far we have come since the early days of the university. It also makes us realize that the organization of even the most highly administered university (the multiversity?) has not had a chance to adapt in an evolutionary sense to this set of implied promises and commitments.

WHICH WAY ADAPTIVE EVOLUTION?

The above examples of dilemmas and difficulties are merely illustrative. There are others both related and of comparable importance.

University administrators often find it hard to forecast a balanced future for their own institutions when the allocation of resources for growth is subject to centrifugal control by peers or determined by a mission that clearly transcends that of the particular university. Academic scientists and engineers often find it more rewarding to advise federal or even international agencies than to work with those at the state and local levels. We have lived so long with the coexistence of two concepts — that of the university as an elite institution and that of economy of scale — that we are hampered in thinking clearly about how or whether the ambiguous slogan of "universal higher education" can be institutionalized meaningfully.

Thus the trinity of progress — science, technology, and the university — finds that not only has it acquired many new concerns and pressures but that it also has outgrown its earlier conceptualizations. We hear voices, raucous and shrill, but also sensitive and apparently thoughtful, proclaiming that they have lost faith in progress and that they are opposed to further advances in science and technology. But even those who feel that the human condition will not profit from a moratorium on all scientific and technical progress are puzzled. Which is, indeed, the most adaptive path for science, technology, and the university in their present state of strong coupling to society?

There are those who together with Weinberg[18] suggest that certain types of intellectual pursuits — in particular, those that relate to problems with both social and technological aspects — can best be solved in institutions that are not part of universities. In making this suggestion, Weinberg and other like-minded critics of the contemporary university feel that if universities were to become mainly problem-oriented institutions they would risk deterioration from the viewpoint of their traditional purpose, which is higher education. They might lose their role as guardians of disciplinary standards, as social and intellectual critics.

We live in a society that badly needs a balanced "ecology" of knowledge-related institutions, institutions that can acquire and accumulate knowledge, that can disseminate it, and that can integrate it successfully for social purposes. Such institutions must relate meaningfully to universities and yet, traditionally, universities find it difficult to incorporate their several expected roles into their present structure.

Thus, we find a need for new types and new groupings of institutions that reflect the extent to which ours has become a knowledge-dependent society. The required adaptation process will involve a good deal of institutional differentiation. In addition to the "knowledge industries," which have already exhibited such differentiation, we need — especially in the area of human services, in contrast to the area of the production of goods — institutions that will assist universities in "coupling" themselves to public needs while, at the same time, "buffering" themselves against being completely absorbed by societal tasks. Medical schools have, in some sense, succeeded in doing so through the system of teaching hospitals. While nobody would want to claim that our health system is satisfactory, few would disagree with the statement that teaching hospitals, the community hospitals, and the related neighborhood health centers that are coming into existence constitute elements of a workable ecology of health institutions.

Perhaps, in addition to institutions that can be responsible for the delivery of "care" (be it medical, urban, or environmental), for the education of practitioners, and for the acquisition of new knowledge, we need new types of "multisector" or "bridging" institutions. Such institutions could bring together government at all levels, industry, consumers of a variety of human services, and the university in flexible and even transitory arrangements that could mobilize a broad spectrum of technical know-how in the public interest. In these areas of societal problems few, if any, institutions now exist that could conduct R and D operations and, at the same time, be able to extend the range of operation to a chain that includes $R - D_1 - D_2 - E - F$. Here R and D_1 stand for the conventional R and D links of the chain; D_2 refers to a demonstration, or model, of a new system; E refers to the evaluation of performance of the system; and F stands for the social feedback that relates to goals and values which may be in need of error-correction.

When universities found that a single institution was unable to provide certain facilities, various types of consortia came into existence to operate a special facility, such as a big nuclear machine or a computer network. What is suggested here is a different type of consortium among institutions (or parts thereof) that are not all of the same kind. This type of consortium would provide both for complementary competences and a bridging function to other societal institutions or communities whose characteristics make it difficult for them to manage the whole innovative chain.

These bridging institutions ought to be so designed that they are coupled to higher education in the traditional sense (i.e., of the young) as well as with a kind of continued higher education of both adult individuals and existing institutions. For without this latter component we shall neither keep our society "s-and-т literate," nor be sure that s and т remain aware of what the impact of new knowledge upon our society might be.

This balance between the creation of new knowledge and a concern for its consequences of course is not new, but the concern for the mismatch gets more and more poignant as man's environment grows more s-and-т-dependent. The structure of the university seems to optimize the creation of new knowledge, hence a serious concern for its consequences can hardly be pursued without relation to the university. Centuries ago, Bacon told us that the search for truth was for both the greater glory of the creator and the relief of man's estate. Recently Weisskopf[19] has eloquently reformulated this complementarity of compassion and curiosity in relation to the human condition.

At this stage of man's history, science, technology, and the university must adapt to this essential complementarity.

CONCLUDING COMMENT

The past quarter-century has been characterized by the massive growth of what were formerly élite activities and institutions, to wit science, technology, and the university. The university, in technically advanced societies, has emerged as a key institution in the realms of both knowledge acquisition and social change.* Within it, the "specific gravity" of science and technology has increased dramatically under the stimulus of broad federal support. This has resulted in an entirely new scale and style of university research and has been the major contributor to the growth of the graduate and, in particular, of the postdoctoral population.

These occurrences have had a major impact upon all elements within the university, from curriculum reform to institutional leadership, and have clearly influenced its internal structure as well as its relation with the external world. These changes had their beginnings in the apparent magic of science and technology, which modified profoundly the expectations of government officials, of lay citizens, and of students alike for university contributions to social change and human welfare. These were the attitudes of the 1950s and they were not to continue into the 1960s. During the latter decade, the earlier and almost naive faith in the goodness and effectiveness of science and technology was largely replaced by disenchantment because of many poorly foreseen side-effects of technological advance.

In consequence, the university and science and technology now find themselves in a state of crisis of which funding is only one aspect. Society is no longer so sure that the kinds of knowledge universities can acquire uniquely well, and the kinds of education they conventionally dispense, are together truly relevant to current societal needs. This uncertainty is reflected, in combination with certain demographic and political realities, in the outlook of the labor market and in the career choices of the young.

Further, as institutions, the University, Science, and Technology must adapt to an age wherein the former mystique of science has been largely lost but wherein the goal of "higher education for all"[21] provides an opportunity to render both individuals and institutions in our society literate with respect to science and technology. Within such a new setting, science and technology as institutions must learn concern for a finite, complex, man-made globe in which the more we uncover at the "endless frontiers"[22] the broader the venture that is before us. Further, the institutions of the intellect face the task of differentiating themselves to a degree that is commensurate with the intellectual capital that has been amassed. But they must also find ways to strike a meaningful

* The university itself has not been an agent of social change deliberately,[20] but the university's educational and intellectual "output" has provided indispensable ingredients for such change.

balance between the search for new knowledge and the application of knowledge to satisfy societal needs.

Because science and technology are increasingly pervasive of human activity, they must accommodate themselves to the knowledge base, to the institutions wherein they can be contained, and must adjust themselves to the values that are associated with these institutional activities (and vice versa). Thus science, technology, and the university have major new tasks before them: (1) the adaptation of the institutions of the postindustrial society to the potential of man's brain and the hardware and software it creates; (2) the self-renewal of science, technology, the university, and the professional products of these environments; (3) the critical examination of the consequences of human thought and action, so as to distinguish between that which is technically feasible and that which is socially desirable or at least acceptable.

REFERENCES

1. Wolfle, D. (Editor). Symposium on Basic Research. AAAS, Publication No. 56, 1959, pp. 1-15.
2. Meeting Manpower Needs in Science and Technology: Graduate Training in Engineering, Mathematics and Physical Sciences. E. R. Gilliland, Chairman. (Report to the President's Science Advisory Committee by the PSAC Panel on Scientific and Technical Manpower.) U.S. Government Printing Office, December, 1962.
3. Kennedy, J. F. A Century of Scientific Conquest. *In* The Scientific Endeavor. Rockefeller Institute Press, 1965.
4. Federal Funds for Academic Science, Fiscal Year 1970. National Science Foundation 72-301, Washington, D.C., 1972.
5. Wolfle, D., and Kidd, C. V. The future market for Ph.D.'s. *Science* 173:784-793 (1971).
6. Hollomon, J. H. America's technological dilemma. *Technology Review* 73:30-40 (1971).
7. Heyns, Roger. The academic community. *The Graduate Journal* 8 (No. 1):9-20 (1968).
8. Weiss, Paul. Science in the University. *In* The Contemporary University (R. S. Morison, Editor). Houghton Mifflin, Boston, 1966.
9. Nisbet, Robert. The Degradation of the Academic Dogma. Basic Books, New York, 1971.
10. Rosenhead, J. University science for sale. *New Scientist* 43:582-584 (1969).
11. Ravetz, J. Ideological crisis in science. *New Scientist* 51:35-36 (1971).
12. Rose, S., and H. Social responsibility III: The myth of the neutrality of science. *Impact of Science on Society* 21 (2):137-149 (1971).
13. Perkins, J. Commencement address, Cornell University, June, 1969.
14. The Research System: France, Germany, United Kingdom. Vol. 1. Organisation for Economic Co-operation and Development, Paris, 1972, pp. 61-143.

15. Science, Growth, and Society, a New Perspective. Report of the Secretary-General's Ad Hoc Group on New Concepts of Science Policy. Organisation for Economic Co-operation and Development, Paris, 1971.
16. Wolfle, D. The supernatural department. *Science* 173:109 (1971).
17. R.L.E. 1946 + 20. Research Laboratory of Electronics. Massachusetts Institute of Technology, 1946, pp. v + 1-52.
18. Weinberg, A. M. The scientific university and the socio-technological institute in the 21st century. *The Graduate Journal* 8 (No. 2): 311-316.
19. Weiskopf, V. F. Physics in the 20th Century. M.I.T. Press, Cambridge, Mass., 1972, pp. ix and 364.
20. McDermott, W. The University as an Agent of Change. *In* Community Medicine, Teaching, Research and Health Care (W. Lathem and A. Newbery, Editors). Appleton-Century-Crofts, New York, 1970, pp. 5-15.
21. Prospectus for the Seventies. Presented by H. Cleveland, University of Hawaii, January 1970, pp. 1-39.
22. Bush, Vannevar. Science, the Endless Frontier. (A Report to the President on a Program for Post-War Scientific Research). U.S. Government Printing Office, Washington, D.C., July, 1945.

VI · *Support of Research and Graduate Education in the United States*

IVAN L. BENNETT, JR.

To avoid monographic proportions, this presentation is limited to a consideration of federal government support of academic research and graduate education in science. The acute fiscal ischemia created by the abrupt restraints on the federal science budget in 1966, far from being a transient phenomenon, has become a chronic, debilitating disorder, manifested by progressive atrophy of many segments of the nation's scientific endeavor.

In 1969, when it was becoming evident that the fiscal pause of 1966 was likely to be prolonged indefinitely, Dr. James A. Shannon pointed out that any new public policy for science must reflect the differing assessments and requirements of a series of "publics," including: the working scientist; the institutions that house him and lend him institutional support; the technologist concerned with the application of science; the program director of a federal agency; and the society at large in its perceptions of the benefits to be derived from sciences.[1]

He then went on to state and to justify three "propositions" concerning science in the United States. These are:

1. The most important strengths of U.S. science are its broad scope and general excellence, and these are due, in no small measure, to a support system characterized by pluralism.
2. The most important weakness of U.S. science is derived from the progressive decoupling that has occurred between research and education. Such decoupling results in part from the mechanisms utilized in support of academic research and from the lack of sufficient concern for the institutions of higher education.

IVAN L. BENNETT, JR. Director and Dean, New York University Medical Center, N.Y.

3. A second important weakness results from the progressive disenchantment of society with science, there being too little general understanding of the relation of much of the nation's substantial research undertakings and their ultimate social purpose.

I would like to comment briefly on this last point. The scientific community still faces a major task in reeducating the American public and their elected representatives about science, particularly basic research. We must devote our efforts to reorienting their expectations by fuller explanation and by avoiding overpromise for the short run.

The public's main source of information concerning science has been through newspapers, magazines, television, and other mass media. With notable exceptions, these have dwelt largely upon the short-term, practical results of applied research and technology as a series of isolated, newsworthy spectaculars.

Of course, the progress of science is not a series of discrete events, and to portray it only in this fashion is to miss the essential process — the continuous infrastructure of investigation and experiment by many individuals with many ideas, exploring many pathways in many disciplines. This, the heart of the scientific enterprise, is not now generally regarded as newsworthy. Consequently, the tendency of laymen to evaluate scientific endeavor on the basis of practical results alone is constantly intensified. The results are the only part of the continuum that anyone bothers to explain in understandable terms. I am in no way derogating science writers and reporters or detracting from the importance of their efforts. As a group, their genuine attempts to understand what science is really about are extremely impressive. The reluctance of the scientist to explain what he is doing is a far greater problem for them than it is for the man in the street. It does not suffice to depict basic research as analogous to an art form or a cultural activity. "Science for the sake of science" now sounds dangerously like "science for the sake of scientists." We must find ways of portraying the articulation of basic research and social and economic goals. We must demonstrate that while the short-term value of much basic research is measurable only in what economists call externalities, the results, in the longer run, open the way to social and economic benefits of the kind that the public understands and appreciates.

I believe it is no accident that present federal moves to increase support of research and development are limited almost entirely to such programs as the National Science Foundation's IRRPOS (Interdisciplinary Research Relevant to Problems of Our Society) and RANN (Research Applied to National Needs) programs, the Conquest of Cancer, and promised assorted technological initiatives to solve domestic social problems and to restore our balance of payments. Despite disclaimers and qualifying statements in small print, all of these create new expectations for the public that are unlikely to be fulfilled in the short run.

I now address the great weakness of the existing support system for academic science that Dr. Shannon has identified as "the progressive decoupling that has occurred between research and education." Along with others, I have said elsewhere much of what follows,[2] but it bears repetition. Some of the statistics are not completely updated, but the trends they represent have not changed significantly.

This discussion is limited to academic science and touches on applied science, development, and technology only in passing. Academic science encompasses research in the physical, biological, engineering, and social sciences that is carried out in the nation's universities and colleges and the related educational programs, predominantly at the graduate and professional level. Some of this research can be classified as basic* and some as applied** A small proportion of the work can properly be termed technological development.†

The determination of the exact proportion of each of these three subclasses of scientific investigation within the mix of academic science is a semantics problem and has no importance for overall policy. The important point is that after more than two decades of experience, academic science has come to include a varied array of scientific activities, concentrated in the basic sector, that can be carried out willingly, appropriately, and effectively in institutions of higher learning. Some 10 per cent of the total federal budget for research and development has supported research in colleges and universities (excluding federal contract research centers) during recent years.

It should be pointed out that academic science is responsible for about one-half of the nation's basic research, the most innovative segment of our overall scientific effort, often referred to as its "cutting edge." Gen-

---

* Systematic, intensive study directed toward fuller understanding of the subject under consideration, in which the primary aim of the investigator is an increase in scientific knowledge without regard to any utility of the knowledge gained.

** Systematic, intensive study directed toward fuller understanding of the subject under consideration, in which the primary aim of the investigator is practical use or application of the scientific knowledge gained.

† Systematic use of scientific knowledge for the production of useful materials, devices, systems, or methods, including design and development of prototype processes. Quality control and routine product-testing are not included.

erally, however, the nature, methodologies, and objectives of academic research are not qualitatively different from those of research performed in many nonprofit institutes, in municipal, state, and federal laboratories, or in industrial laboratories. It is not any peculiarity of scientific content that prompts consideration of academic science as an entity. Rather, it is the association of this portion of the nation's research endeavor with institutions of higher learning and its resulting effects, direct and indirect, upon higher education that create problems which should be of particular concern to the federal government and to the nation.

Graduate education is the culmination of the formal process of preparing individuals for teaching and for research and technical endeavor at the frontier of expanding knowledge and technological innovation. The graduate and professional schools of the United States now include a predominant portion of the intellectual resources that assure this country of a continuing capability to advance knowledge, to extend the base for technological progress, to influence the social, cultural, and economic quality of national life, and to exert intelligent and effective leadership in world affairs.

Graduate and professional programs are far more expensive for universities than is undergraduate education. Because they are so dependent upon federal funding, they were affected early by limitation of resources from the national government and, by now, appreciable reductions in students entering graduate programs in various disciplines are apparent.[3]

Training to the doctoral level no longer suffices to launch most scientists upon their careers as fully qualified researchers or teachers. Postdoctoral training has become a critical component of higher education, although it is not yet fully embedded in the academic structure. While federal budgetary stringency appeared at first to strike hardest at this important new area of advanced education in the sciences, the numbers of such students continue to increase, although the most recent survey by the Office of Scientific Personnel of the National Research Council[4] indicates that an increasing number of such appointments are going to individuals as a "holding operation" when they cannot find employment elsewhere.

At this stage in the evolution of federal programs of support of academic science, the following aspects of the situation are giving rise to problems:

Federal funds now support more than 75 per cent of all academic research. By far the greatest amount of this money ($1.235 billion of a total of $1.455 billion in FY 1967 and $1.359 billion of a total of $1.617 billion in FY 1971) is provided by the various "mission agencies"* as "project" or "program" grants or contracts for research in specific fields by individual faculty members or faculty groups of an institution. Each agency supports research in those areas (including mission-related basic research) that are relevant to its overall mission. Judgments of relevance were rather broad in the past, but tightening of budgets and such actions as the so-called Mansfield amendment have tended to lead to reassessment and stricter definition of "relevancy" by both the agencies and the Congress. Only 15 to 16 per cent ($218 million of a total of $1.455 billion in FY 1967 and $258 million of a total of $1.617 billion in FY 1971) of support has come from the NSF, the one agency authorized to support the advancement of knowledge in *all* fields of science. This fraction is estimated to rise to 20 per cent ($379 million of a total of $1.896 billion) in FY 1972, but much of this is a result of the NSF's commitment to applied research in the RANN program. The financial inability of the NSF to play a more significant role in funding university research during a time when mission-agency funds are dwindling and the range of their support is narrowing has posed severe and unprecedented problems in maintaining a *balanced* national development of the various branches of science for the future.

The growth of support for science from multiple federal sources for many years, plus the present retrenchment, now is posing increasing difficulties for the nation's institutions of higher learning in planning for *all* of their functions and activities.

Institutions of higher learning are hard-pressed to sustain all of their activities in the face of falling enrollments, increasing difficulties in securing additional funds from public and private sources, resistance to increasing tuition, demands that they undertake additional important service activities for localities, states, and the nation, and rising costs.

Academic research is so intimately interwoven with graduate and professional education in science and engineering that it is virtually impossible to consider federal support of research or the federal support of graduate and professional education in isolation, because any significant change in one is immediately reflected in the other.

Federal funds for research have become an important component of the overall financing of higher education in science (with the significance of the funds varying widely from institution to institution), because the graduate and professional schools are the source of the scientific and technical manpower so essential to the entire nation as well as to federal programs.

Total national expenditures for higher education have been increasing rapidly — from $11.2 billion in 1963-64 to $18.3 billion in 1967-68. Federal funds for higher education rose during this period from $3.2 to $4.4 billion. The proportion of total expenditures accounted for by federal funds more than tripled —

---

* This total was distributed among major federal departments and agencies in 1967 as follows: HEW, 48%; DOD, 17%; NSF, 15%; NASA, 7%; AEC, 6%; Other, 14% (includes Agriculture, Commerce, Housing and Urban Development, Interior, Labor, State, Transportation, Agency for International Development, and Veterans Administration).

from 7 to 24 per cent — between 1939-40 and 1967-68 (Table I). By 1980 the federal government may be supplying as much as 40 per cent of the total cost of higher education in the United States. The U.S. Commissioner of Education in 1969 predicted a total public outlay of $100 billion for all education by 1980 (about twice the present amount) and said that the federal government "obviously must bear a much more substantial share of the cost than at present." (Reported in the *N.Y. Times*, July 9, 1969).

The major trends in financing higher education are clear despite the disruption of the present general economic recession. The total cost of higher education has risen rapidly. The component covered by federal, state, and local governments is increasing. Academic science funds are now about 15 per cent of the total funds spent for higher education, but nonscience federal expenditures will soon exceed the science expenditures. In terms of national policy, federal expenditures for academic science must be considered in light of their general effects on colleges and universities, as well as in terms of their effects in the realm of science.

This brief description of the broad trends and status in financing higher education, the federal component, and the academic-science portion, portrays the general significance of federal funds for academic science to universities. They make it clear that the volume of funds for academic science, the stability of funding, and the terms and conditions under which the funds are available have important repercussions on colleges and universities — even those which are not critically dependent on these funds. In particular, it is evident that unless there is a pervasive continuing effort to avoid impeding, disrupting, or unbalancing the process of graduate and professional education for science and technology, serious problems will be created for the future.

During the past 10 years, the legislation that accounts for the sharp

TABLE I

Source of Funds for Undergraduate and Graduate Education in the U.S.

Source of Funding	1939-40	1967-68	1979-80
Total	100%	100%	100%
Institution (including tuition)	43	39	27
Donation and endowment	19	11	8
Public funds	38	50	65
Federal	(7)	(24)	(40)
State and local	(31)	(26)	(25)

Source: Office of Education, HEW, 1979-80 figures from American Council on Education. (Note: Figures on income for higher education differ slightly according to various sources. The Office of Education figures used here have been challenged, but the *general trends* that are important to this discussion exist, no matter what statistical source is used.)

increase in the flow of nonscience funds to universities (subject, of course, to the vagaries of Congressional appropriations and executive apportionment) represents the first step in the emergence of a new policy — an implied responsibility of the federal government for underwriting the support of universities, including their educational, service, and research functions. Logical proposals for revising federal programs for support of academic science can be framed, therefore, only by assuming explicitly that the federal responsibility thus far expressed in legislation and appropriations may be extended to general federal underpinning for higher education. It is becoming increasingly evident that there is real danger that any measures intended to strengthen and stabilize academic research and graduate education in science that neglect to consider all other functions of the universities can create further bias and imbalance within the higher educational system.

It is useful, I believe, to look at where we are and how we got here in the development of present federal programs of support for academic science. Soon after World War II, it became clear that pursuit of national objectives in health, agriculture, atomic energy, and defense would require an expanding effort in science, the principal resource for which was in the nation's universities. Federal action during the next two decades featured the development of many programs designed to utilize and to enlarge this capability in institutions of higher learning.

The country has benefited enormously from this close association of university capability and national purposes in several discrete areas. (1) The vigor and excellence of American science placed the United States in the vanguard of scientific and technological advance. It is still the envy of and the emulative model for the world. (2) Science was brought into more sensitive and responsive relationship to urgent public needs and national goals. (3) The entire framework of research and graduate education in science was strengthened and broadened, and the nation's resources of scientific manpower were substantially increased and enhanced. (4) The process of undergraduate education also benefited, through the enrichment of the academic environment, the quality of teaching, and the improved content of curricula that resulted from these developments. (5) The pluralistic system of federal support for academic research evolved and served the nation well. The principle of pluralism is basically sound and should be sustained, but it should now be modified and supplemented along lines to be suggested later.

Federal mission agencies have increasingly called on universities to perform research. Until 1966, the annual growth in federal funds for this purpose was nothing less than spectacular, averaging 22.7 per cent per year between 1956 and 1966 (see Table II).

TABLE II
Federal Funds for Research and Development in Universities*

Fiscal Year	Total Federal Funds** (millions of dollars)	Percent increase from pervious year
1955	144	—
1956	176	22
1957	224	27
1958	288	28
1959	367	27
1960	459	25
1961	585	27
1962	755	29
1963	900	17
1964	1,077	20
1965	1,194	11
1966	1,350	13
1967	1,455	7
1968	1,490	2.4
1969	1,526	2.4
1970	1,473	−3.5
1971	1,617	9
1972 (Estimated)	1,896	17

* Does not include federal contract research centers and AEC educational research centers.
** Figures for 1955-67 from NSF Federal Funds for Research, Development and Other Scientific Activities, Vol. XVII, 1968. (Later figures obtained from the Office of Science and Technology.)

It is hardly surprising that the nation's universities became highly dependent upon federal research funds. While it was obvious to all that this high annual rate of expansion of all federal funds for academic research could not continue indefinitely, the unexpected abruptness of the change in FY 1967 and the subsequent failure to provide the funds needed even to maintain the existing effort have created unforeseen and unintended difficulties for many institutions.

Federal funds for research and graduate education now come predominantly through mission agencies, whose responsibility and authority for supporting academic science are defined in terms of the tasks of the agency. Thus, the bulk of support for academic science is provided as a derivative and partial activity, largely through devices directed toward such discrete and limited segments of university activity as research projects and special training programs.

All of the federal agencies that support academic science have been more or less concerned with the effects of their activities on colleges and universities, and most have taken steps to provide a measure of institutional support. These initiatives, however, have been and will continue to be limited to the field for which the agency has responsibility — defense, health, space, etc., and, in the case of the NSF, for science totally. Even the NSF cannot provide funds not related to science or science education.

When the NSF was established in 1950, the National Science Board and the Director were assigned responsibility for: supporting basic research and scientific education so as to assure the continued health and vitality of the country's scientific resources and to serve the general welfare and interest; and developing and encouraging national policy for science and research.[5]

The NSF, for a variety of reasons, has been unable to fulfill its intended role. During the years when mission-agency budgets were growing rapidly, the broad objectives of the NSF were inadequately supported by the executive branch, the Congress, and the scientific community, except for a slight post-Sputnik flurry. Consequently, the abrupt drop in rate of growth of mission-agency budgets in FY 1967 found the NSF without the means to offset the uneven effects of the curtailment of funds for academic science. Indeed, even as late as FY 1969, the reduction by Congress of the NSF's proposed budget was the severest suffered by any of the agencies which finance academic science. The NSF is the only agency that Congress had established for the specific purpose of assuring the integrity of academic science. Yet, this agency was effectively prevented by Congress from fulfilling its function on the first occasion in history when the agency had become truly essential for the support of academic science.

The pattern of diffuse and subordinate attention to the overall needs of science, scientific education, and the universities as institutions is also reflected in Congress. Responsibility for the several federal agencies that furnish the principal support for academic science is divided among many committees and subcommittees in both the House and the Senate. This complicates the task of directing attention to the problems of the basic academic functions of universities in a context distinct from their usefulness to mission programs or the research interests of individual faculty members.

During the period of rapidly increasing budgets, the devices used by the various federal agencies were productive and flexible. But as the rate of increase has slackened, limitations of the system that were not evident during the earlier period have become very apparent. Means for insuring stability of support for academic science within individual institutions have proved to be inadequate, and means for assisting universities to deal with fluctuating levels of support are equally inadequate.

Several salient features of the existing support system are relevant to the further evolution of national policy and action. The dominant national urgencies were first perceived in areas demanding progress in the physical and biomedical sciences. Thus, the flow of federal science funds for research and graduate education has been almost exclusively directed to the natural sciences, with only limited and latterly recognition of the needs for expanding effort in the social sciences.

As mentioned, federal funding of universities for purposes other than science (Table I) has been increasing steadily. The science funds tend to be highly concentrated and the nonscience funds tend to be widely dispersed, so that the shifts in funding are not compensatory for individual institutions.

Federal support for research expanded rapidly as a means of achieving national goals. No other sources of funds were able or could have properly been asked to foot the bill, and there is no realistic prospect that academic research will cease to be dependent upon federal money. Private sources, while important, simply cannot bear the bulk of the cost. State and local funds are important in providing basic support for many colleges and universities, but this growing burden, plus other demands on their limited resources, prevents them from assuming the support for academic science that has evolved as a federal responsibility.

For several reasons, the effects of leveling or decreasing federal research budgets have not been distributed uniformly among universities and among parts of universities. The universities hardest hit seem to be: (1) those with low reserves, shaky state appropriations, or slender current endowment income; (2) those that have relatively new programs of research and graduate education; (3) those that receive a high proportion of their total research support from one or two federal agencies, particularly the NSF; (4) those that have made heavy commitments of their own funds in expectation of receiving federal funds that will not, in fact, be available.

Over the years, an accretion of onerous administrative requirements has proliferated red tape, unduly complicated relations between universities and federal agencies, and increased costs of operating the system. Federal funds for science can and should be administered more simply without reducing accountability for proper use of public funds.

The capacity of most institutions of higher learning to adapt has been nearly exhausted during these lean years and a continuing lack of growth in federal support of academic science research will affect programs of higher quality and scientists of higher competence.

The tightness of federal funds for academic science has demonstrated the urgent need to increase the capacity of colleges and universities to set policy and to make decisions of two types. The first is to establish general institutional goals that place scientific research soundly within the context of the total array of functions of the institution. The second is to reach a sound balance between two important objectives that are difficult to reconcile — on the one hand, maintenance of economy, efficiency, accountability, and order and, on the other hand, maintenance of the important values of academic freedom for schools, departments, and individuals. This is primarily a problem for the institutions, but the task could be made easier by proper federal policy.

It is now clear that a system designed fundamentally to meet the needs of federal agencies for science and technology is not an adequate means of meeting the emerging responsibilities of the federal government for support of higher education. Many of the questions now raised with respect to the "adequacy" of the federal system for support of academic science are, in reality, directed to the more fundamental question of the nature of the responsibilities of the federal government for the support of universities and, particularly, for the support of graduate education. We must recognize that the agencies which compose the network supporting academic science serve essentially as separate conduits for funds to support research, training, or institutional development, but, in concert, they do not function as a system responsive to the needs of universities in general because they were not intended or designed to constitute such a system.

Forging a new and more logical relationship between federal support for academic science and the emerging federal role in total support of higher education is a major task for the next decade. This process will require major changes in approach, in the structure of the executive branch, and in legislation over a wide front. This overall policy area is more significant and far less well-defined than are the policy questions relating to academic science as a discrete problem.

During the past two years, as a result of constraints on federal funding of academic science and research training, constraints on funding of all R and D, curtailment of procurement in national defense and aerospace programs, and the general economic recession, there has been sizeable unemployment among scientists and engineers. In addition, newly graduated Ph.D.'s in many scientific (and other) disciplines have experienced difficulty in finding employment that fits with their ambitions and hopes. This has generated political heat, has been used as an argument for further reductions in federal fellowships and training grants and has resulted in a spate of studies and publications concerning future short-ages and surpluses of manpower in science and engineering.[6]

I have reviewed much of the literature listed in Reference 6 in detail and have participated in a few studies and innumerable discussions of these problems. This is not to imply that I understand all of the argu-ments that have been set forth, particularly by economists who look at the market mechanism for scientists and engineers and who discuss "ex-ternalities" and the differences between private and social rates of "time discounting," and so forth. Indeed, I would much prefer to avoid com-pletely the whole set of issues and arguments in this presentation. As it is, however, I will limit coverage to a list of my personal convictions and conclusions at this truly rudimentary stage of development of real under-standing in this area:

1. The subject is important and massively complex. It deserves intensive study and research.

2. We now lack the information base, the theory, the methodologies, and the predictive models to allow conclusions that can form a valid basis for major changes in mechanisms, funding, or policy for support of graduate education in science.

3. It would probably be a good thing for the country if federal policy for support of science, support of education, and the nation's long-term "require-ments" for skilled manpower eventually could be coordinated or, at least, rationalized.

4. Science and technology will continue to be important to the nation, and the annual erosion of the financial base of the "production system" for trained scientists and engineers, a system with a lag-time of several years, is a most dangerous form of false economy.

5. Finally, I would point out that we are in a time of enormous pressures to rationalize reductions in federal spending for both economic and political reasons. To take an example, it is argued that federal support of research train-ing creates expectations on the part of the trainee that place the government in a position of responsibility to meet these expectations. There is no reason to believe that support of research training raises any more expectations than does support of research itself. The reductions in federal support for research and training that began five years ago for reasons of budgetary stringency alone have now led (and hardly unexpectedly) to a situation in which there are evi-dences of a "surplus" or of "underutilization" of scientific personnel. To use this as the basis for a new policy for further reductions or major changes in mechanisms of training support is hardly conducive to confidence that anything other than budgetary expediency is being considered seriously as a criterion for action.

The foregoing statements admittedly are tinged with a note of per-sonal frustration with current federal attitudes and actions, but, in fair-ness, it must be said that the eventual solution of the problem is far from being a simple governmental matter. One of the best statements of what might be involved is the summary by Wolfle and Kidd[7] of a conference sponsored by the Association of American Universities in April, 1971, which I can do no better than to quote:

> While universities ought to maintain much individuality, and while freedom of scholarly effort is a value to be preserved, some problems are too big to be handled by universities acting independently. Controlling the flow — which need not mean dropping below present levels but which would probably mean both slowing the rate of growth and reorienting some of the educational programs — would require collective action. Complete freedom of choice by each university and each college that wishes to become a university would mean that the sum of individually defined interests would add up to a national disservice. A proportionate reduction over all universities would not be the wisest procedure. Yet collective controls which grant continued opportunities for graduate education to the already well-established universities and deny that opportunity to institutions that have high aspirations but not yet reputations or facilities will inevitably create interinstitutional tensions. Somehow, within this difficult situation, efforts should be made to agree upon the desirable flow of new doctorates and upon the universities that can best prepare them. Because large amounts of federal funds will be involved, the federal government should be a partner in the planning. But the universities had better also try to be partners. There will be more shocks in the market place and much lively debate before controlling mechanisms are adopted, but we think it essential that universities move toward a state in which their graduate offerings are conducted within the guidelines of a national pattern.

> Even if agreement on "Solutions" is reached, the processes of adjustment will be difficult. More stringent admission standards, quotas, reduced financial support, incentives, or other means of controlling the number of doctorates will challenge established values, frustrate many students and many professors, exacerbate tensions among established and emerging institutions, aggravate the uneasy relationships between universities and government, complicate faculty-administration problems, and accentuate differences between older and younger faculty members. Some academicians will no doubt be inclined to the view that difficulties in the job market for young doctorates created by a laissez-faire approach are moderate compared with the difficulties that will be generated by efforts to adjust supply and demand.

> We are of the opinion that these problems must be faced, and that the long-range imbalance, inequities, and strains arising from ignoring the problem will far outweigh the stresses generated by efforts to cope with it.

SUMMARY OF NEEDS AND PROBLEMS

More Money for Academic Science

The responsibility of the NSF must be matched by congressional willingness to make sufficient resources available for "balancing" the system, the magnitude of which is defined, in large measure, by the demands placed by the other agencies upon the universities. The NSF simply will be unable to perform the function without sizable budget increases and the present pattern of increases for applied programs in the NSF is inappropriate to meet this need.

More Than Money

Additional funding alone, however, within the existing pattern and under existing policies, will merely postpone, rather than solve, the problems of academic science. These problems include: inconsistencies among agencies in policies, procedures, and practices in day-to-day dealings with institutions that have become major sources of dissatisfaction and irritation; difficulties raised by the pressure of many mission agencies to narrow the range of their support of academic research as a result of continuing budgetary constrains or changes in their mission needs; obstacles that these actions by the mission agencies cause the NSF in trying to "fill the vacuum"; the need for agencies to allow universities the maximum flexibility in administering limited funds; the repeatedly recognized need for sustained, flexible, long-run institutional support to minimize the disruptions produced by fluctuations in project support.

New Policy and New Structure for Academic Science

The existing policy structure for academic science in federal government can best be described as a loose network lacking a prime mover and without a strong center for long-range planning or evaluation. Present support is fractionated and there is no really effective focus of responsibility.

In sum, there is a need for a better focus of organizational responsibility and a system for fuller, prospective, "horizontal" consideration of the budgetary requirements of academic science among the programs of the many agencies involved in utilizing the resources of the universities.

Finally, there is a need for a better system for examining and setting ultimate goals. These have been well stated by Don K. Price[8]:

We have to learn how to support an educational and scientific establishment including private as well as public institutions, without either destroying its freedom or leaving it in a position of privileged irresponsibility. We have to learn how to fit the research interests of free scientists into a pattern of public policy and to take account of the need for balanced national development while building up our existing centers of high scientific quality. And we need, equally obviously, to devote our knowledge to the service of human welfare, as effectively as it has been enlisted in the service of national defense.

A Means of Reconciling Goals
for Academic Science and Higher Education

The existing arrangements for evolving strategies for academic science or for appraising the interaction of the natural sciences with the humanities and social sciences are inadequate. The present arrangement displays only ad hoc organization for communication and consultation within the federal components of the system and externally with academic institutions and their intermediaries. Under the theory that has prevailed until now, advance consultation among agencies to adjust proposed actions that will affect higher education and academic science should be effective.

It is time to strengthen the federal organization for planning, balancing, and communicating between the function of supporting academic science and the emerging federal function of general support for higher education. Therefore, any structural remedy must go beyond a concern for academic science alone and place research and education in a unified perspective.

RECOMMENDATIONS

I. Establish more stable funding for academic science.
   A. Prepare a three-year "indicative plan" for federal support of science, including minimal projections for funding by all the agencies that now support academic research.
      1. Any change could be an add-on and the plan could be extended yearly.
   B. Increase the research budget of the National Science Foundation.
II. Continue and strengthen the existing system of pluralistic support.
   A. Mission-oriented agencies should continue to finance academic research and advanced training that are related to and part of their missions.
   B. Enhance the "flexibility" of federal support of colleges and universities by making funds available on an institutional basis for those research-related activities they select.
      1. The key to such funding is employing a formula that will alleviate imbalances.
III. Improve administration of federal academic-science programs.
   A. Reduce administrative inconsistencies.
   B. Cushion the shock of unexpected restriction of funds through arrangements to "phase out" support over a reasonable period of time.

1. The NASA approach — a three-year grant with two years of initial funding on a 1 $2\!/\!3$ to $1\!/\!3$ basis — is an example.

IV. Improve the organization of the Executive Office for science and education.

   A. Leadership and coordination of the departments and the establishment of policy to be performed properly in a number of agencies can be undertaken effectively only in the executive office.

or

   B. Establish by legislation a statutory Council of Advisers in Education and Science, the members of which would be presidential appointees.

      1. The Council would consider the complex problems of education (particularly graduate education) and science (particularly academic science).

      2. The Council would interpret to the Congress an understanding of the facts and of administrative positions on national goals in science, technology, and education, reporting to pertinent congressional committees on progress in both public and private bodies.

      3. The Council would not be responsible for carrying out programs, but would be influential through its relationship to the President, to the Office of Management and Budget, to the Cabinet, and to the Congress.

      4. The Council would examine interactions of science with social development, international relations, technological advances, and economic growth.

or

   C. Broaden and strengthen the Office of Science and Technology.

      1. Redraft the OST charter to include graduate education, and ratify it by legislation.

         a. Such legislation would help to generate congressional support and the understanding that OST is responsive to the Congress, although it is responsible to the President.

         b. Definition of function should be made by presidential action.

(NOTE: As between a new statutory council and a revision of the charter of OST, I recommend that a council be established by law, although either alternative would result in marked improvement of the capability of the Executive Office to serve the President and to help the Congress. The reasons that I prefer the statutory council are these:

1. Science and education are now as significant to the national welfare as economic development, and the federal role in these areas is expanding and becoming more complex. It is important that the Congress ratify this estimate.

2. A new statutory council would avoid the strong coloration of science and technology that would follow from putting the combined functions in OST.

3. The council form would provide for the expression of varying philosophies by persons with dissimilar backgrounds.

4. Establishment of a council by law would expose issues to broad public debate and would ratify the operation in the eyes of the Congress.)

or

D. Consider the establishment of a new cabinet post, the Department of Higher Education.

   1. It is desirable to place as many functions of the executive branch as possible in operating departments and agencies to help reduce presidential responsibility.

   2. Questions presented by this action:

      a. Should the federal government be organized so that responsibility for higher education is separated from other education?

      b. Should responsibility for science be separated from responsibility for technology?

      c. Might it not be advisable to consider establishing a broad Department of Education and a separate Department of Science?

      d. Should the education function be split off from the health and welfare functions, involving a significant shift in the philosophy underlying the existing Department of Health, Education and Welfare?

It is my conclusion that the next practical steps involve changes short of the establishment of a new cabinet department. It is, in fact, highly probable that the establishment of the proposed statutory Council on Education and Science would serve adequately for the foreseeable future the functions that have been suggested for a new department, because the key functions are those that can be performed effectively only as part of the presidency.

REFERENCES

1. Shannon, J. A. Centralization of Federal Science Activities. (Testimony before House Subcommittee on Science, Research, and Development, 91st Congress, 1st Session.) U.S. Government Printing Office, Washington, D.C., July 30, 1969.

2. Bennett, I. L., Jr. Research in the Service of Man. (Application of Biomedical Knowledge; The White House View). Senate Subcommittee on Government Research. U.S. Government Printing Office, Washington, D.C., 1967.

—— Future of federal support for the biological sciences. *Fed. Proc.* 26 (No. 5): 1281 (1967).

—— Research in the Service of Man. (Testimony before Senate Subcommittee on Government Research, 90th Congress, 1st Session.) U.S. Government Printing Office, Washington, D.C., 1967.

—— National Commission on Health, Science, and Society. (Testimony before Senate Subcommittee on Government Research, 90th Congress, 2nd Session.) U.S. Government Printing Office, Washington, D.C., 1968.

—— Centralization of Federal Science Activities. (Testimony before House Subcommittee on Science, Research, and Development, 91st Congress, 1st Session.) U.S. Government Printing Office, Washington, D.C., 1969.

—— Support for Biomedical Research: A View from OST. *Fed. Proc.* 28 (No. 5): 1592 (1969).

3. Science Resources Studies. Recent Trends in Enrollment and Manpower Resources in Graduate Science Education, 1969-70. National Science Foundation (NSF 71-14), Washington, D.C., May 26, 1971.

4. Employment of New Ph.D.'s and Postdoctorals in 1971. Office of Scientific Personnel, National Research Council, Washington, D.C.

5. NSF Report to UNESCO on U.S. Science Policy, 1968.

6. Resources for Biomedical Research and Education. Report No. 16, USDHEW, PHS, NIH, March, 1969.

Graduate Student Support and Manpower Resources in Graduate Science. National Science Foundation, NSF 70-40, September, 1970.

Issue Paper on The Training Programs of the Institutes of the National Institutes of Health, Part I. USDHEW, NIH, October, 1970.

Impact of Changes in Federal Science Funding Patterns on Academic Institutions. National Science Foundation, NSF 70-48, December, 1970.

Education and Employment Patterns of Bioscientists. Office of Scientific Personnel of National Research Council, National Academy of Sciences, February, 1971.

Cartter, A. M. Scientific Manpower for 1970-1985. *Science* 172: 132 (April 9, 1971).

1969 and 1980 Science and Engineering Doctorate Supply and Utilization. National Science Foundation, NSF 71-20, May, 1971.

Terman, F. E. Supply of Scientific and Engineering Manpower: Surplus or Shortage. *Science* 173: 399 (July 30, 1971).

Employment of New Ph.D.'s and Postdoctorals in 1971. Office of Scientific Personnel of National Research Council, National Academy of Sciences, August 1, 1971.

Wolfle, D. and Kidd, C. V. The Future Market for Ph.D.'s. *Science* 173: 784 (August 27, 1971).

7. Wolfle, D., and Kidd, C. V. op. cit.

8. Orlans, H. (ed.). Science Policy and the University. Brookings Institution, Washington, D.C., 1968, p. 38.

THE FEDERAL SUPPORT
OF SCIENCE

VII · *The Physical Sciences: Bellwether of Science Policy*

HARVEY BROOKS

IT IS APPROPRIATE that our discussion of public policy and the federal support of science should begin with engineering, mathematics, and the physical sciences, which, for convenience, I will call EMP. It is in these three fields that the general pattern of federal science policy has been set during the quarter century since the end of World War II. Although it is true that the spectacular growth of the biomedical sciences after 1956 set a somewhat different style from EMP, it was still an adaptation, rather than a radically new departure. More recently, the rapid expansion in support of the social sciences has tended to follow a similar pattern.

No history of American science policy can be told without an understanding of the deep and pervasive influence of the military. This is not peculiar to the postwar period, but has been true throughout the history of the Republic. The greatest periods of scientific development have tended to follow military crises, during which new scientific institutions were created, ostensibly to meet an emergency. Subsequently, these institutions were turned towards the fostering of fundamental science, and the diffusion and "civilianization" of technology originally developed for a military purpose. This is the history of the National Academy of Sciences, the National Research Council, the National Advisory Committee for Aeronautics (NACA), the Atomic Energy Commission (AEC), the National Aeronautics and Space Administration (NASA), and even, in some measure, the National Science Foundation, which was patterned in part after the Office of Scientific Research and Development (OSRD).[1]

Nevertheless, I shall begin this account with World War II, because this was a real turning point in the formation of an American science

HARVEY BROOKS Dean, Division of Engineering and Applied Physics, Harvard University, Cambridge, Mass.

policy and a sharp departure from the past, in respect to the permanent and irreversible involvement of the federal government in the support and management of the national scientific enterprise. One cannot understand either the weaknesses and strengths of what exists today or the salient issues for the future without an appreciation of the historical origins of our present national scientific and technological establishment, which, except in the universities, is overwhelmingly dominated by EMP.

"SCIENCE, THE ENDLESS FRONTIER"

During the period between World War I and World War II, military research and development was severely contracted along with all other military activities of government. In 1938, more than 40 per cent of the federal funds for research were expended by the Department of Agriculture. In 1936, an Army General Staff report stated that "the Army needs large quantities of excellent equipment that has already been developed" but that "the amount of funds allocated to research and development in former years is in excess of the proper proportion for the item in consideration of the rearmament program."[2] Thus, the military services entered World War II as reluctant recipients of new technology, an attitude in sharp contrast to the later euphoria about advanced technology, which reached its culmination in the science-fictional plans of the U.S. Air Force in the early 1960s.

The imminence of World War II generated a mobilization of the leaders of American science in advance of American participation in the war. The story has been graphically told by Conant[3] and Bush[4] in their memoirs. Through the lobbying of the scientists, first the National Defense Research Committee (NDRC) and later the OSRD were created as civilian agencies reporting directly to the president, with an extremely open-ended charter to do military R and D wherever the need was foreseen by scientists themselves. Whereas technical advances in World War I had been generated largely from existing military needs, many of the World War II advances were born in the laboratory, almost as solutions looking for problems. Their military application was evolved as military strategy and technology were developed in tandem, with scientists and the military in equal partnership. As Professor Warner Schilling of Columbia University has recounted,[5] scientists "were eventually able to persuade the soldiers to inform them of the general military problems involved in order that the scientists might reach their own conclusions about the kinds of weapons and devices the military would need to meet those problems." Unlike the situation in World War I, science in World War II was mobilized under civilian tutelage, with the leaders of the scientific community having direct access to the president and to the congressional appropriations committees, if necessary over the heads of the military.[5]

The experience of World War II had a profound impact on both the political and scientific leadership and crucially influenced the position of science relative to government after the war. The wartime experience of our scientific leadership was crystallized in the report *Science, the Endless Frontier,* which Bush induced President Roosevelt to ask him to prepare in November, 1944, before the end of hostilities, and which was published in July, 1945.[6]

The main points made in the Bush report can all be recognized in recent and current thinking about national science policy. They can be summarized in the following quotations:

1. Science can be effective in the national welfare only as a member of a team, whether the conditions be peace or war. But without scientific progress no amount of achievement in other directions can insure our health, prosperity, and security as a nation in the modern world. (p. 5)

2. If we are to maintain the progress in medicine which has marked the last 25 years, the Government should extend financial support to basic medical research in the medical schools and in universities. (p. 6)

3. It is essential that civilian scientists continue in peace-time some portion of those contributions to national security which they have made so effectively during the war. This can best be done through a civilian-controlled organization with close liaison with the Army and Navy, but with funds direct from Congress, and the clear power to initiate military research which will supplement and strengthen that carried on directly under the control of the Army and Navy. (p. 6)

4. . . . new products and processes are not born full-grown. They are founded on new principles and new conceptions which in turn result from basic scientific research. Basic scientific research is scientific capital. Moreover, we cannot any longer depend upon Europe as a major source of this scientific capital. Clearly, more and better scientific research is one essential to the achievement of our goal of full employment. (p. 6)

5. If the colleges, universities, and research institutes are to meet the rapidly increasing demands of industry and Government for new scientific knowledge, their basic research should be strengthened by use of public funds. (p. 7)

6. To provide coordination of the common scientific activities of these governmental agencies as to policies and budgets, a permanent Science Advisory Board should be created to advise the executive and legislative branches of Government on these matters.

7. The real ceiling on our productivity of new scientific knowledge and its application in the war against disease, and the development of new products and new industries, is the number of trained scientists available.

The Government should provide a reasonable number of undergraduate scholarships and graduate fellowships in order to develop scientific talent in American youth. The plans should be designed to attract into science only that proportion of youthful talent appropriate to the needs of science in relation to other needs of the Nation for high abilities. The most immediate prospect of making up the deficit in scientific personnel is to develop the scientific talent in the generation now in uniform. (pp. 7-8)

8. The Government should accept new responsibilities for promoting the flow of new scientific knowledge and the development of scientific talent in our youth. . . .

Therefore I recommend that a new agency for these purposes be established. Such an agency should be composed of persons of broad interest and experience, having an understanding of the peculiarities of scientific research and scientific education. (pp. 8-9)

In relation to the "peculiarities of scientific research," Bush's committee spelled out five basic principles which "must underlie the program of Government support for scientific research and education." These were summarized as follows:

1) Whatever the extent of support may be, there must be stability of funds over a period of years so that long-range programs may be undertaken.

2) The agency to administer such funds should be composed of citizens selected only on the basis of their interest in and capacity to promote the work of the agency. They should be persons of broad interest in and understanding of the peculiarities of scientific research and education.

3) The agency should promote research through contracts or grants to organizations outside the Federal Government. It should not operate any laboratories of its own.

4) Support of basic research in the public and private colleges, universities, and research institutes must leave the internal control of policy, personnel, and the method and scope of the research to the institutions themselves. This is of the utmost importance.

5) While assuring complete independence and freedom for the nature, scope, and methodology of research carried on in the institutions receiving public funds, and while retaining discretion in the allocation of funds among such institutions, the Foundation proposed herein must be responsible to the President and the Congress. . . . The usual controls of audits, reports, budgeting, and the like, should, of course, apply to the administrative and fiscal operations of the Foundation, subject, however, to such adjustments in procedure as are necessary to meet the special requirements of research. (p. 33)

The eight recommendations and the five basic principles together constitute a charter of national science policy, and have supplied the implicit premises on which most federal support of science, particularly in the universities, has been undertaken in the past 25 years. Nevertheless, reality has diverged from the blueprint in a number of significant respects.

First, the report had envisioned a fairly monolithic organization for research support that was to have a division of medical research, a division of military research, and a division of natural sciences. In the event, the functions of the first division were taken over by the independent National Institutes of Health (NIH), an almost autonomous unit within the Department of Health, Education, and Welfare (HEW). The functions of the second were assumed initially by the Office of Naval Research, and later shared among the "OXR's"* of the three services and the Advanced Research Projects Agency (ARPA). Of these, only ARPA followed the recommended pattern of full civilian management. The functions of the third division were assumed initially by the Office of Naval Research (ONR) and the Atomic Energy Commission, which were later joined by the other research agencies of the Department of Defense (DOD), the National Science Foundation, and, to a partial extent, NASA. Even within the disease-oriented National Institutes of Health, a new institute of General Medical Sciences was created to support biology not uniquely related to a particular disease. Even the fellowship and educational functions were split among several agencies, including the National Science Foundation, the Office of Education in the Department of Health, Education, and Welfare, and to some extent NASA, the NIH, and the AEC.

This pluralism made the problem of stability of policy and funding much more difficult, and although the functions apparently envisioned for the Permanent Science Advisory Board were nominally assumed by the President's Science Advisory Committee (PSAC) and the Office of Science and Technology (OST), it proved impossible in practice to secure more than partial coordination of such a far-flung empire against the internal priorities of agencies whose primary concern was not necessarily with the health of scientific research and education as such. Even in the case of academic research, the NSF's share of total federal support has reached only 20 per cent, whereas for federally supported basic research as a whole, the NSF's share is only a little more than 10 per cent. Thus, the span of policy and budgetary control by a group whose primary concern was the effectiveness of science was always limited.

Nevertheless, the system worked surprisingly smoothly as long as total resources were increasing, as they did with few interruptions from 1946 through 1966. For example, in the period 1957 to 1964, total support for biomedical research in medical schools increased at the rate of 23 per cent a year. During the same period, nonbiomedical academic research grew at 14.5 per cent a year, and the annual growth rate of federal support for such research was 16 per cent. In such a period, ques-

---

* OXR is a generic term, in which X = N (naval), X = A (army) or X = S (scientific, air force).

tions of relative priority received little overt attention, because worthy new projects and new investigators could be supported with comparatively little detriment to work already under way. Basically, the system was manpower-limited throughout the postwar period, as indicated by the fact that the United States was importing foreign scientists and engineers, including graduate students, at an accelerating rate through almost the entire period.

Since about 1967, however, the scientific enterprise has faced an entirely new situation. Direct support for academic research as a whole has declined about 17 per cent in real terms from its peak. On a national basis, the total federal R and D outlays have declined from $12.7 billion in 1967 to $9.6 billion in 1972, as measured in 1958 dollars of R and D purchasing power.[7] Real support of federal R and D is less than in 1963 and has thus declined about 24 per cent from its peak in real purchasing power. This decline has probably fallen most heavily on EMP, because about 7/8 of the federal money is in these areas — mostly, of course, in industry, government laboratories, and captive contract research centers. Significant unemployment has appeared among scientists and engineers for the first time since the Great Depression, and is worst among physicists. Although the rate of unemployment is considerably lower among Ph.D.'s than among less-trained people, and lower than in the general labor force, its impact on the morale of the scientific community, and particularly on young scientists, has been disastrous. It has engendered bitterness, disillusionment, and hostility toward government and the science "establishment."

The disruption has been produced primarily by governmental actions and policies. Privately financed industrial research continued to grow at a steady rate throughout the 1960s, and only leveled off with the recession of 1970 and 1971. Because of the acceleration of inflation, however, there has been a decline in manpower supported by industrial research. In effect, three crises have coincided: the collapse of the market for science faculty, especially in the leading unversities; the shrinkage of the aerospace and electronics industries, the two largest industrial employers of R and D manpower; and the industrial recession, combined with inflation, which has cut into real private R and D spending. Although graduate enrollments declined in response to declining employment prospects, it will be four or five years before this affects the output of Ph.D.'s appreciably. In addition, a large "holding pattern" of postdoctoral scientists has accumulated in the universities, especially in physics, which hangs suspended over the employment market.

It must be remembered that there was an element of "boot-strapping" in the growth of faculty and graduate enrollment, especially in the 1960s.

The growth in enrollment generated a demand for faculty, which created more job prospects for faculty, which attracted further graduate enrollment, even though external demand for scientists in industry and government began to decline after 1965. Thus, for example, in the physical sciences and engineering, initial employment of new Ph.D.'s by industry declined from 44 per cent in 1958-60 to 30 per cent in 1964-66, while initial academic employment increased from 39 per cent to 48 per cent in the same interval.[8] Total employment of physics Ph.D.'s in industry and government together declined from 37 per cent in 1960 to 30 per cent in 1970.[9]

There now is a sudden sense that the "endless frontier" has come to an end, like the geographical frontier of a century ago from which it draws its name. EMP. seems to face a glum future, no longer tied to any overriding national goal and faced with political reaction against the goals with which it had been sold to the electorate in the recent past. The contraction of the prospects for political and financial support in the physical sciences, especially in physics, astronomy, chemistry, and mathematics, occurs at a time when, to the practitioners in these fields, the scientific accomplishments and opportunities are more exciting and extensive than ever before.

In many ways, the prospects faced by the physical sciences are unprecedented. Even during the Great Depression, support for science in the universities and for R and D in industry and government was growing substantially, except for a brief retrogression in 1934. On the average, over the decade 1930 to 1940, funding of academic science grew by 6 per cent annually, while R and D funding as a whole grew nearly 9 per cent annually. Despite widespread unemployment among Ph.D.'s, young scientists were entering the system, and the nation's capability for doing science was growing.[10] Even though there was much bemoaning the sad state of science, and many were blaming underemployment on the automation resulting from advancing science and technology,[11] the system remained basically healthy, and the number of employed scientists and engineers continued to grow as a proportion of the professional and technical work force.

THE SPECIAL CHARACTERISTICS OF EMP

The physical sciences and engineering share certain characteristics that have a bearing on their role in science policy. First, physical scientists and engineers are employed in industrial research and development to a greater extent than are other technical groups. Furthermore, the fraction of Ph.D.'s employed outside academic institutions is higher than for other disciplines, ranging between 50 per cent and 70 per cent, with chemistry having the highest nonacademic representation. As a consequence, the competitive standards both for salaries and for support with instrumentation, materiel, and technician help tend to be set by the nonacademic sectors.

Second, those subfields of the various disciplines that are cultivated in universities have been strongly influenced by job prospects outside of academia, particularly in engineering. That engineering schools have concentrated on electronics and aerospace subjects is not surprising when it is considered that, between 1959 and 1965, 80 per cent of all the growth in industrial R and D employment occurred in just two industries — aerospace, and electrical equipment and communications.[12] The rapid relative growth of engineering Ph.D. output, as compared with other scientific fields, has been responsive to high salaries and good employment prospects for people with advanced degrees in these high-technology industries, which are also heavily dependent on federal R and D funding.

Third, EMP has a unique relationship to military and space technology. This has been especially true of physics and engineering, less so of chemistry. In 1968, the number of physics Ph.D.'s in jobs involving federally supported research was 62 per cent of all physics Ph.D.'s, as compared with 43 per cent for Ph.D. scientists as a whole.[13] Throughout the 1960s, the percentage of federal R and D expenditures in space technology and national defense hovered at 90 per cent, and fell only gradually to 78 per cent in 1972.[14] Until recently, 38 per cent of the support of the physical sciences in universities came from the Department of Defense and NASA, and for the best-known engineering schools, the figure was as high as 65 per cent. Because of the importance and growth of biomedical research in universities, the percentage of space and defense support for academic research as a whole was much smaller than for EMP.

Fourth, the physical sciences are characterized, more than most fields, by large projects organized around unique equipment and facilities. This is particularly true of nuclear physics, particle physics, astronomy, and space science. In such areas, a higher fraction of the support necessarily goes into just keeping the facilities in operation, which means that the research productivity of such facilities is much more sensitive to small changes in funding levels than is the typical individual project, characteristic of other areas of research.

The above point is illustrated by the situation in elementary particle physics. In 1971, the operating and staffing costs of eight major facilities and of accelerator development consumed 73 per cent of the federal funds allotted to the field. Yet 76 per cent of the Ph.D. physicists conducting research in particle physics were situated in universities, mostly as members of user groups that were designing, performing, and interpreting experiments at the major centers.

Finally, the physical sciences have the highest degree of "codification" of any of the experimental sciences. According to the definition of Merton and Zuckerman,[15] "codification refers to the consolidation of empirical knowledge into succint and independent theoretical formulations." This characteristic leads to a unity of the physical sciences that also embraces most of engineering and has an important bearing on the relationship of theory to practice and basic research to application. This is because detailed empirical knowledge can be subsumed under general principles from which details to fit specific situations can be regenerated at will. It is in this sense that basic research in the physical sciences is "scientific capital."

UNRESOLVED ISSUES

I would now like to turn to several unresolved issues of science policy. These are not all unique to engineering, mathematics, and the physical sciences, but generally they have been raised first or most acutely in one or more of these fields.

Overspecialization

Until 1965, it was widely believed that massive support of space and defense technologies by the federal government resulted in extensive benefits to the civilian economy, a process known as "spin-off." This view was also widely popularized in Europe by such writers as Servan-Schreiber[16] and was taken up by European politicians under the slogan of the "technology gap."

There is no question that defense and space spending have accelerated the commercialization of a few key technologies, such as computers, solid state electronics, jet aircraft, and satellite communications, in which the United States dominates the international market. However, this achievement has come at a price — a price that is only just beginning to be appreciated. Excessive demands for highly skilled technical and managerial manpower raised the cost of R and D relative to that of our foreign competitors and probably helped to price innovation out of the market for the more mature or traditional industries, such as steel or textiles. Thus, R and D has lagged in the United States, except in a few highly sophisticated technologies. The United States has maintained a large favorable trade balance in high-technology products, amounting to about $9 billion, about $7 billion of which is with less-industrialized countries. But, at the same time, the balance of trade in low-technology products — and even in the more "mature" products of high-technology industries, such as radio and TV and automobile components — has gone heavily against us.[17] The rapid diffusion of new technology, and the fact that technological know-how can be purchased and adopted by technically sophisticated countries at much lower cost than it can be developed, make even our superiority in a few products a rapidly wasting asset. That asset can be maintained only by continual development and commercialization of new or superior products not yet made by foreign manufacturers.

Not only has the United States possibly overspecialized in a few technological areas, but large amounts of technical manpower have been channeled into end-item developments, such as the Apollo program, which have little generic significance. Most spin-off comes from the more basic and generic and less particularistic aspects of these developments, the part that costs relatively little. For example, the theory of automatic controls and methods for optimizing industrial process control have benefited from advances in control theory stimulated by the needs of space and missile programs. The concepts have also found application in economics and in inventory management.

Outside of space, defense, nuclear energy, and agriculture, the United States government devotes less R and D funds to civilian industrial technology as a proportion of gross national product than do most other industrial nations. This also applies to most of the missions of government other than defense and space.

On the industrial side, we face growing problems with environmental protection. These may require drastic modification of such older technologies as paper making, mining, electric-power generation, and the internal combustion engine. Many of these problems are long-range, and perhaps are beyond the financial capacity or the time horizons of private industry. Their solution may require new forms of governmental intervention, such as taxing the cash flow of major industries to finance environmental or safety research in a centralized way, either directly, through government, or by new types of regulated monopolies analogous to the Bell Laboratories.

More directly, the government is likely to take steps to encourage productivity-related R and D in industries that are lagging in international trade.[18] Although some economists argue that unfavorable trade balances can be accommodated by proper currency revaluation, the growing dependence of the United States on imported raw materials and fuels will make this ever more difficult. From the standpoint of science policy, we are likely to see much broader involvement of the federal government in industrial technology, as indicated by recent statements of politicians in both parties.[19]

Centralized vs. Pluralistic Management

Science is both a common resource and a pervasive tool in virtually every sector of government and the private economy. In the United States, each mission-oriented agency has been responsible for generating or acquiring from other agencies the scientific knowledge it needs to carry out its mission. This has resulted in close coupling between science and technology and agency functions, but is not always best for the sustained health and vigor of science itself or for the development of technological capabilities that will find application beyond the time horizons of typical government agency planning.

A more centralized system of management and support of science and technology may be more efficient for the progress of science and for the development of radically new technological capabilities. However, such centralized resource allocation may also be less responsive to the more immediate needs and operating problems of agencies.[20]

A comparison of the United Kingdom and the United States is illuminating in this connection. In the United States budget for fiscal year 1972, the National Science Foundation — the only part of the government not tied to a specific extra-scientific mission — accounted for only 5.2 per cent of nonmilitary research and development expenditures, or about 2.5 per cent of all R and D expenditures. By contrast, the Department of Education and Science (DES) in the United Kingdom accounted for 28.4 per cent of all British nonmilitary R and D expenditures. Even if the recommendations of Lord Rothschild's report[21] were adopted, the British would still be supporting 20 per cent of their nonmilitary R and D through the DES. This is about four times the percentage that the United States spends through the National Science Foundation.

Because the United States lacks any centralized science and technology establishment, there has been a tendency to create separate, new agencies, such as the AEC, NASA, or the National Oceanographic and Atmospheric Agency (NOAA), to foster particular new technologies. This scheme has often worked well in the early stages. However, after such agencies mature, they tend to lose their sense of mission and begin to behave like solutions looking for a problem.[22]

The Place of EMP in New National Priorities

When space and defense were at the forefront of national missions, the physical sciences were at the forefront of scientific attention and public popularity. The basic disciplines tended to be carried along with the tide of technological application. A major science-policy question for the 1970s is whether research at the conceptual frontiers of the physical sciences and mathematics has a continuing place in the new scheme of social priorities.

In a long-term sense, several of the most fundamental problems that mankind faces will depend for their solution on the physical sciences. One of them is certainly the future supply of energy — its generation, transmission, and efficient utilization, as well as the associated problems of waste-heat management. Here the most obvious applications are those of high-temperature plasma physics to controlled fusion, the transmission of electricity by means of underground superconducting transmission lines, and the magneto-hydrodynamic extraction of power from heated ionized gases. But the very fact that we can foresee such applications, however speculatively, may mean that they are already "over the hill" with respect to their relationship to the current frontiers of physics research. Many of the key physics problems are already definable in terms of the requirements of the system; on the other hand, the successful realization of practical systems may well depend on ancillary technology growing out of basic physics research.

Although these technological applications may have already fallen back from their close relationship to contemporary physics, they will require continuing participation of physicists. As time goes on, the physicists will act more and more as quasi-engineers, used more for their familiarity with new techniques than for their knowledge of contemporary physics. This has already happened in such areas as nuclear-fission power, or radiation physics in biomedicine.

Another long-term "mission" of the future will be the organization, management, and communication of information. Many of the future problems of meeting the "collective" needs of society in such fields as health-care delivery, education, and municipal public services in general have a large information-handling component.

Only in the fields of computer technology and telecommunications are there institutional arrangements adequate to elicit and carry forward the necessary innovative activity in the information field across the full range from fundamental research to large-scale systems applications. This industry draws its scientific inspiration mostly from two fields — solid-state physics and applied mathematics (or its derivative, computer science). In fact, solid-state physics is the only subfield of fundamental physics that derives less than half of its support from federal sources. The maturation of computer and communications technologies as they have assimilated the solid-state electronics revolution has been accompanied by declining support of basic solid-state science by industry.

In the field of optical technology, derived from the laser, most commercial applications lie fairly far in the future, and the same applies to most applications of superconductivity. Nevertheless, the promise of important technology from both of these fields is such that they should prosper in industry, given an expanding economy and reasonable prospects of long-term future demand.

Many other areas of information technology are lagging, however. A particularly prominent example is the system of information storage and retrieval — the system of libraries that constitutes the collective, long-term memory of mankind. This is in a sad and deteriorating state, with rising costs, much hand labor, a highly fragmented organization, and no system for placing an economic valuation on various services that might serve to allocate more efficiently the inadequate resources available.[23] Unlike the fields of communications, transportation, and energy, no large private cash flow can be tapped to finance a coherent program of system development or even to develop the underlying technology. It is possible that the whole concept of libraries as currently constituted is obsolescent, although nobody can really foresee either the form of a new public memory system or where the initiative might come from to undertake its development. Should this field of technology be revitalized, however, it could help to sustain a justification for research in several areas of physics, particularly those that might be related to large-scale, low-cost information storage, and to inexpensive graphic displays or transformation of format, as in automatic character reading.

Of course, it is implicit in the above discussion that very few civilian missions in either government or industry have developed a sense of responsibility for the basic technology and even less for the basic science on which they ultimately depend. Only in the areas of industrial chemicals, communications, computers, electrical equipment, pharmaceuticals, and agriculture is there really a system of continuing and comprehensive technological innovation. Yet in these industrial areas, economic forces seem to have discouraged long-term research recently. Thus, the employment of physics Ph.D.'s in industry increased from 2,450 in 1960 to 3,800 in 1970, but the absolute number of physicists engaged in basic research actually declined. The increase was entirely in development and in non-R and D activities, such as management. By 1970, two-thirds of the Ph.D. physicists in industry were engaged in activities other than basic or applied research. A generally similar pattern is discernible in government laboratories and research centers.[24] Funds used by industry for basic research declined from a peak of $550 million in 1966 to about $435 million in 1971 — less than in 1962[25] — and in real terms the decline was much greater, to about 63 per cent of the 1966 level in 1971.

The reasons for these changes are complex. The increase in the volume of basic research in universities undoubtedly led mission-oriented institutions to concentrate a greater percentage of their efforts in development. There was a growing realization that, although the general social payoff of basic research might be large, it could not, for the most past, be recaptured by a single firm, unless it were in a virtually monopolistic position. Finally, during the long period of shortage of highly trained scientists and engineers, basic-research opportunities had undoubtedly been offered as a non-monetary fringe benefit to attract the most talented young scientists. This was especially true in the aerospace industry and in the government-supported segments of other industries, where a good deal of basic research effort could be carried as overhead on government contracts and where a company's technical capability was often assessed by government procurement officers on the basis of the distinction of its roster of scientists. Whatever the cause, industry felt less responsibility to support the science it needed in the long run, relying increasingly on science from other sources.

In the past, science has furnished the soil in which new technology could grow and develop. In the future, it is likely to be equally important as a source of knowledge for the evaluation and management of technology and hence, ultimately, for its rational social control. Technology often can be generated on a trial-and-error, or empirical, basis — simply trying one thing after another until it works — and this is frequently as efficient as waiting to acquire the necessary theoretical understanding to approach development or design in a more "rational" way. But in evaluating the safety or the potential environmental effects of technology, greater theoretical understanding is essential.

Without a body of theory — for example, an understanding of the mechanism of the action of various chemicals on the physiology and biochemistry of the organisms with which they may come in contact — we cannot hope to anticipate all the potential side-effects of either existing or new technologies. In fact, with a sufficiently good theory, we can afford to leave much essential information stored in the "library of nature," because theory enables us to know precisely where to look for the critical information we need when we require it.

Critical Size vs. Dispersion in Research

Even relative to its size, the research effort of the United States is probably more dispersed both geographically and among institutions than in any other developed country. One consequence is the paradox that, in certain fields, one can find single laboratories in some European countries that are better-supported and better-equipped than any single laboratory in the United States, even though total United States support for the field may be much larger.[26] The issue of concentration vs. dispersion in research has become an increasingly difficult one, as the total share of the federal government as a supporter of research has increased. Politically, this is almost inevitable, given the geographically and regionally oriented nature of political representation in the legislative branch of the government, combined with the strong egalitarian and populist currents in American politics.

The conflict has become more acute between "equity" in the distribution of research funds, both institutionally and geographically, and the necessity for a "critical mass" of people and facilities to operate at the frontiers of many scientific fields. The problem has been especially difficult for physics and astronomy and, within physics, for nuclear and particle physics. It reached one of its many dramatic climaxes in the competition for site selection of the new 200-Gev. particle accelerator, which was finally built at Batavia, Illinois, near Chicago. This had followed a bitter quarrel over the failure of the Johnson Administration to fund the high-intensity accelerator proposed by the Midwest Universities Research Association (MURA). During the middle 1960s, a series of Congressional inquiries raised questions about the concentration of research support in Eastern private universities and the West Coast public institutions.[27]

On the other hand, it is easy to exaggerate the degree of "over-concentration." There has been a steady trend toward wider institutional distribution of research funds since the beginning of extensive federal support of academic science. For example, in fiscal year 1950, eleven academic institutions received 50 per cent of all academic R and D funds. The number had increased to twenty by FY 1963 and to more than thirty by FY 1970. In FY 1963 the first 100 institutions received 90 per cent of academic R and D funds, but this had dropped to 85 per cent by FY 1970. Furthermore, in FY 1970 these same institutions received only 82 per cent of the funds for academic science, and 71 per cent of total federal obligations to academic institutions.[28] These last numbers are probably more representative of the dispersion of support, because in 1950 and also largely in FY 1963, R and D support was almost the only kind of federal subsidy available.

Recent actions by the federal government in reducing the number of federally funded traineeships and fellowships have differentially hit the research-oriented schools, especially the highest-quality private universities, most of which have experienced nearly a 50 per cent reduction in entering physical science graduate students during the last four years as compared with the peak, which was reached about 1968. This has taken place even while some of the "developing" schools have continued to grow in graduate enrollment.

Not everybody agrees that this is an unhealthy trend; some would assert that the graduates from the less prestigious schools are psychologically better prepared to accept more applied and operational jobs, involving work under supervision in hierarchical structures. The dispersion of some able graduate students into many institutions is thus said to be matched to the lower career aspirations that are now appropriate for the growing majority of students — those who can no longer expect to attain positions in major universities or industrial or national laboratories that offer extensive opportunities for basic research. On the other hand, at a time when the critical mass for doing research at the frontier in the physical sciences is increasing, it is questionable whether the shrinkage of the leading institutions is a desirable trend for the health of science in the United States.

The critical-mass problem is well illustrated by nuclear structure physics, projections for which have recently been made by a panel of the National Academy of Sciences.[29] This field is in the midst of a transition in scale, in which accelerators at the most advanced frontiers of current research capability will, within the next few years, probably consume most of the available funds and force a cutback in the number of active laboratories from about 93 to about 30 within five years. For the most part, this cutback is to accommodate new advances in intermediate energy nuclear physics and heavy-iron physics. With level funding in real terms, the total professional manpower in the field would drop about 30 per cent as a result of the closing of many laboratories. The choice is a hard one; if the United States effort in the field is to remain competitive in the most significant frontier areas of nuclear structure research, much of the research capability created in the last twenty years will have to be liquidated. Even with an increase in funds sufficient for full utilization of available manpower, the number of laboratories still would be reduced to 50 or 60, and the available scientists would have to be concentrated in fewer installations in order to retain critical size in the most important efforts.

This may have serious repercussions for institutions. Academic scientists will have to spend much more time off campus if they are to continue in nuclear physics; teaching and course schedules will be disrupted. A much greater fraction of the research will be carried out in the "user-group" mode of operation now typical in elementary particle physics and in both optical and radio astronomy. The life style of several fields of academic science will change and in ways that may make it less attractive to the best younger scientists with young families, because they will have to spend much time away from home or commuting to research facilities.

Moreover, the gradual but steady trend toward greater concentration of effort in many areas of the physical sciences will be a continuing source of controversy and tension within the physical-science community, especially in physics. In the next decade, national decisions will have to be reached as to which laboratories will be supported and which phased out or at least tapered off. Unless these hard choices can be rationalized by internal consensus in the relevant scientific communities, they will tend to spill over into the arena of administration and congressional politics, as happened in the case of MURA, the Los Alamos Meson Facility, and the National Accelerator Laboratory.

Where there have been plausible scientific reasons for certain choices of location for a facility, as in astronomy and many of the environmental sciences, there have been and will continue to be less of a problem. However, in most fields of science the scientific community must develop more effective means of settling its arguments away from the public eye and presenting a more nearly united front to the political process. The cumulative price of repeated appeals to the political process would be high in terms of damage to the integrity of the resource-allocation process for science. The mechanism of the reports of the Committee on Science and Public Policy (COSPUP) of the National Academy of Sciences has helped in this regard, but has not wholly solved the problem.[30]

There is also a real intellectual problem in the proper balance between concentration and dispersion of effort in a given research area. Too much dispersion leads to many subcritical efforts, each unable to acquire the modern research tools or the diversity of scientific skills necessary for effective progress. But too much concentration can lead to intellectual monopoly of a field by a few dominant personalities or organizations.

The complementarity of large and small facilities is well-expressed in a recent report of the National Science Board[31]:

The balance between necessary regionalization and centralization on the one hand and the many necessary autonomous research groups on the other is very difficult to establish in practice. Smaller facilities, readily accessible to local faculty and students, are very important in the design of experiments and in optimizing them before making use of major facilities. The high cost of experimentation with frontier research facilities makes careful preliminary design and testing mandatory. Thus, the decision between national facilities and local research support is not a case of one or the other. An extreme in either direction makes for a less productive scientific enterprise. Local facilities, moreover, usually have a much quicker response time in following up new opportunities and new discoveries made with major facilities.

Integrity of the Self-Regulatory Systems of Science

In the currently fashionable parlance, science is a highly "elitist" activity. The funds for research are distributed in an unequal manner among institutions and among individual principal investigators within institutions. For example, a study made of NSF basic-research project grants for FY 1963 showed that about 12 per cent of the total funds went to 1.4 per cent of the grants, 18 per cent to 3 per cent of the grants, and 59 per cent to 24.5 per cent of the grants.[32] The Westheimer study of chemistry[33] showed that in the aggregate of university chemistry departments studied in FY 1963, of the 2,300 faculty members of sufficient rank to supervise thesis research, 27 per cent had no external research support and 40 per cent had support of less than $5,000 annually, while 17 per cent had support in excess of $100,000 per year. Even among faculty actually supervising thesis research, 25 per cent had support of less than $5,000 per year. Recent cutbacks in federal support for academic research have resulted in a decrease of the percentage of university faculty members in the natural sciences who perform sponsored research from about 69 per cent to 57 per cent; the drop among younger scientists has been from 64 per cent to 50 per cent.[34]

That inequalities in distribution of government funds is politically viable in the American system is, in part, the consequence of public confidence in the integrity and fairness of the selection mechanisms for research grants and fellowship awards. For the most part, the public and the scientific community share the belief that the institutional selection mechanisms of science guarantee the recognition of the people and projects most capable of advancing the scientific enterprise. In addition, they believe that the criteria of recognition are both objective and objectively applied, i.e., applied largely without reference to personal relationships, institutional loyalties, or imputed status.

Within the scientific community it is an article of faith that the system of selection of research-project proposals by "committees of peers" in the scientific field concerned is the key to quality and continued progress. The working members of the scientific community are highly skeptical of any modification of the research-project support system that tends towards the delegation of quality judgments either to government administrators or to local university management. These principles were forcefully articulated in a report published by the Committee on Science and Public Policy of the National Academy of Sciences in 1964, as indicated by the following excerpts:

The use of project support as the principal means of aiding basic research has advantages of great practical importance. Through the project system the Federal Government can finance research in institutions of higher learning in the way that relates the award of funds as closely as possible to scientific merit and minimize the effects of political pressure. . . . The decisions on individual awards can be made with the advice of professionally qualified specialists in the various disciplines, so that each scientist's application is judged by a panel of his peers; and thus no one, in the name of the Government, makes an administrative or political decision on the fate of a college or university as a whole. Thus, this competition avoids the perils of overcentralization of planning and management. . . . We are therefore convinced that, for the foreseeable future, the major emphasis in the Federal Government's support of basic research in science in institutions of higher learning should continue to be given to the project system.[35]

A significant question exists, however, as to whether the project system is still a sufficient guarantee of the integrity of scientific choice under today's circumstances. In the first place, the growth of national centers and national and international programs has created a new system of research support that is partly outside the peer-evaluation system. This is necessitated by the nature of the research, which requires a large amount of advance planning and coordination among several institutions and research groups. National Academy committees and similar devices have been created to assist quality control in these programs and a continued pluralistic input from the scientific community. The effectiveness of these methods of managing research in comparison with the project-grant system is hard to measure, because of the broadly varied types of research. In some instances, the caliber of scientists involved in these national programs is not uniformly equal to that in the typical university project grant, but this does not necessarily mean that the programs as a whole are of lesser quality. Frequently, the success of the larger programs depends on the dynamic leadership of a few outstanding individuals working with a large group of technically capable scientists who may be less original, but who also are more willing to work in a coordinated effort, deferring to such leadership. In other words, the program actually may be more successful than it would have been if all the participants were prima donnas, each going his own way, no matter how brilliantly.

The image of the scientific peer system may be becoming tarnished even within the scientific community itself. Professor S. M. Lipset, a Harvard sociologist, has recently conducted an opinion survey of academic natural scientists and engineers as one of the studies sponsored by the Carnegie Commission on Higher Education.[36] This survey included some questions on strictly academic matters. Some of the results are disturbing. For example, more than 60 per cent of the scientists surveyed in the most prestigious institutions agreed with the proposition that professors exploit their graduate students to advance their own research and scientific prestige. Nearly 50 per cent agreed with the proposition that the most successful professors were "operators," rather than true scholars, and more than 30 per cent agreed with the opinion that large research grants "corrupt" their recipients. The respondents apparently included many of the "corrupted" scientists themselves.

It is difficult to assess the real import of such surveys. In part, the opinions no doubt reflect a kind of academic romanticism, easy to affect when one is responding to general propositions rather than to inquiries about the performance of individual investigators. The survey conclusions seem to contrast strongly with other studies, such as those of Merton and Zuckerman, on the operation of the referee system of the *Physical Review,* which indicate a surprising degree of objectivity in the anonymous referee reports on articles submitted for publication by authors with various characteristics.[37] However, an increasing number of voices within science is questioning the integrity of the scientific choices that are being made through the peer system, and this comes less from disgruntled outsiders than from successful scientists whose eminence is so secure that they can afford to consider themselves above the battle.

Typical of a widely expressed view are the following words of J. M. Ziman[38]:

> . . . the consequences of flabbiness [in science policy] are all too sadly evident in all quarters of the globe — the proliferation of third-rate research which is just as expensive of money and materials as the best, but does not really satisfy those who carry it out, and adds nothing at all to the world's stock of useful or useless knowledge.

Or the words of P. A. Weiss[39]:

> . . . the question remains as to whether all that flood is necessary and justifiable, or whether some of it is not the product of a sorcerer's apprentice's obedient, but thoughtless, broom being let loose.

Despite these sour observations on the self-policing system of science as it is exhibited in publication, the only empirical studies of which I am aware suggest caution in drawing too sweeping conclusions about the trivial, or "pebble-picking," character of the scientific literature. Herring[40] reports a sample study in the field of solid-state physics in which a panel of experts was asked to rate a random selection of single-author papers in the field. Of all the papers rated, only 8 per cent were judged worthless by any single one of the experts and 33 per cent were judged by at least one scientist on the panel to contribute something of lasting value and conceptual interest. The other 59 per cent of the papers were of value, but were considered either pedestrian or likely to be soon superseded.

The question of how well the self-regulating system in basic research is working must be considered as still moot. It is perhaps unfortunate that there have been no retrospective studies by competent referees of the quality of publications resulting from funded research grants in the physical sciences in comparison with the evaluation of the corresponding grant applications by screening panels before the fact. A study somewhat along these lines was conducted of grants supported by the NIH; this was reported by a panel of the President's Science Advisory Committee in 1965.[41] It was concluded that not more than 5 per cent of a sample of grants selected on the basis of a random dollar would, in retrospect, have been judged unworthy of support. (In the random dollar method, projects were chosen for intensive review at random, with a probability-weighting proportional to their annual dollar expenditure. Thus, a large project had a higher probability of being chosen for review than a small one.) One would have anticipated an even better record in the physical sciences because of the generally greater degree of consensus that appears to obtain among referees in this more highly codified area.

Alternative Methods for the Support of Graduate Education

As indicated in the preceding section, federal involvement in the support of higher education arose as a spin-off from the support of research projects. The system of support was inherited largely from the philosophy and procedures developed by the private foundations in the early part of the twentieth century. The two primary mechanisms were the project grant and the nationally competitive individual fellowship, both at the predoctoral and postdoctoral levels. In the words of John T. Wilson[42]:

In the quarter century since the end of the Second World War, the Federal government, guided largely by the scientific community and working from what it hoped were successful models for progress in science, has placed major emphasis on research in contrast to education and on the individual investigator in contrast to the institution.

The main rationale for this approach was the half-articulated political perception that only by focusing on individual scientific merit would it be possible in the long run to prevent the erosion of universities and other scientific institutions by political interference and the injection of nonscientific criteria into the distribution of funds and ultimately even of scientific appointments. During the middle 1960s, the situation began to change as new mechanisms of support were tried. Indeed, change had been foreshadowed by the introduction of the research training grant and the general research support grant by the National Institutes of Health at the end of the 1950s. These two mechanisms, respectively, attempted to redress the balance between research and education, at least at the most advanced training level, and to restore some flexibility and intellectual initiative to the institution to offset the independent entrepreneurship of the individual investigator.

Later, institutionally administered traineeships and so-called institutional development grants were introduced by several agencies, including the NSF, with the motive of increasing the geographical dispersion of awards and of encouraging the qualitative upgrading of institutions. In both instances, the funds were made available to the central administration of the institution and the awards were based on the evaluation of institution-wide plans, including the competence and commitment of the administration itself. In both programs, the beneficiaries were not underdeveloped or low-rank institutions. Rather, they were those just below the first rank which were judged most capable of substantial self-improvement. The most noticeable effect, however, was to increase the total output of Ph.D.'s. It is still a matter of debate whether this acceleration was caused by the new programs or whether their effect was to improve the research environment for students who would have flocked to these institutions in any case because of demographic and social pressures.

My own belief is that the new federal policies did little to affect total numbers, but that the primary effect was on the quality of training available to a larger pool of able students, who could not have been accommodated in the first-ranking institutions in any case. However, subsequent federal policies of the late 1960s and early 1970s appear to have been predicated on the assumption that the earlier policies had been aimed mainly at quantity rather than quality and, because there was no longer a national need for numbers, the programs were phased out as rapidly as possible without breaking commitments to individuals already in the pipeline. The true answer will probably never be known; it is impossible to do a controlled experiment and so many other social changes have taken place concurrently that it is difficult to sort out cause and effect.

At all events, current government policy seems to be reverting rather rapidly to the situation that existed at the beginning of the decade, with institutional and student support being largely derivative from research projects. Between 1967 and 1970, R and D rose from 57 per cent to 67 per cent of all academic science support, and the trend accelerated in 1971 and 1972. In addition, research itself is becoming more categorical, less responsive to the interests of the individual scientist.

In 1969, the National Science Board issued the first of a series of reports mandated by the 1968 amendments to the National Science Foundation Act under the title, "Towards a Public Policy for Graduate Education in the Sciences."[43] Although aimed primarily at the sciences, the report treats all graduate education fairly comprehensively. It proposes a radical transformation of current modes of support of graduate education, in which research-project grant support is to cover only direct expenditures by investigators and exclude faculty salary support, graduate student support, indirect costs, and general departmental expenditures. These are to be covered by other types of institutional or departmental grants specifically designed for these purposes and administered according to a central plan, probably by a single federal agency charged with responsibility for graduate education. The report estimates that if FY 1966 expenditures for project research had been divided in the way recommended, only $426 million out of the $1,246 million spent by all federal agencies on academic research, or about 35 per cent, would have represented direct costs of research in the sense defined in the report. The remaining 65 per cent would have been divided among the various other categories of institutional, departmental, and student support.

The publication of the first statutory report of the National Science Board came at a politically inopportune time. It appeared on the scene just when the professional analysts in the Bureau of the Budget had concluded that the federal policies of the early 1960s were generating a surplus of science and engineering Ph.D.'s and that steps had to be taken to pull back from the growing federal commitment to the broad support of graduate education. Indeed, the publication of the report may have helped to stimulate a counter-reaction in the Bureau, because it spelled out in detail the long-range fiscal implications of a policy which the federal government had been creeping up to in small bites over many years. By 1980, according to the Board projections, expenditures for graduate education would increase from $6 billion annually in 1968 to $20 billion annually in 1980, with a rising share coming from federal sources.

However, the report found a more sympathetic hearing in the Congress. The Subcommittee on Science, Research, and Development of the

House Science and Astronautics Committee took it quite seriously indeed, and in the following year issued its own report under the title, "The National Institutes for Research and Advanced Studies (NIRAS)."[44] This report followed fairly closely the recommendations of the National Science Board. It advocates centralization of federal responsibilities for basic research and graduate education, defined as "those scientific activities which are carried out in universities or similar institutions, and which are closely related to the total intellectual operations of higher education and advanced study." Education programs at the undergraduate level were to be transferred to the Office of Education in the Department of HEW, and NIRAS was to become a sort of super-NSF, with a total budget corresponding to an aggregation of activities authorized for FY 1970 amounting to $2.3 billion — more than 75 per cent of all federal activities in this category. On the other hand, the report urged that the "mission agencies continue to support basic research both in their own laboratories and in the universities" and expressed the opinion that "the establishment of a NIRAS would by no means lessen the need for close liaison and actual contracts and grants between the universities and the mission agencies."

Although not spelled out in the report, it was apparently envisioned that the mission agencies would cover only direct costs of research, while, as in the National Science Board report, other types of grants from NIRAS would cover institutional, departmental, and student costs. One consequence of this system of support would be that mission agencies could procure research from universities for about 35 cents on the dollar, because 65 per cent of the costs already would have been covered by the NIRAS subsidies.

The reception of these two reports was mixed, even in the scientific community. The new system of support, according to the NIRAS report, was seen as assuring "stable, continuous, predictable funding of academic science and higher education on which the welfare of the United States depends." On the other hand, many scientists were apprehensive about the loss of exposure to sharp peer evaluations of more than $\frac{2}{3}$ of the total funds expended — that is, the 65 per cent covered by the NIRAS subsidies. In the words of a minority of the National Science Board: "It is much more difficult and perhaps less meaningful to rate an entire department, and such evaluations may tend to be based on non-objective judgments influenced by out-of-date information."[45] Furthermore, the minority felt that departmental grants, in particular, appeared as "an intrusion on the individuality and into the internal policy of universities." If the Board report were to be implemented, about 78 per cent of all the federal funds flowing to academic science would come from a single agency, whose vulnerability to political accidents and personalities in the administration or the Congress would become a matter of serious moment.

The proponents of a multiplicity of granting mechanisms also argued from pluralism. Although the source of funds would be monolithic, the criteria of scientific choice would become more decentralized and pluralistic, because each mechanism would emphasize different criteria and would be applied at different levels and places in the institutions involved. Departmental and institutional grants would permit greater recognition of local talent not yet identified on the national scene, for example, while stable institutional funding would permit the university to regain collective control of its own scientific priorities. This would lead to greater diversity and less following of scientific fashions, such as were alleged to be encouraged by the national peer-evaluation system in various disciplines.

Recent trends in the Congress to tie more and more restrictions to federal funds have led many people to reconsider the desirability of the NIRAS class of proposals. Within the last three years, amendments to appropriations bills have been introduced to cut off payment of government funds to fellowship holders accused or convicted of "disruption" on campus. In 1972, a ban on training military officers at institutions which have eliminated ROTC has actually been passed. There are threats of a ban on all Department of Defense funds to institutions that have banned ROTC.[46]

The present plurality of sources of support is felt to provide some protection against across-the-board federal intervention in the internal policies of universities, as a result of actions within the power of a single federal agency or congressional committee.

One mechanism of support which has not been explored, except to a limited extent in the biomedical field, is that of long-term support for outstanding individuals, not on the basis of project proposals, but simply on the basis of demonstrated accomplishment over an extended period. The nearest thing to such support is the career-investigator awards made by several of the voluntary health associations, such as the American Cancer Society, and a similar award tried for several years by the National Institutes of Health. The theory underlying such an award is that there exists a small minority of scientists of such outstanding brilliance and originality that society can do no better than to provide them with unencumbered research funds for whatever they choose to undertake. Once such an individual has sufficiently established himself in the eyes of his peers, no amount of pre-screening of his research ideas can be particularly useful, and the necessity of preparing grant proposals is an unconstructive diversion of his effort. The selection and support of a few outstanding individuals of this type could help to establish standards in a field and would be a form of recognition more meaningful than a monetary prize going to the individual personally rather than to the support of his research. The recognition of such individuals might provide a guide to supporting agencies and academic administrators as to where the most significant current intellectual frontiers are.

While support should not be automatic for an entire career, it should be for a sufficiently long period and sufficiently large in amount so that the individual would not normally have to apply for additional grant funds and could plan a long-term research program without the necessity of continually rejustifying his progress. The support would be renewable indefinitely, but would be subject to rigorous, retrospective, peer review prior to renewal — say once every seven years.

Relation Between United States' and World Research Efforts

On an average, the United States accounts for about one-third of the world's scientific publications, and the variation of this fraction from field to field of basic science is rather small. Among seven principal subfields of physics, for example, the United States is the largest single producer of papers except in nuclear physics, where it is surpassed slightly by western Europe as a whole. The production of scientific papers bears an almost constant ratio to gross national product among the advanced nations. This is indicative of the highly international character of the communications system of basic science. New developments and research interests diffuse with remarkable rapidity throughout the world, especially in the physical sciences.

Little information is available on the *quality* of the scientific effort in the United States relative to that of other countries. Such fragmentary information as exists supports the conclusion that scientists in this country produce a somewhat larger share of major discoveries — perhaps 50 per cent rather than 30 per cent — than their proportion of papers would indicate, judged on the bases of citation studies, Nobel prizes, and other internationally recognized awards. In the last 25 years, the United States has been especially adept at following up on major discoveries made initially in other countries. Striking examples are the Mössbauer effect, the chemistry of xenon compounds, optical pumping, and the tunnel diode and associated phenomena. Nevertheless, concepts of "ahead" and "behind" in basic science are misleading, and become more so with time. Science is a universal enterprise; the rate of progress of science in the United States depends on that of world science, and vice versa.

Some fields are more completely internationalized than others. Probably the most complete internationalization has occurred in the disciplines that require the most expensive and complex facilities, particularly elementary particle physics. This applies to the circulation of both information and people. At any one time, dozens of foreign scientists are engaged in active research in major laboratories in this country, and Americans flock every year to such major European centers as CERN near Geneva, Saclay near Paris, Frascati near Rome, the Bohr Institute at Copenhagen, and the German nuclear center Deutsches Elektonen-Synchroton (DESY) near Hamburg. A whole new research area of long base-line interferometry has been developed in radio astronomy, involving elaborate cooperation among observers and instrumentation in many countries.

During the 1950s and 1960s, scientists often talked their governments into financing major scientific facilities by using arguments of international competition or relative national prestige. This rationale for science is losing its lustre, not only in the United States, but elsewhere in the world. However, there is increasing recognition of the significance of international science as a path-breaker for other forms of international cooperation and even for political contacts on sensitive issues. The contacts between the United States and Russia that led to the partial nuclear test-ban treaty, the nonproliferation treaty, and the new arms accord with the Soviet Union reached in the SALT talks were significantly furthered by informal extra-governmental contacts among the scientists of the two nations. The well-known Pugwash meetings are one example.

Most recently, world-wide concern with environmental problems and cooperative applied science aimed at managing them has grown rapidly. The climate of opinion in government is now such that the possibility of furthering international cooperation has become an important argument in persuading national governments to undertake major scientific programs. The recent reversal of the British government's decision not to participate in the European accelerator project was, in large part, the result of the political and public appeal of this giant new cooperative scientific venture. The United States and Russia have announced specific plans for collaborative efforts in space and in certain areas of biomedical research, and are about to embark on much broader joint programs.

The decade of the seventies is likely to be one of spectacular progress in the further internationalization of science. What the political effects will be is hard to forecast. Cooperation in science is certainly not enough by itself to counteract long-standing political divisions, but it can be a powerful accelerating agent when the climate of public opinion becomes ripe for a more collaborative approach to the world's problems. Furthermore, once established, scientific contacts can weather periods of political storm to serve as a basis for renewed contact in the political sphere when the climate once again improves.

REFERENCES

1. Brooks, H. Impact of the Defense Establishment on Science and Education. *In* National Science Policy Hearings before the Subcommittee on Science Research and Development of the Committee on Science and Astronautics. U.S. House of Representatives, H. Congressional Resolution 666, No. 23, 1970, Appendix E, pp. 931-963.
2. Dupree, A. Hunter. Science in the Federal Government. Belknap Press of Harvard University Press, Cambridge, 1957, p. 367.
3. Conant, James B. My Several Lives; Memoirs of a Social Inventor. Harper and Row, New York, 1970.
4. Bush, Vannevar. Pieces of the Action. William Morrow, New York, 1970. *Also*: Book review of above by Brooks, H. in *Technology Review*. April, 1971, p. 16.
5. Schilling, Warner. Scientists, Foreign Policy, and Politics. *In* R. Gilpin and C. Wright (Editors), Scientists and National Policy Making, Columbia University Press, New York, 1964. Cf. especially p. 155.
6. Bush, Vannevar, et al. Science, the Endless Frontier. (Reissued as part of the Tenth Anniversary Observance of the National Science Foundation 1950-1960.) National Science Foundation 60-40, Washington, D.C., 1960.
7. Estimated academic R. and D. direct price trends 50 per cent higher over decade 1961-1971. *In* Science Resources Studies Highlights, National Science Foundation 71-32, Washington, D.C., November, 1971.
8. Doctorate Recipients from United States Universities 1958-1966. Pub. # 1489, National Academy of Sciences, Washington D.C., 1967.
9. Manpower in Physics: Patterns of Supply and Use. *In* Physics in Perspective, Vol. I, Chapter 12, Fig. 12.12, p. 843. National Academy of Sciences (ISBN 0-309-02037-9), Washington, D.C., 1972.
10. See ref. 6, Table 1, p. 86.   *
11. Weiner, Charles. Physics in the Great Depression. *Physics Today* 23 (No. 10):31-39 (1970).
12. Research and Development in Industry. Full-time Equivalent Number of R and D Scientists and Engineers, by Industry and Size of Company, 1957-1970. Table B-12. National Science Foundation 71-18, Washington, D.C., 1969.
13. American Science Manpower 1968. National Science Foundation 69-38, Washington, D.C., 1969.
14. An Analysis of Federal R. and D. Funding by Budget Functions. Surveys of Science Resources Series. National Science Foundation 71-25, Washington, D. C., 1971.
15. Zuckerman, H., and Merton, R. Patterns of evaluation in science institutionalization, structure, and functions of the referee system. *Minerva* 9 (No. 1):66-100 (1971).
16. Servan-Schreiber, J. J. The American Challenge (Ronald Steel, translator). Atheneum, New York, 1968.

17. Beretsky, M., Concerns about the present American position in international trade, *Technology and International Trade*, National Academy of Engineering, Washington, D.C., 1971, pp. 18-66; Branson, W. H., and Junz, H. B., Trends in U.S. trade and comparative advantage, *Brookings Papers on Economic Activity* 2:285-345, 1971; Committee on Science and Astronautics, *Science, Technology, and the Economy*, Hearings in the 92nd Congress, July 27-29, 1971, U.S. Government Printing Office, Washington, D.C., 1971; Brooks, H., What's happening to the U.S. lead in technology? *Harvard Business Review*, May-June, 1972, pp. 110-118.

18. Science and Technology, The President's Message to the Congress, March 16, 1972. Weekly Compilation of Presidential Documents, March 20, 1972.

19. Committee on Science and Astronautics. *Science, Technology, and the Economy*. Hearings in the 92nd Congress, July 27-29, 1971. U.S. Government Printing Office, Washington, D.C., 1971, p. 17.

20. Brooks, H., et al. Science, Growth, and Society: A New Perspective. Report of the Secretary General's Ad Hoc Committee on New Concepts in Science Policy. Organisation for Economic Co-operation and Development, Paris, 1971, pp. 66-68.

21. A Framework for Government Research and Development (British Government "Green Paper"). HMSO, Com. 4814, Nov. 24, 1971; *also* Brooks, H. Rothschild's recipe in the United States. *Nature* 235:301 (1972).

22. Brooks, H. The Government of Science. The M.I.T. Press, Cambridge, 1968, Chapter 3.

23. Libraries and Information Technology, a National System Challenge. A report to the Council on Library Resources, Inc., by the Information Systems Panel, Computer Science and Engineering Board, National Academy of Sciences (ISBN 0-309-01938-9), Washington, D.C., 1972.

24. Manpower in Physics: Patterns of Supply and Use. *In* Physics in Perspective, Vol. I, Chapter 12, Figs. 12.24 and 12.25, pp. 879-880. National Academy of Sciences (ISBN 0-309-02037-9), Washington, D.C., 1972.

25. National Patterns of R. and D. Resources, 1953-1972. National Science Foundation, NSF 72-310, Washington, D.C. 1970, pp. 26-27.

26. National Science Board. The Physical Sciences. U.S. Government Printing Office, Washington, D.C., 1970, cf. pp. 53-54.

27. Statistical Review of Research and Development. Report of the Select Committee on Government Research of the House of Representatives, 88th Congress, Second Session, under the authority of H. Res. 504, as amended by H. Res. 810, Study Number IX, Union Calendar No. 833, House Report No. 1940. U.S. Government Printing Office, Washington, D.C., 1964.

28. Federal Support to Universities, Colleges, and Selected Nonprofit Institutions, Fiscal Year 1970. National Science Foundation 71-28, Washington, D.C., 1971. (U.S. Government Printing Office, Stock No. 3800-0100.)

29. Weneser, J., et al. Preliminary Report of the Nuclear-Physics Panel of the Physics Survey Committee. National Academy of Sciences, Washington, D.C., 1971.

30. Ezrahi, Yaron. The political resources of American science. *Science Studies* 1 (No. 2):117-133, 1971.

31. See ref. 26.

32. Personal analysis of unpublished NSF grant data, 1965.

33. Westheimer, F., et al. Chemistry Opportunities and Needs. A Report on Basic Research in U.S. Chemistry by the Committee for the Survey of Chemistry. (Publication # 1292). National Academy of Sciences, National Research Council, Washington, D.C., 1965, pp. 205-206.
34. American Science Manpower 1970. A Report of the National Register of Scientific and Technical Personnel. National Science Foundation, NSF 71-45, 1972.
35. Federal Support of Basic Research in Institutions of Higher Learning. Publication #1185. National Academy of Sciences, Washington, D.C., 1964, p. 76.
36. Ladd, E. C., Jr., and Lipset, S. M. Politics of academic natural scientists and engineers. *Science* 176: 1091 (1972).
37. See ref. 15.
38. Ziman, J. M. Public Knowledge, the Social Dimension of Science. Cambridge University Press, Cambridge, U. K., 1968, p. 361.
39. Weiss, P. A. Within the Gates of Science and Beyond. Hafner, New York, 1971, p. 135.
40. Dissemination and Use of the Information of Physics. *In* Physics in Perspective, Vol. 1, Chapter 13, p. 934. Report of the Physics Survey Committee, National Academy of Sciences, National Research Council (ISBN 0-309-02037-9), Washington, D.C., August, 1972.
41. Wooldridge, D., et al. Biomedical Science and its Administration. A Study of the National Institutes of Health, Report to the President. The White House, Washington, D.C., February, 1965, p. 30.
42. Wilson, John T. A dilemma of American science and higher education policy: the support of individuals and fields versus the support of universities. *Minerva* 9 (No. 2):171-196 (1971).
43. Towards a Public Policy for Graduate Education in the Sciences. National Science Board 69-1. U.S. Government Printing Office, Washington, D.C., 1969.
44. Science Policy Research Division, Legislative Reference Service, Library of Congress, *Centralization of Federal Science Activities,* Document # 91-172; Report to Subcommittee on Science Research and Development of the Committee on Science and Astronautics, U.S. House of Representatives, First Session, U.S. Government Printing Office, Washington, D.C., 1969. *Also* The National Institutes of Research and Advanced Studies, *A Recommendation for Centralization of Federal Science Responsibilities,* Document # Serial N, 42-363-0; Report of the Subcommittee on Science, Research, and Development of the Committee on Science and Astronautics, U.S. House of Representatives, 91st Congress, Second Session. U.S. Government Printing Office, Washington, D.C., 1970.
45. Cf. ref. 43, p. 61.
46. The Military Procurement Authorization Bill for Fiscal Year 1973. Title 6, Section 602 of HR 15495. Report # 92-1149, House of Representatives, June 19, 1972.

VIII · *Social Change and Social Science*

HENRY W. RIECKEN

IT IS BANAL, BUT ACCURATE, to remark that these are times in which social turbulence has reached a high point in its cycle. The winds of change blow everywhere, and they have begun to loosen some of the cherished and apparently stable structural members of the scientific establishment in the United States. The comfortable assumptions of the sixties about federal support for scientific research; about the dedication of professors and graduate students to the life of the mind; about the fundamental importance of the pursuit of truth through pure research — all these and more have been shaken. Instead of being the private business of a select few, science and technology have now become the preoccupation of politicians, of leaders of the ecology movement, young radicals, and old conservatives. The prominence which many scientists yearned for in the fifties and sixties has turned into an unpleasant notoriety in a very perplexing way. Even scientists themselves have begun to raise questions about the legitimacy of some of their work, and have suggested that rather than the eternal search for pure truth, science might well try discriminating between knowledge that is worth having and that which is dangerous to produce. Some aspects of high technology are called oppressive by young people, and they do not mean simply the impersonality imposed by punch-card equipment. Others object to research which "invades privacy"; and they express concern about violation of human rights, which they believe experimentation on human beings may involve.

Although the bulk of the outcry has been directed so far at the technologies of physical science and, more lately, biomedical science, the

HENRY W. RIECKEN Center for Advanced Study in the Behavioral Sciences, Stanford, California. *Present address*: School of Medicine, University of Pennsylvania, Philadelphia.

behavioral sciences are themselves not exempt. They do, of course, have a smaller technology and hence are less likely to be objurgated. Nevertheless, various groups have taken aim at intelligence and personality tests and have stigmatized testing as an instrument of oppression. Economists are also coming in for their share of criticism from those who decry the gross national product and the national income accounts as a measure of the well-being of the total society. Nevertheless, behavioral scientists are somewhat better able to shelter from wrath because they have exposed fewer targets to the revolutionaries.

To be sure, the correct object of protest should not be technology per se, which is almost always neutral, but rather the social system, which is responsible for the way in which technology is used — the system of rewards and penalties that characterizes our "postindustrial" society, the kinds of institutions that have grown up around the system, and the kinds of stakes that the members of organizations have in perpetuating the present system. In a very literal sense, then, not only is the analysis of the revolt against technology a social-scientific question but, indeed, social science should be concerned with the adjustment or amelioration of those features of this high-technology society that cause objection.

In many ways, the revolt against technology is a revolt against aspects of human nature. Technology is, after all, instrumental; it is the means by which human beings may be able to achieve their wishes. The greater the efficiency of technology, the more achievable are the aims of those who control it. Some problems seem to arise because of technology, but that usually means that something that was already there has been raised to the status of a problem because an activity previously carried out badly can now be carried out well. For example, the invasion of personal privacy has been a matter of some concern throughout civilization, but that concern has increased since the technological means of invading privacy have improved. If there were no bugs, no taps, no hidden cameras, if the job of surveillance was still performed by the application of the human ear to the hotel-door transom, there would be less public concern about the right to privacy.

To be sure, any right that has only the fragile protection of inefficiency is perpetually in jeopardy. The almost automatic response of the engineer is to devise technological counter-measures, thus leading to an escalation of sophistication in machinery, but perhaps only to a stalemate in solving the problem. A sounder, long-run solution lies, perhaps, in some sort of social invention that would make the illegitimate penetration of privacy so penalizing to the invader that he would not undertake it. Legal protections and public opinion are, in the long run, probably more efficacious than mechanical or electronic devices. But social devices seem to be much more difficult to develop.

Why should that be so? Why should it be so much harder to produce social than technological change? There are many reasons, including the very subject matter of social science and the fact that it intrudes much more directly upon the domains of political and economic power than physical technology appears to do. The social consequences of technology are vast and pervasive, but they are also subtle. No one in the business world or in the political one was foresighted enough to envision anything like the social and economic consequences of the automobile. Its vast, truly revolutionary, effects upon the way Americans live were completely unanticipated. It looked like "simply" a better means of transportation; and, in the beginning, not even that. In contrast, the antipoverty programs of the mid-sixties immediately provoked widespread discussion, opposition, second-guessing, and predictions about dire consequences to the society, the economy, and indeed to human character itself. So far, the evidence suggests that they have been very much less powerful than the indirect effects of technology, for example, in displacing black farm-workers from the rural south to the industrial north. Like any direct and proximal attempt to alter social structure and the performance of the social system, however, the antipoverty programs were challenged and fought. This is partly because they violated, as any social program is bound to, the assumptions of some part of the population that they knew best how to deal with poverty.

One of the grave difficulties of the social sciences is that they deal primarily with a subject matter that is "everybody's business." Everyone knows something about human behavior and society because he is a participant in it and he believes that his view, his analysis, his image of the way society works and human beings behave is the correct image. It is necessary that he believe this for his personal stability and self-respect, even though he may be wholly wrong. When a deliberate and self-conscious attempt is made to alter the social system or human behavior, one of the things it encounters is this established set of beliefs, which are likely, in some respects, to run counter to the proposed action.

Despite the difficulties, attempts to induce social change peacefully and to change personal behavior therapeutically are increasing at a faster rate and on a larger scale than at any time since the beginning of the New Deal. It is not an accident of history that, a generation of political leadership later, the same purposes, the same aspirations for a "better" society, for the elimination of social injustice and economic inequity, should be focused on contemporary versions of persistent social and behavioral problems. The urge toward social reform runs deep in the ethos of America, and belief in the perfectability of man, while frequently shaken, has never been lost. In the mid-1960s, the administration and the Congress began to shift attention and emphasis away from international political and military competition toward domestic distress and untranquillity. Compare, for example, the rationales offered for two important federal programs in education: the National Defense Education Act in 1958 was inspired by and directed toward improving the nation's human capital stock in order to "stay in the race" with the Russians; the Elementary and Secondary Education Act of 1965 turned inward upon national concerns for its justification and for its political basis. The important point of the examples is the nature of the symbolism, the context of the argument for the support of education.

Among the effects of this rising concern with social problems has been a sharpened challenge of the justification of science for its own sake, manifested as a growing impatience with the classical rationale for supporting "basic research" (i.e., that undirected inquiry guided by scientific interest alone will inevitably, albeit unpredictably and distantly, lead to useful results and practical applications); and, second, the beginning of disenchantment with physical and biological technologies (or, more properly, with their personal, social, economic, and "environmental" effects). Third, there has been a turning toward the behavioral and social sciences, especially in their applied aspects, in the hope and expectation that these sciences may be able to aid and forward the current impetus toward social reform and personal improvement.

Thus the National Institute of Mental Health has turned its attention not only toward alcoholism and drug addiction — classical, if neglected, problems of psychiatry — but also toward crime and delinquency, and metropolitan studies. The National Science Foundation in its programs for Research Applied to National Needs has oriented about one-third of that budget for studies of "social systems and human resources," which includes such topics as criminology; municipal systems and operations; social data and community structure; and methods for the evaluation of social programs.

It is relevant that a recent RANN grant (of $1.5 million) was made to the Center for Advanced Study in the Behavioral Sciences for the purpose of investigating Problems of Science, Technology, and Society. While the project will involve distinguished biological and physical scientists — Joshua Lederberg, for example — the activity will be housed in and oriented through an interdisciplinary, semiautonomous center whose principal mission for seventeen years has been the advancement of social science.

There has also been a substantial increase in the funding of applied social research in the Department of Labor, principally for manpower and training studies. The Office of Economic Opportunity has had large increases for experimentation on welfare schemes and for inquiry into other aspects of poverty, as well as for research on education and housing. The largest increase (more than $30 million between 1970 and 1971) occurred, not surprisingly, in the applied social science research budget of the Department of Health, Education, and Welfare.

The total federal agency budget for research in the social and behavioral sciences has grown, over the last four fiscal years, from about $250 to about $398 million, with three-quarters of that increase occurring between FY 1970 and FY 1971 and 80 per cent of it in *applied* social and behavioral research (Table I). That is, between FY 1968 and FY 1971, while federal support for basic behavioral and social research grew by about 16 per cent, applied-research support nearly doubled. The federal government's expenditures in these sciences may seem large at first glance, although it is small compared to the total scientific research budget of the government — about 6 per cent. This fact is perhaps less surprising when one examines the character of the behavioral and social sciences, their size and their place in the community of science. Three features stand out. First, the United States literally leads the world in the size, activity, and sophistication of its social science community, and, with a few exceptions, the intellectual leadership and methodological influence of the United States presently dominates the social and behavioral sciences in virtually all parts of the world. Nevertheless, these disciplines are small and uninfluential in the United States as compared with the physical and biological sciences.

There are more than 110,000 chemists in the United States, and more than 60,000 biologists, but fewer than 35,000 psychologists, no more than 20,000 economists, and fewer than 15,000 genuine professionals in anthropology, political science, and sociology *taken together*. There are about

TABLE I

Federal Funds for Research in the Behavioral and Social Sciences*
(Millions of Dollars)

	FY 1968	FY 1969	FY 1970	FY 1971 (Est.)
Basic research	116	127	122	141
Applied research	134	148	206	257
Total: Behavioral and Social Sciences	250	275	328	398

* Adapted from *Federal Funds for Science*.[1] Includes all psychology and all social science. Rounded to nearest million.

four times as many physical, biological, and engineering scientists on United States university campuses as there are behavioral and social scientists.

Not only is the absolute size of these disciplines small, but much of it is very recent growth. The ranks are thin, and even thinner is the array of experienced, middle-aged, and elder statesmen who so often are called on to advise government. A small number of people, then, are faced with a rapidly rising set of demands for help — knowledge, advice, research assistance, program evaluation, and so on. What the social and behavioral sciences do have, in common with other scientific disciplines, is a large body of young Ph.D's, trained in the 1960s. In fact, between 1960 and 1970, while graduate enrollment in all fields of science and engineering increased by 109 per cent, the increase for the social sciences was 163 per cent. Many of the students entered these fields because of practical interest in social problems and ameliorative purpose. If their experience as graduate students did not dispel such notions, some of them, at least, may be interested in careers in applied social research. Another factor working in this direction may be the structure of the future labor market.

A number of forecasts of demands for scientific manpower during the next two decades are in agreement with each other in their overall conclusion: that the openings for holders of the Ph.D. in academic positions at institutions that traditionally have employed them will be smaller than the expected supply of trained individuals. The rate of growth in new jobs is predicted to be much smaller in the future than it has been in the recent past, owing to changes in the apparent size of cohorts of future college-level students. This fact, coupled with a very recent tendency toward an increased rate of graduate study, leads to gloomy forecasts of unemployment or underemployment among holders of the Ph.D. in the 1980s. Many, it is said, will be forced into occupations of an administrative character or into teaching at the community college or high school level, which would not fully utilize their scholarly competence.

Such a picture has been broadly sketched for all fields of science. One may assume that the forecast applies more or less equally to the social sciences in particular, with one additional stricture: the relative dearth of alternatives to an academic career in the social sciences, outside of psychology and economics. There is, in addition, some evidence of modest unemployment or underemployment at the present time, although the situation currently appears to be slightly more favorable for the social than for some of the physical sciences.

A second major feature is that the social and behavioral sciences have only recently become differentiated from ethical and moral philosophy and, hence, from a position in which they were not empirically grounded sciences, but only one more doctrinaire opinion in a cacophony of conflicting views. In terms of the span of the history of science, this emergence bears a dateline of "yesterday." It is perhaps only in the last two or three decades that any substantial number of scholars has been practicing social *science* rather than social opinionating, and the difference is at least as great as that between chemistry and alchemy.

In part because their development as sciences has been recent, the behavioral and social sciences have accumulated a relatively small knowledge base and do not yet have as sophisticated knowledge-getting techniques as the physical and biological sciences. Therefore, the contribution of social and behavioral sciences to the solution of practical problems has been less than it should be and, as a further consequence, these disciplines have not been called upon much in the past to assist in the solution of the problems of governing the nation. (When they have been called upon, the effectiveness of their response has been uneven and erratic — with some substantial successes as well as a number of failures.)

Finally, for the reasons just cited, the social sciences have not yet achieved the place for themselves in the information and advice structure of United States' scientific affairs that the physical and biological sciences have won. To be sure, the position is gradually shifting. Social scientists have been serving on the President's Science Advisory Committee for a few years, and there is evident intention to increase their number in the National Academy of Sciences. Perhaps social scientists should not legitimately expect to be as influential in the absence of demonstrated equality of achievement, but that is not the point. Rather, the point is that a place in the information-advice network will, per se, help the social sciences to develop strength and competence in the solution of practical problems at this stage in their history. A deeper knowledge of government agency needs; advance notice of new programs; participation in the making of long-range and far-reaching plans; an awareness of probable future developments in physical science and technology; an opportunity to join with physical and biological scientific colleagues in the disciplined examination of the problems of the society — these are some of the advantages that would accrue to the social sciences if they had a more central place in the network.

If there is any moral for the social and behavioral sciences in this abbreviated, but frank, assessment of their state, their capacities, and their limitations, it surely is the admonition: "Don't oversell." Don't promise more than can be fulfilled and don't encourage overzealous support and advocacy on the part of well-meaning friends who hope that deliverance from all social ills can be found in the application of more social science. Many of the problems to which social scientists are being asked (or will be asked) to address themselves are intractable and some are frankly impossible of solution in the near term. Social science cannot save us any more than any other science can.

Yet that does not mean that there is nothing to be gained from trying to work scientifically on social problems, or from trying to improve the social sciences. On the contrary, there will be some fundamental and significant gains from such strategy.

One important gain will be simply better knowledge about the current state of society and more accurate and detailed information about particular social problems. As Alice Rivlin has cogently pointed out, when the "war on poverty" was conceived in the mid-sixties, policy makers literally did not know who the poor were. There was no really *available* information about their social, occupational, racial, and demographic characteristics. As Rivlin says:

In late 1963, when the launching of the war on poverty was under consideration, those who made the decision had only the vaguest notions about how many people were poor and who they were. [An arbitrary and simple definition of poverty was adopted.] At that time however a more sophisticated definition could not have been used even if it had been available. No technical capability existed for estimating quickly from the census, or any other source, the characteristics of the poor according to more complex definitions.[2] (p. 10)

This is not elaborate, high-powered social science. It is merely essential information — but information that can best be gathered, analyzed, and used for planning, through social scientific methods.

The need for basic, descriptive data that are both up to date and available has been recognized again in the numerous proposals and extensive discussion of "social indicators" during the last half dozen years.[3,4] The notion of a set of frequently repeated series of measures of the state of a society surfaced much earlier in the form of a presidential commission, appointed in 1929 by Herbert Hoover, which in 1933 published a volume entitled *Recent Social Trends*.[5] The report consists of 29 monographic chapters, covering such topics as population characteristics, health, education, welfare, race and ethnic groups, religious behavior, and "social attitudes."

The authors of the monographs felt keenly the inadequacy of the statistical data they had to work with, and that complaint, like many other matters touched upon in the introduction to the volume, dismayingly resembles current comment about the social scene. For example, the Commission was concerned about the role of women outside the home; about "the sprawl of great cities"; about crime and racketeering; about "the consumer and his perplexities"; about poverty; and about the "dearth of physicians in rural areas." Some problems do *not* decay with time.

For a few years after this publication appeared, an attempt was made to keep selected series up to date through publication in a sociological journal, but the venture was not enduring. The idea reappeared in the early 1960s and has been extensively examined in several recent books. It was also tried out, so to speak, in pilot form through the staff of the Assistant Secretary (of HEW) for Planning and Evaluation, who published *Toward a Social Report* in 1969.[6] This slim volume modestly attempted to illustrate what "social indicators" might show about the state of society by assembling and interpreting readily available quantitative data about seven areas of society: health and illness; social mobility; the physical environment; income and poverty; public order and safety; learning, science, and art; and participation in and alienation from society.

The interest of social scientists in social indicators and a social report was inspired in part by the apparent success of economic indicators in keeping surveillance over changes in economic growth and, at least in the early 1960s, in helping to predict the economic future and to make effective recommendations for public policy in fiscal and monetary actions. It is clear that many social scientists (and perhaps even more nonscientists) are interested in developing indicators of noneconomic phenomena. This is because they hope that both the "bookkeeping" and the forecasting functions of such indicators could enlighten our understanding of social change and assist in the development of public policies for social intervention in such matters as health, employment, education, welfare, and so on.[7,8]

Because the term "social indicator" has accumulated a number of meanings, it may help to define it as a quantitative measure of the performance (or, as economists say, the "output") of a facet of the society. Ideally, a set of social indicators would be conceptually integrated into a system of statistics that, in a fashion analogous to the National Income and Product Accounts, would provide comprehensive coverage of the performance of major institutions and subsystems such as education; health; crime, justice, and rehabilitation; employment; and welfare. (The analogy is rough; it is *not* intended to imply the development of an aggregate index similar to the gross national product.) Such a fully articulated set of indicators presumably would be able to show the gross response of social institutions to changes in inputs, hence enabling better judgments to be made about the effects of social programs. The ideal system will be difficult to build and its accomplishment is far in the future. For a considerable time, policy makers and social scientists will have to be content with much more fragmentary, disaggregated, and unarticulated series; and even developing these will be a considerable labor, whose beginning should not be delayed.

It is important to draw the distinction between the usefulness of social indicators for "bookkeeping" purposes, on the one hand, and their usefulness for forecasting the effects of proposed public policy (or measuring the effects of specific social interventions) on the other. Social indicators can be quite useful right now for what Herbert Simon has called "scorecard purposes." That is, they can give us some idea of how various aspects of society are changing and can call attention to problems as they arise. They can play a role in drawing up an agenda for social action, for the first step in social problem-solving is to identify the problem and bring it into public awareness. Some indicators may help to diagnose how well or how poorly various institutions of society are working — education, law enforcement, justice, and health care, for example — and how their effectiveness is changing over time, provided that series are collected on a large sample base that will allow meaningful differentiation among age, ethnic, geographic, and other categories. Finally, social indicators can provide much-needed evidence for arguments and viewpoints that usually have been hard to substantiate. For instance, conflict between economic growth and conservation of the natural environment often appears one-sided because conservationists are unable to summon enough hard evidence to support their cause. A system of quantitative indicators that would enable conservationists to measure changes in the quality of the environment would raise the level of debate to a point at which rational choices could be made.

The arguments for the establishment of a national system of social indicators are strong, but that should not lead to the conclusion that such indices, even if fully perfected, will satisfy all the needs of designers engaged in developing new social practices. In addition to the problems of analyzing serial data statistically, indicators suffer from the deficiencies of all observational and retrospective forms of study. The trouble is inherent in the observational method itself, for, in any natural situation, a large number and variety of forces are at work, making the causative relations obscure and hard to disentangle.

An even more formidable defect is that there is no general theory of (noneconomic) social systems, no conceptual or mathematical model of how the society works that is capable of being matched with available data. What is missing is a comprehensive idea about the dynamics of the social system and the interconnectedness of its parts. Hence, it is difficult to decide how to choose indicators that would give valid estimates of changes that result from particular social interventions.

Some beginnings have been made along these lines, however, and a few are exciting and promising. For example, a team at the Urban Institute has been developing a model of income distribution which they expect will enable them to simulate interactions and transactions between persons, families, and institutions in respect to sources and uses of income. The model is based in part upon data from the Survey of Economic Opportunity, augmented by other data for more well-to-do segments of the society. The model is "policy oriented" by design — that is, it focuses on those aspects of consumer-investor behavior that can be affected by actions which lie within the realm of deliberate public policy, such as taxation, welfare payments and other income transfers, the support of education, and so on. The outputs of the main model are changes in the use of income — for consumption or saving and, within consumption, for such various purposes as housing, education, recreation, and others. There are also "side models" being designed to articulate with the main model, but focusing on special areas of behavior, such as health behavior.

This ambitious attempt to conduct what amounts to computerized experiments with alternative policy options is heavily dependent on the correctness of the underlying structure that is built into the equations. If that corresponds to the real structure of the social system, and if the input data are correct, the simulation will permit alternative policies to be tested in a neat and clear fashion.

These are two very large conditions, and few social-system models meet them. Much social data is of poor quality or is unavailable. Many of the major dynamic relationships among components of the social system are poorly understood.

Attempts to improve on social data through the social indicator route must go forward. Attempts to improve theoretical understanding of societal dynamics through model-building and simulation may be a viable alternative to "pure" theoretical work or to the foot-slogging approach of intuitive-empirical "cut and try" attacks on the available data. Experience suggests that improving the data collected; pure theoretical work; and simulation will contribute mutually to understanding. The three approaches should go forward together.

Yet it is debatable whether, in the short run, a system of social indicators can be developed that would be sufficiently sensitive to detect the effects of specific social interventions and, at the same time, broad enough in scope to serve other descriptive and analytical functions. Because social phenomena and social systems are characterized by strong interactions, it is difficult to isolate the social situation under study from its contemporary context and almost impossible to isolate it from historical influences, owing to human memory and to cultural traditions. As Cronbach and Suppes remark:

The essential difficulty in research on social processes is the interaction of variables. . . . A teaching method that works for one child will not necessarily work for another. . . . Brownell and Moser . . . found that a meaningful presentation of subtraction was ineffective for children who had been taught until then by a rote method; the children simply had not learned to make use of meaningful connections.[9] (p. 141)

For all these reasons, it seems likely that, at least in the short run, until more powerful social-system theory as well as better measurements are perfected, progress in assessing and forecasting the effects of social interventions (and hence in guiding public-policy recommendations) is likely to be made through controlled and focused experiments that examine the outcomes of social programs on the persons and social systems directly involved in them.

The notion of experimenting directly upon parts of the social system is a bold one, as well as an ambitious one. Yet the conclusion is unavoidable that such experiments are necessary in order to get more dependable knowledge about the effects of deliberate social interventions. There are serious limitations upon the yield of information from laboratory experiments, in which the researcher attempts to abstract what he considers the essential features of a real-life situation and to reconstruct it in miniature. The limitations arise from the strong and pervasive interactions of which Cronbach and Suppes speak. In the present state of social science knowledge, it is extremely difficult to design an adequately representative laboratory experiment to study a complex series of social processes. Much more can be learned from deliberately planned experimental programs that intervene in actual social processes, even though on a small scale. Such experiments must be designed to yield dependable information through random assignment of subjects and through reliable measures of the relevant variables — both the "inputs" of the social program (the treatment) and the "outputs" (the behavior it is intended to affect, as well as its unintended consequences).

Genuine social experiments are infrequent for a number of reasons. They are technically difficult, expensive, in some cases ethically problematical, and they almost always require more time to mount, conduct, and analyze than policy makers are willing to invest. There are, of course, a number of different kinds of ventures that go by the name "experiment." These include pilot studies, demonstrations of one kind or another, and the sort of laissez-faire variation in program that some legislation permits or even prescribes (e.g., Title III or Title I of the Elementary and Secondary Education Act of 1965). Such ventures are ordinarily not true experiments, in that they fail to meet the essential criterion of social experimentation, namely: that the subjects of the experiment are assigned randomly to different treatments and that measures of the behavior being studied are made both before and after the treatment. This experimental model resembles that used in agricultural experimentation, although the social experiment does not often attain the precision of the agricultural one. However, some current examples illustrate how close social science can come to meeting the requirements of the experimental model and also illustrate some of the problems and difficulties referred to earlier.

The New Jersey Graduated Work Incentive Experiment (usually known as the Negative Income Tax Experiment) is being conducted for the Office of Economic Opportunity through the Institute for Research on Poverty at the University of Wisconsin and MATHEMATICA, Inc. The experiment was launched in 1968 to test the impact of a welfare system on intact families of employable poor. A sample of such families was obtained by interview and, after screening to determine eligibility, families were assigned randomly to a control group or an experimental group. The control group is stratified into eight different treatments which differ in respect to the "guarantee level" — that is, the level of benefits provided by the scheme, and in respect to the "tax rate" — namely, the rate at which benefits are reduced as other income increases. Ignoring the details, the net effect is to produce eight variations in the relationship between welfare benefits received and income earned in order to study the effect of income guarantees on motivation to work. Of course, ancillary observations can be made, such as the impact of the scheme on health, on borrowing and spending behavior, on family stability, attitudes toward work, children's school performance, leisure-time activities, and so forth. The experiment involves more than 1200 families (about 60 per cent in experimental treatments) in urban areas of New Jersey and Pennsylvania. Final results will not be available until June of 1973. Preliminary results from a year and a half of experience with part of the sample show no evidence indicating a significant decline in weekly family earnings as a result of the income-assistance program.[10] Thus, the guaranteed income seems not to have reduced the beneficiaries' propensity to work, at least so far.

This experiment illustrates very well some of the difficulties of social experimentation mentioned earlier. Most of the technical problems, including those of design and random assignment of subjects, seem to have been handled with both dexterity and good fortune. In social research, this is a major achievement. Perhaps because it was frankly an experiment and was not linked to any immediate policy proposal for welfare reform, and certainly because the agency funding the research had a professional sympathy for and understanding of the requirements of experimental design, the social scientists were able to avoid the kind of political and humanitarian pressures that sometimes beset those who are conducting experiments. Often there seems to be a sentiment that subjecting individuals to experimental and control treatments is somehow basically unfair. If a program has benefits, then all human beings should be equally eligible to receive them. The difficulty here, of course, is in being able to demonstrate the "benefits" of a particular program without the experimental evidence to show that, in fact, they are benefits and not penalties or mere illusions. The legitimacy of experimental procedure is not always well understood or, indeed, received with sympathy.

The design of the study includes measures of indirect effects of the scheme. Here the investigators ran into another technical problem, for although they could easily measure changes in family earnings, there was some difficulty about attitudes toward work and other social-psychological measures. "Off-the-shelf" technology was simply not available and they had to devise their own measures, whose validity and reliability have not been established.

While technical problems were formidable, resources were available for their solution. The experience of trying to organize field operations, however, revealed the even more formidable requirement of managerial skill to execute the design in the field. The essential combination of scientific skill, supervisory talent, and administrative savoir faire is very hard to find. The project was successful in locating an excellent field manager, but in the course of looking for him discovered how rare this combination of talents is among social scientists. He was required not only to assemble and train a field staff but to make sure that their performances as interviewers adhered to the standards of quality and adhered to these standards consistently, which is required to obtain objective, unbiased information from respondents. He had to be sure that the machinery required for calculating benefits and changes in them in response to other income functioned accurately. He had to keep track of families that moved and take other measures to reduce the attrition rate in the sample. He had numerous other managerial tasks of central importance to the outcome of the study, but perhaps none was more trying than managing the data-processing system itself. The accurate and rapid processing, the compact storage, and the accessing of complex longitudinal information in great quantity is a technology that is, as yet, underdeveloped in social science. In this respect, too, there is a shortage of personnel, and the occupational role and career line is only beginning to be defined. The kinds of skills and their combinations needed for the conduct of large-scale and longitudinal experiments in social research is still an ill-defined matter. This is especially true for paraprofessionals, for whom there is almost no formal training available (partly because the role requirements are so ill-defined), but it is also true for professionals, because the career of field-research management is so new and opportunites in it as yet are so limited.

Earlier, I referred to questions of cost and time with regard to experimentation. A rough estimate for the New Jersey Work Incentive Experiment suggests that its total cost during a five-year period (including three years of actual payments to subjects) will be in the neighborhood of $5 million. This is an unprecedentedly large scale in the social sciences, although it certainly looks tiny by the standards of NASA, ESSA weather modification, AEC underground tests, or the perinatal collaborative study.

The value of the information returned from this investment is difficult to calculate, partly because of the time factor. When the experiment was being planned in 1966 and 1967, its designers certainly must have thought they were at the forefront of social planning.[2] As Alice Rivlin has pointed out, a negative income tax was only one of several proposed attacks in the war on poverty during the mid-sixties; it had the endorsement of some academic economists, but it appeared to have little popularity in the Congress or the Administration. Even in 1968, when the experiment went into the field, there seemed little likelihood that the negative income tax would be considered seriously in Congress. Yet, in the summer of 1969, the President suggested "the family-assistance plan," which was, in effect, a negative income tax for some families. The matter subsequently began to receive the most serious attention from the Congress, and hearings held by the Ways and Means Committee of the House in the winter of 1969-70 virtually forced the experimental project to analyze the first year's results.

The House inquiry also pushed the bounds of interest wider, since by that time it had also become concerned with day-care programs, and the Committee wished to know the effect of income maintenance programs on incentives for women to work. This feature had not been considered important in the original planning of the New Jersey experiment, and hence insufficient provision was made in selecting the sample for measuring the work behavior of female heads of households and females who were secondary wage earners. Furthermore, the demand of the Congress for information and the importance of the answers to their questions suggested that the experiment should have been planned and executed on a larger basis in the beginning, perhaps costing even three or four times as much as the actual one. By the end of the 1970 fiscal year, the experimenters surely must have felt that the ground had moved under their feet. From being a pioneer venture on an unprecedented scale in a daring design, they had become a research project that was rather slow-moving, too small, and too narrowly conceived to meet the demands that the Congress and Administration, as well as the public, were imposing on this significant area of American life.

The demand for information did not, indeed, stop with the Congress. In fact, demands for information about the project posed one of the most serious ranges of ethical problems with which the experiment has had to deal. Its managers were beset by requests from the major news media for interviews with the participants; with demands from both administrative and congressional groups to examine individual records; and with a similar request from state agencies, which accused certain of the participants of "welfare cheating." Without going into the details of any of these requests, it is clear that they came as unexpected demands for which the project was ill-prepared because of the almost total absence of any sort of legal or conventional precedent for dealing with such matters. Neither statute nor common law has caught up to the point that social research has reached in dealing with individual and personal matters; nor have the social science associations done much more than begin to consider the questions of the invasion of privacy, protection of the confidentiality of data, the rights of subjects, and the need for information.

It is not possible to enter into a serious discussion of these matters here. They are complex and, like all value-laden choices, involve elements of arbitrariness, as well as of power. Perhaps the most hopeful thing to be said is that the debate has been opened and is being carried on at a reasonably public level. But social scientists ought to be concerned about certain features of the situation that currently are being exaggerated. On the one hand, there seems to be a degree of overzealousness in the popular movement to "protect the rights of the subject" of experimentation. For example, the doctrine of "informed consent" has serious limitations. It is impossible to legislate what informed consent is, and its genuine implementation depends upon the investigator's own ethical sense being developed highly enough to insure his voluntary compliance with the intent of the doctrine. At the same time, it is true that inexperience, overeagerness, and unforeseen consequences are traps for the investigator; and he benefits on these counts from having review committees of intellectual peers, who should be diverse in background, rather than all from the same field. Appealing as is the doctrine of "informed consent," it is sometimes simply unworkable in practice because the subject cannot be made to understand all of the complexities involved in the research procedure, whereas at other times the explanation of the research seems not to be heard at all or to be quickly forgotten. Memorable is the example of John Lofland, who, in studying a millennial group as a participant observer, was a model of openness and fair dealing. He explained to the leader and the membership why he wished to reside in their communal house while they waited for the next Coming and was apparently understood to be a sociologist in pursuit of a research goal. Yet, at the end of a year, when he had not announced his conversion and taken up the beliefs of the group, he was angrily abused by some of them for having deceived them.[11] Evidently his protestations were not believed, although they were understood. So much for "informed consent."

There is also a great deal of concern abroad about the psychological damage done to subjects in experiments and other research projects of a social, as well as a medical, character. In this realm, both popular and professional ignorance is overpowering. There are only the most general and vague intuitive notions about what constitutes psychological damage and there is, except in rare instances, very little evidence to show that experimental procedures have been responsible for psychological or emotional damage to subjects. There are outrageous cases to the contrary, but these are, in general, a small minority of all experiments, conducted under conditions in which professional peer surveillance seems to have been inadequate.

On the opposite side, social scientists should be concerned about the eagerness of legislators, police officials, and other guardians of the law and public morality to obtain and use research data about individuals as if they were subpoenable records that could be put to an "official" purpose. Social scientists are especially defenseless in this realm. Their needs and deeds have no precedent in common law and they do not enjoy its understanding. They are not statutorily protected in any state. Social science records have been subpoenaed both for criminal and for civil actions at the state level, as well as by committees of the Congress at the federal level. The social science community needs to organize for concerted action in this realm. It needs better-articulated codes of conduct and standards of ethical behavior to which its members subscribe wholeheartedly. It needs to provide better ethical and procedural inculcation for practitioners, especially in applied research. More than anything else, it needs some sort of legal recognition of its special problems and protection from the onslaughts of those who would severely restrict the conditions of data collection or the kind of data that may be gathered, and of those who would exploit whatever data exists for their own purposes, to which the subject has not given prior consent.

One ethical question that needs more attention than it has yet received arises with particular cogency in connection with social experiments in which the experimental treatment has a substantial and lasting effect on the life situation of the subjects. For example, the negative income tax experiment certainly will provide some families with income payments upon which they will come to depend. How should this dependency be managed when the experiment is over? To take another example, at least two field experiments in Central America are concerned with the relation between nutrition and the mental development of children. The experimental treatment in both cases is to provide a protein-calorie food supplement free of charge to the experimental subjects in order to remedy their dietary deficiencies in childhood. In one study, the supplement is to be provided to individual households in a large city.[12] In the other experiment, an entire village (of several hundred inhabitants) receives either the experimental or the control treatment, which means that upward of 100 pregnant women, and children under 12 are fed a supplementary diet twice a day at a community center.[13] The urban families in the first example live at such a level of poverty that the amount of the supplementary food to be given them would, in effect, considerably increase their total income and perhaps affect the way they spend their cash. Over the course of the five years during which the study is proposed to run, the urban families will not only have received the benefits of better diet, but will have had a sharp increase in their whole standard of living. In the rural example, not only are diet and (presumably) income allocation changed, but a new community institution has been created in the center where the diet supplement is mixed and served, where families gather twice a day in sociable discussion and play, and where medical examinations and health care are offered freely. These changes have substantial impact on individual lives.

From the viewpoint of the experimenter, the question is how he can terminate the experiment humanely and ethically. He surely is responsible for having changed the life situation of some subjects; equally surely, he cannot assume responsibility for sustaining that change indefinitely. A completely satisfying solution for the dilemma does not exist, but some measures seem reasonable.

Unquestionably, the experimenter first must explain to the subject of an experiment as clearly as possible what she is being invited to do. To be sure, there are serious limitations on the effectiveness of informing the subject in advance. Over a four- or five-year period of experimentation, subjects surely become habituated to the treatment and forget it is a time-limited experiment. Or they wishfully believe that benefits will continue despite the experimenter's warning. On the scientific side, there is also the possibility that the generalizability of the experiment will be limited because subjects will adopt strategies oriented toward the time-limited nature of the treatment. This possibility may attribute more rationality and foresight than most people are able to muster, but there is very little evidence on the point.

A second suggestion for getting the experimenter out ethically is that termination should be gradual and with as much forewarning as possible. When the technical needs of the experiment have been met, a period of termination and withdrawal should begin. The transition should not be abrupt. The planning of the experiment should include provision for the withdrawal period as an ordinary and necessary administrative cost, and the experiment should not be considered to have been satisfactorily concluded until it has gone through an effective withdrawal procedure.

Third, during the withdrawal period, every effort should be made to help the experimental subjects to continue to enjoy the benefits the treatment has brought them. Sometimes this may be done through shifting responsibility to an agency that ought to have borne it anyway — for example, by persuading the national government health-service agency to provide the amount and quality of care which the experimental treatment offered or by persuading a private charitable agency to give the food supplement. More desirable than perpetuating dependency is, of course, helping the individual family or community to organize itself to provide the benefit. Training or counseling the head of the family, or encouraging the formation of community organizations, with material assistance provided at the outset, may be efficacious ways of discharging the experimenter's responsibility.

These suggestions are only a beginning of discussion of the problem. The ethical problems of conducting the experiments described above, and particularly the problems of withdrawal, are being given the serious consideration they deserve by the investigators concerned. But they are venturing into an area that is new, whose properties are not fully explored, and whose management will surely benefit from responsible and sober public discussion.

There has been opportunity to touch only upon some of the more salient features of the current scene as they affect the development of the social sciences. The coverage is narrow and the analysis less penetrating than a fuller treatment would have permitted. Some things should be repeated in summary about the present state of the social sciences and their relationship to the rest of American society.

In the first place, it is clear that, more than ever before, a great deal of attention, funding, and expectation of help in solving social problems is being directed toward the social scientist. This poses both unusual opportunities and some dangers — the dangers principally being those of overexpectation followed by disappointment and overselling. Social scientists themselves can avoid the latter, but only nonsocial scientists the former.

Second, it is apparent that the social sciences are relatively small in size and that they need encouragement to grow in both size and quality. Any public policy that serves to increase the amount of social science manpower is a useful one, provided that it also increases the level of quality of talent drawn into the field. A major effort should be made to attract better young people earlier and so, through their addition to the corps of workers, to raise the intellectual level of all the discipline.

Third, it is apparent that some new descriptive and analytic approaches to the study of social problems are at hand. Both social indicators and social experimentation are feasible, although they are expensive and difficult to develop. Each technique has its place and jointly they may serve as instrumentalities for gathering the kind of information and providing the kinds of insights that are necessary for rational development of public policies in the social area.

Fourth, the current forecast indicates a shortage of posts in the traditional academic sector where basic research is the vehicle of choice for advanced training and for the development of scholarship in social science. Academic institutions have not ordinarily (with certain outstanding exceptions) made special efforts to build and maintain operating capacity for applied social research. In fact, most academic departments consider such work to be outside their proper sphere, and the interstitial units of the university structure (research institutes or centers-for-the-study-of-) have usually been fragile, short-lived, and easily deflected from applied research purposes.

One may raise the question, then, whether this may not be the time to begin a more serious effort to implement some of the recommendations made by the National Science Foundation's Commission on the Social Sciences and by the Behavioral and Social Sciences Survey. The former body recommended the establishment of problem-centered research institutes devoted to the application of social science methods to the solution of social problems. The BASS survey recommended the establishment of Schools of Applied Behavioral Science for the education of just such professionals as would be needed to staff such institutes. If there will be a shortage of openings for social scientists in traditional occupations, and if government and private funding seem to be converging on means of wider utilization of social science, then perhaps the time has come to use these forces to make some beginnings in the direction endorsed by these two bodies which so recently examined the social sciences and their usefulness to society.

Finally, it is clear that as social scientists move out of ivory towers, libraries, laboratories, and other sheltered niches of the academic world and into the commission of acts of applied research, they need both to develop some additional standards of conduct and to achieve some protection from those who would exploit, as well as those who would restrict, their technical possibilites of accomplishment. It is none too soon to begin.

REFERENCES

1. National Science Foundation. Federal Funds for Science, Vol. 20. U.S. Government Printing Office, Washington, D.C., 1972.
2. Rivlin, A. Systematic Thinking for Social Action. The Brookings Institution, Washington, D.C., 1971.
3. Bauer, R. A. (Ed.). Social Indicators. MIT Press, Cambridge, Mass., 1966.
4. Sheldon, E. B., and Moore, W. E. (Eds.). Indicators of Social Change: Concepts and Measurements. Russell Sage Foundation, New York, 1968.
5. President's Research Committee on Social Trends. Recent Social Trends in the United States, 1933 (2 Vols.). Greenwood Press, Westport, Conn. (reprint, 1971).
6. Department of Health, Education, and Welfare. Toward A Social Report. U.S. Government Printing Office, Washington, D.C., 1969.
7. Ferriss, A. L. Indicators of Trends in American Education. Russell Sage Foundation, New York, 1969.
8. Ferriss, A. L. Indicators of Change in the American Family. Russell Sage Foundation, New York, 1970.
9. Cronbach, L. J., and Suppes, P. (Eds.). Research for Tomorrow's Schools. Macmillan, New York, 1969.
10. Office of Economic Opportunity. Further Preliminary Results of the New Jersey Graduated Work Incentive Experiment. OEO Pamphlet 3400-4, Washington, D. C., May, 1971.
11. Lofland, J. Doomsday Cult. Prentice-Hall, Englewood Cliffs, N.J., 1966.
12. Latham, M. C., Cobos, L. F., Rueda-Willliamson, R., and Stare, F. J. Nutritional and ecological factors in intellectual deveopment of Colombian children. Paper delivered to the VIII International Congress of Nutrition, Prague, 1969.
13. Klein, R. E. Performance of malnourished in comparison to adequately nourished children (Guatemala). Paper presented to the annual meeting of the American Association for the Advancement of Science, December, 1969.

IX · *Biomedical Sciences*

JOSEPH S. MURTAUGH

THE CONSIDERATIONS SURROUNDING federal support of the biomedical sciences are in some respects similar and in others markedly different from those of science generally (Figure 1). The basic pattern approximates that for the support for all research, with these differences: (1) there was no perturbation during the Korean War period (1950-1955); (2) the large annual budget increases for the biomedical sciences began in fiscal year 1957 and is clearly pre-Sputnik I; (3) the growth rate was sharper (1955-1965); (4) the post-1965 slowdown in support was less severe; and (5) evidence of a beginning recovery is more clearly evident. The discussion that follows is largely based on the background and implications of these differences.

The rapid growth in the federal support of biomedical research is primarily the consequence of a set of events and forces that had as their base a belief in the value of research in the definitive solution of a number of important medical problems. Such a set of concerns derived from the internal social aspirations of the nation and are domestic in origin. Much of the growth of research and development in other areas has been engendered by considerations of national technological prowess and international tensions. Only very recently has major emphasis been given to domestic social purposes in the federal support of nonbiomedical research.[1]

The nature and magnitude of biomedical research support has been modified by the constraints imposed by the protracted and controversial evolution of parallel federal roles in health education and health services. An expanding set of national purposes in these latter areas became clearly apparent only in the post-1965 period. This delay engendered a framework for federal support of biomedical research during the 1950s and much of the 1960s that, while well-adapted to the conditions and

---

JOSEPH S. MURTAUGH Director, Dept. of Planning and Policy Development, Association of American Medical Colleges, Washington, D.C.

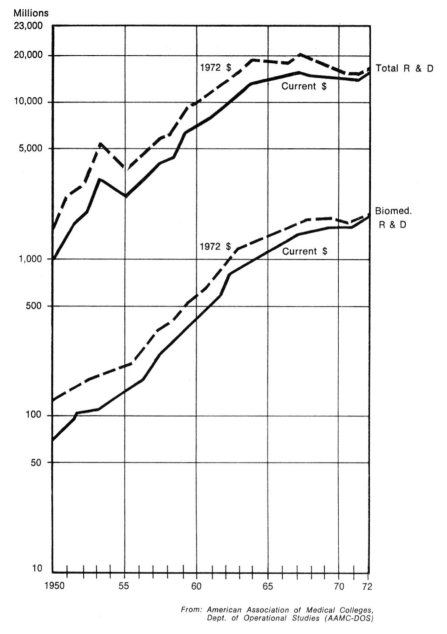

From: American Association of Medical Colleges,
Dept. of Operational Studies (AAMC-DOS)

FIGURE 1.   Federal obligations for research and development, both total and biomedical, in current and 1972 constant dollars, 1950 to 1972.

purposes of that period, is showing increasing inadequacies in the context of the broadening scope of federal health efforts, the current stage of development in biomedical science, and the total requirements of educational programs and academic institutions.

In the opening chapter of this book, Caryl Haskins refers to the significant transformation in American attitudes toward science that appears to be associated with the "depression" in federal support of science in the latter half of the 1960s. That a transformation has taken place there can be no doubt, despite differing views on its nature and cause. One view of this rather abrupt and general curtailment is that it marked the end of the period when federal support of research was aimed at urgent and special purposes, without important regard for the other social needs of the nation or the significant relationship of research to the processes and institutions of higher education. The direction of current events reflects an emerging coalescence of science-policy discussions with these other two broad areas of national concern. This chapter is one perception of these developments as they relate to the biomedical sciences.

THE GROWTH OF THE NATIONAL INSTITUTES OF HEALTH

It is appropriate to examine the events and forces that influenced the growth of the federal role in the biomedical sciences in the context of the development of the programs of the National Institutes of Health. It is similarly convenient, but perhaps more arbitrary, to deal with biomedical science largely in terms of research carried out in academic medical centers and institutions intimately associated with them. This is reasonable because the bulk of federal funds for biomedical research has been channeled through NIH programs and because a significant proportion of the resulting activity has been in these institutions.*

The growth of the programs of the NIH are summarized in Figure 2. Much has been written about the sequence of events and the program and policy action that constituted this "billion dollar success story," as President Johnson once described the NIH.[2] Despite the complexity of the contributory events, the sustaining force behind the growth has been

* Activities related to health, including research, are ubiquitous within the executive branches of the federal establishment. There are also many institutions and agencies concerned with the performance of biomedical research. These include, in addition to the medical and dental schools and directly related institutions, a number of federal agencies, the more general university counterpart of the professional schools, freestanding research institutions, nonprofit and not-for-profit research institutions, and, finally, a massive industrial activity centered largely in the pharmaceutical and chemical industries.

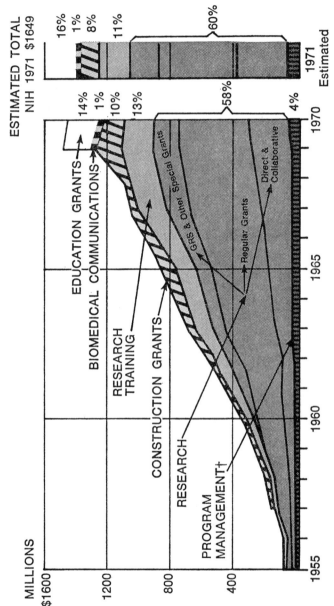

FIGURE 2. Estimated NIH obligated funds by function for fiscal years 1955 to 1971, excluding programs that have been transferred out. (Transfers: NIMH and community programs. Also excludes foreign currency program. Includes Bureau of Health Manpower Education and National Library of Medicine from FY 1969 on. †Includes buildings and facilities from FY 1969 on, but chart excludes direct construction for prior years.)

centered in a basic social need — the improvement of the health of the nation.

The Beginnings

Increasing and urgent national concern for health beyond conventional attitudes toward "public health" became evident in the 1930s as reflected by the initiation of the venereal disease program, the National Health Survey of 1935, and, explicitly for biomedical research, in the passage of the National Cancer Act in 1937.[3] This Act provided the basic ingredients for many later developments: (1) a major disease problem was singled out for concentrated attack; (2) the support of research in nonfederal institutions through project grants was authorized; (3) fellowships for advanced study and training were initiated; and (4) a substantial role in the guidance of research and training was given to an advisory council composed of nonfederal lay and professional leaders. These basic ideas, later extended to include other major disease problems, initiated the basic program structure for the postwar development of the National Institutes of Health.

The growing and controversial involvement of the federal government in the broad social and economic problems of the nation was interrupted by World War II. At its termination, efforts to extend the social legislation of the depression thirties were rejected. The national mood of the postwar period was one of conservatism. This mood, together with an increasing concern over the emerging role of communist ideologies in the world scene, was reflected in a tendency to view as dangerously socialistic proposals for many new federal initiatives in domestic problems.

The strength and effect of these views is perhaps best epitomized in the congressional action on proposals for a compulsory national health insurance program, developed in the late forties by Oscar Ewing, Administrator of the Federal Security Agency (the forerunner of the Department of Health, Education, and Welfare). Although supported by President Truman, these legislative proposals were denounced in the Congress as a plan to socialize American medicine.[4] The rejection of these proposals reflected an attitude that was to dominate the federal role in health for the better part of the next 20 years. Not until 1965 was this restraining grip on national health policy partially modified through the passage of the Medicare and Medicaid amendments to the Social Security Act. In keeping with these conservative views, efforts to engender concern over the precarious financing of medical schools in the 1950s did not survive the prejudice against a direct role for the federal government in education.[5] Not until 1963 did legislation dealing directly with medical education, albeit limited to construction, emerge from the Congress, despite repeated efforts in the intervening years.[6]

In contrast to restrictive limits on the federal role in health and education, few restraints were placed on the federal support of research. The war experience resulted in a new comprehension of the significance of science and technology in national affairs. Atomic energy, the "wonder drugs," and electronics clearly held high promise for a new way of life. The role of academic science in extending this promise, as demonstrated by the success of the wartime Office of Scientific Research and Development (OSRD), generated a ready acceptance of a broad federal role in the support of research in universities.[7] Disagreement was basically limited to differing views on the desirable organizational form and setting for a national effort in science, as reflected in the legislative struggle preceding the creation of the National Science Foundation (NSF) in 1950.

The delay in establishing the NSF resulted in no single agency being concerned solely with science when the OSRD was terminated in 1946. In consequence, the residual OSRD contracts were distributed to existing federal agencies with scientific competence — in biology and medicine to the National Institutes of Health, and in the physical and mathematical sciences to the developing Office of Naval Research. These determinations, in association with a continuation of the broad research programs of the Department of Defense and the burgeoning program of the Atomic Energy Commission, placed broad support for academic research in the mission-oriented agencies long before the debate over the role of the National Science Foundation was completed. Largely as a consequence of these events, the dominant method for the federal support of basic research continues to be through mission-oriented agencies.

Between 1946 and 1950, successive legislative enactments, modeled after the Cancer Act of 1937, made explicit the categorical structure that now comprises the NIH. This concept envisaged that each institute would be concerned broadly with all the problems of an important set of related diseases and that its programs should encompass support of research, research and specialty training, disease control, and public information. The progressive concentration of those categorical efforts on the research and research-related aspects of disease problems has had an important bearing on current events, as will be noted later in this chapter.

In the early 1950s, the Korean War imposed a delay in program expansion for NIH, but this was helpful; it permitted attention to be directed to the development of sound operating concepts. Two determinations had particular influence on subsequent developments.

1. It was concluded that the biomedical knowledge available was inadequate for a direct assault on the major disease problems. This judgment resulted in support of broad and far-ranging programs for research in the relevant fundamental biomedical sciences.

2. A commitment was made to the concept of scientific excellence, and a peer-review mechanism was refined to limit support to those projects that met rigorous standards of scientific merit.

Thus, by the early 1950s, the stage had been set legislatively and administratively for what was to be one of the more remarkable developments in the federal relationship to science. Although there were to be important legislative enactments affecting the NIH in subsequent years, these were basically elaborative, except for the General Research Support Amendments in 1960. It was not until the passage of the Health Professions Education Assistance Act of 1963 that a significantly new federal dimension became available in the health field.

Substantial Growth

The Congress provided effective impetus for the period of rapid program growth, which, beginning with decisions in the fall of 1955 and spring of 1956, was to continue for more than a decade. Enlightened and powerful leadership in the Senate and House, in the persons of Lister Hill and John Fogarty, combined with the appointment of James Shannon as Director of the NIH, joined an extraordinary set of political and scientific capabilities. This combination was reinforced by full and purposeful use of citizens' testimony before the congressional appropriations committees. This latter device provided the Congress with views and concepts that had been unrecognized or ignored in the executive branch of the government.

It is important to note, however, that in the summer and fall of 1965, under the leadership of an able Secretary, Marion Folsom, the Department of Health, Education, and Welfare (DHEW) recognized both the need and the opportunity for scientific advances in medicine, and an effort was made to attain a significant initiative in the presidential budget submitted in January of 1966.[8] The subsequent budget constraints of a conservative administration became overriding, and the opportunity for positive executive-branch influence in this development was lost. Thus, the pace, scope, and direction of NIH program growth was almost entirely dominated by congressional appropriation action.

Underlying Policy Influences

Among factors underlying the massive growth of NIH budgets (Table I, page 172) through the remaining fifties and most of the sixties was the growing force of national aspirations for better health. The increasing support for biomedical research was accompanied by a continued rejection of efforts to obtain a substantial engagement of the federal apparatus with significant programs related to medical education and general medical care. Thus, the avenue and mechanisms for a vigorous federal expression in health were limited largely to the categorical research and training programs of the NIH.*

Thus, in many ways, the NIH programs of the 1950s and early 1960s may have served in part as a surrogate for an otherwise inchoate and inherently controversial, but rapidly growing, desire of the country to undertake on a national scale a substantial effort to improve the health of its citizens.

Another set of factors accompanying the expansion of biomedical research was the growing complexity and urgency of the problems surrounding academic institutions and their educational programs. These institutions were increasingly beset with pressures for expanding enrollments and greater public service in the midst of declining support and rising costs. Recognition of these problems began in the late 1950s, but fears overrode the appreciation of need. As in the health area, strong opposition was arrayed against any direct involvement of the federal government in the operating support of any portion of the educational system. This opposition had its roots in adherence to the constitutional assignment of education to the states, the church-state controversy, and the feeling of some academic leaders that federal action might have a deleterious effect on education.[9] These basic attitudes were amplified by the negative attitude of organized medicine toward any proposal for direct federal intrusion into the medical educational scene.

Effect of Policy Constraints on the Conduct of NIH Programs

The long delay in reaching a consensus on a broader federal role in education and particularly in medical education exerted an important constraint on the conduct and development of NIH programs. The legislative language that authorized NIH support programs was rigorously construed to apply only to research and research-related activities. Guidelines for expenditure of grant funds and their audit drew distinctions between research and research training versus teaching and education. When it became clear that expanding research programs would

---

* The set of "disease-oriented" and resource-oriented programs, such as the Hill-Burton program of the Public Health Service, as well as other limited federal health programs in the area of maternal and child health, vocational rehabilitation, and the Veterans Administration, offered neither the scope nor the appeal of the NIH research effort.

require greater numbers of scientists, which could only be achieved through the correlative expansion of graduate education at both the predoctoral and postdoctoral levels, substantial "research-training programs" in the related fields were undertaken, but similar distinctions were maintained.[10]

These programs provided stipendiary support for students and departmental support for the associated institutional costs. About half of the funds made available through such "research-training grants" were expended to meet these latter costs.[11] Although these programs were clearly limited to the training of scientists and science-based medical specialists in areas of shortage, they became a major source of operating funds for the departments involved.*

Similar constraints influenced the development of programs for the construction of new medical facilities. The construction legislation, initially introduced in 1956, authorized support for constructing facilities for both medical teaching and research. But only by striking support for construction of teaching facilities was it possible to secure the passage of what then became the Health Research Facilities Construction Act of 1956.[12] Ingenious broadening of subsequent renewals of this Act to encompass "research and related purposes" made it possible to cover space needs for the graduate education essential to the expansion of research training.

It was apparent in the late 1950s that broad use of the project system of support diminished the effectiveness of the central authority of academic institutions and introduced a substantial element of instability into the academic structure. Increased consideration was directed to the development of some form of institutional support for research that might offset the influences of an increasing dependence upon project grants of the research programs and the faculties of many institutions. The objectives of these programs were quite specific; they were to return to an institution some measure of initiative in the science area and to exert a stabilizing influence. Such a development was urged in a number of reports aimed at federal-university relationships, and was particularly well stated in respect to medical research and NIH programs in the Bayne-Jones Report of 1958.[13] The program of General Research Grant Support[14] was the legislative consequence of the recommendations in this report.

* These arrangements resulted in an anomalous situation. Specialty training in medicine, surgery, and related areas became broadly supported in association with clinical organizations and their research programs. Thus, major departments were aided in their development, but on the unstable base of project grants for both research and "training" that required renewal, usually at four- to five-year intervals.

The limitations on the federal role in education, in contrast to research, also affected this effort to broaden federal support for research beyond project grants and projects. The full-scale development of the GRS program was hampered by attitudes held in two important quarters. Some congressmen felt that the pressures for general research support arose more out of broader institutional need in the educational area, which they were willing to support — but not by an indirect method. On the other hand, the scientists of the nation appeared to favor determinations by national peer groups as the basis for distributing research support, as opposed to bureaucratic decisions within their own institutions. They did not support the program.

The consequence of these several developments was to insure that the formal policies governing the major flow of money from the NIH to medical schools and related institutions continued to be limited largely to the support of research and related needs and objectives through project mechanisms, in the midst of a growing requirement for some form of broad and less restrictive form of institutional support.

Effects Upon Academic Institutions

In the academic institutions, conditions were created that optimized the research elements of the enterprise, but did little to further a more holistic view of the nature of academic activity. With the recognition of an arbitrary division between teaching and research, an activity called "research or research training" could be supported by federal funds; an activity called teaching could not. Viewed from the standpoint of education, there is a dependent relationship between teaching and research in the attainment of educational objectives in a science-based field such as medicine, but that relationship received little recognition as the levels of support for research activity increased. A few academic voices were raised in alarm over this trend, but complaints about federal funding of academic research were dominated too frequently by acrimonious exchanges over the payment system for overhead costs.

The accommodation to arbitrary distinctions between teaching and research reached the point at which the broader concept of "education" became synonymous with the more limited function of "teaching." The latter activity was viewed as an institutional concern and thus a local responsibility. On the other hand, research and research training (which, to a very large degree, consisted of pre- and postdoctoral education) were considered to be federally sponsored activities, related as much to national as to institutional needs and goals. Academic institutions, their administrators, and their faculties bear a heavy responsibility for the degree to which this arbitrary process of separation and distinction was allowed to become an acceptable condition of academic life.*

The massive expansion of federal funds confined to the support of research activities and a relative decline in the support, from nonfederal sources, of other academic activities that later precluded an adequate response by the institutions affected to the social needs of the later 1960s, laid the basis for a fundamental financial instability in the academic institutions involved. This instability engendered even greater dependence upon the flow of research funds in maintaining the total viability of the pertinent institutions.

The response by the NIH to such an unsatisfactory situation was twofold. On a policy level, it continued to press, although unsuccessfully, for the enactment of legislation that more realistically aligned federal responsibility with the general needs of institutions. But, on a practical level, the NIH developed terms and conditions for the implementation of their programs, which, although within the letter of their legislative authorization, made maximal utilization of research funds for more general institutional purposes. Such temporizing devices operated reasonably well during a period of program expansion. However, in the face of a concurrent increase in the rate of inflation and a beginning constraint on federal funding, both evident in the summer of 1967, a number of institutional programs were placed in jeopardy; this at about the same time that general recognition was given to the need to expand greatly the production of physicians.

Such a sequence of events may have been shocking, but it should not have been surprising. In the early sixties, discussion on a national level resulted in the frank recognition of a need to correct the academic imbalance that resulted from the support of a single academic function and from a process of geographic distribution that provided support for some institutions but not for others. The unsatisfactory consequences of these circumstances, in respect both to the broad national interest and the institutions involved, received national recognition. This concern was epitomized in the Memorandum of President Johnson in September 1965 to the heads of federal agencies with academically oriented grant or contract programs. The Memorandum directed that research supported in the furtherance of agency missions "should be administered not only with a view to producing specific results but also with a view

* The problems surrounding federal-university relationships generated by federal programs, as noted here, were articulated cogently by Charles V. Kidd.[15] Certain of these issues were further elaborated in the 1962 report of the Teaching Institute of the Association of American Medical Colleges.[16]

to strengthening institutions and increasing the number of institutions capable of performing research of high quality."

It is obvious that President Johnson's directive was more an exhortation than a basis for definitive corrective action. The latter required new legislation aimed directly at the support of higher education, but no new legislative proposals were forthcoming. In the absence of a broader legislative resolution of the fundamental matter, the financial circumstances of many institutions became increasingly subject to the vagaries of agency funding. And the federal approach to higher education as such was further subordinated to mission-oriented research determinations.

BROADER PUBLIC POLICY CONSIDERATIONS

The postwar cultivation of science by federal agencies whose fundamental objectives and responsibilities arose from broad public purposes that transcended science imposed a major constraint on the formulation of national science policy. However broadly the terms and conditions of the federal support of academic science were articulated, in the final analysis they were limited by the legislative and program restraints of the mission-oriented agencies that provided the support.

The NIH is, in the final analysis, a "health," not a "science," agency; in like manner, the Office of Naval Research is a "defense" agency. In both cases, science and research are means, not ends. Their concern with science is, therefore, derivative from and subordinate to the primary public purpose from which they originated. In this context, broad national issues concerned with science, education, or academic institutions in terms of their direct significance for overall public interest could not be reached or dealt with in a primary, direct, and coherent manner. One could only assemble and assess, in an after-the-fact way, the probable consequences of diverse policy and budget decisions on the research programs of mission agencies as they related to the overall course of science, graduate education, and the institutions involved.

President Johnson's Memorandum, while seemingly motivated by a concern for the health and vigor of educational institutions, did not appear to reflect any understanding of the seriousness of the developing situation that actually precipitated his remarks nor of the distorting effects that the recommended approach would have on agency roles. A basic federal philosophy was expounded nonetheless. Such a view recognized the net benefit that could be derived from the support of research in academic institutions by a diversity of federal agencies, but largely limited the federal responsibility to research and related purposes.

There is no doubt that advantage does accrue for academic enterprises from the federal support of research, and for the individual this advantage is maximized by diversity of support. However, for the institution to obtain the maximal benefit from the support of a large-scale research enterprise, this support must be paralleled by programs that also provide reasonable support for the other essential purposes of the institution and for the stabilization of the institution as an end in itself.

In the medical schools, the absence of such stabilizing institutional programs, the absence of adequate support for education, the leveling-off in research funding, and the accompanying inflation, all clearly apparent by 1967, revealed the true hazards of this basic pattern of federal support to the integrity of institutions. To the extent that these effects were perceivable, the means for any effective corrective action were, to a very large degree, beyond the scope of the individual mission agencies with science programs.

Another important consequence of funding from multiple sources is that it tends to obscure the true scope and nature of federal action required in new program developments in which academic institutions are called upon to serve a key role. This problem was clearly demonstrated in the set of events surrounding the emergence of a beginning federal role in the education of physicians.

Although opposition to a larger federal role in medical education and health as such dominated legislative attitudes during the expansion of support for biomedical research, there was growing apprehension in many quarters of the nation over the increasingly evident deficiencies in health services and medical care. The late 1950s saw increasing discussion of the adequacy of the nation's supply of physicians. In 1958, the report of the Surgeon General's Consultation Group on Medical Education (known as the Bane Committee) called for substantial expansion in the production of physicians through the establishment of 20 new medical schools.[17] It recommended that the federal government initiate a ten-year program of matching construction grants to meet this need. Dr. Shannon was among the few who argued that a construction program would be useless without programs providing parallel support for the educational process. These warnings went unheeded in both the executive and legislative branches of the government and, interestingly, in the academic community that would be affected, as well.

In retrospect, the views expressed in the Bane report on this latter point reflect a fascinating unreality. On the problem of operating support, the report said in part: "Although some schools are now in a serious financial situation, the consultant group was unable to find a satisfactory way in which federal aid could be secured for the support of the operations of these schools." And it concluded: "The continuation of training grants, the payment of full indirect costs for research and the development of federal institutional research grants . . ., would seem to be the best contribution of the federal government at this time."[18]

Legislation providing for a construction grant program was finally passed by the Congress as the Health Professions Education Assistance Act of 1963, with the seemingly implicit condition that the medical schools, as suggested in the Bane report, should look to the NIH research-support programs as the basic source of federal operating support for expanding their educational activity. Not until the amendment of the Act, effective in FY 1966, which provided for a modest program of institutional grants, did some perception of the medical educational need emerge.

The Growing Incongruity

The appropriations that followed the 1966 manpower legislation never matched the manifestly inadequate legislative authorizations, and their role in resolving the financial problems of the medical schools was limited. The financial plight of medical schools worsened. The setting was now one of growing confusion over how well and in what manner the complex public purposes being sought through these institutions were being and should be served. By this time — the latter 1960s — the dialogue over the inadequacies of the delivery of health services had grown increasingly more urgent and more controversial.

Apart from the issues that surrounded the financing of medical care, which had been muted temporarily by the Medicare and Medicaid legislation in 1965, medical manpower shortages were seized upon as the root cause of much, if not all, that was wrong with the delivery of health services. The manpower role of medical schools then came to the forefront of executive and legislative policy concerns. The apparent incongruity between the substantial increase in the flow of federal funds to medical schools during the previous decade and the corresponding negligible increase in M.D. graduates was imputed to reflect the failure, if not the refusal, of medical schools to respond to public need. Preoccupation with research was cited as the controlling influence upon the behavior of medical schools and their faculties to the detriment of their broader educational and service responsibilities. These views were reflected in increasing legislative and executive resistance to further favorable policy and budgetary determinations related to support of medical research.

The real problem, however, was to a large degree obscured by the pattern of support that had developed over the years. The objectives of the NIH programs within their governing legislation were not educational in nature. The purposes of NIH programs were related to the production of new knowledge and the demonstration that it could be applied to the maintenance of health and the treatment of disease. Their educational purposes were largely confined to the incidental provision of a sound base in the biomedical sciences, which was essential for the education of scientists and the development of faculty. It is true that the programs did enrich the environment for undergraduate education, but this was not their primary purpose. Within their authorization, it was quite impossible to use the programs to satisfy the new public purposes being sought, viz., to increase the production of physicians or to make a direct contribution to the improvement in the delivery of health services. As a consequence, the growth of NIH research programs had brought about a distribution of support that basically could not satisfy the multiplicity of academic programs and the financial needs of institutions. Support of research and related functions also could not satisfy the new public purposes now being identified in respect to producing physicians and improving health services.

Eight years after the enactment of the Health Professions Education Assistance legislation, and in the context of increasing public demand for increased production of physicians, less than 10 per cent of the total flow of federal monies into medical schools was directed to the support of the undergraduate educational process (see Table I). Almost 40 per cent of all medical-school expenditures are derived from federal research and research-training programs, and their faculties receive substantial salary support therefrom. This is simple evidence both of the lack of federal recognition of its important role in medical education and of the de facto dependence of medical schools upon research monies for operating support.*

Academic Science and Categorical Research

Another aspect of the NIH program development has come into sharp focus recently. The early judgment that significant progress toward

* Medical education in the United States, 1970-71. *JAMA* 218 (No. 8) Nov. 22, 1971, Tables 10 and 31. This distribution of support may be modified somewhat under the new Comprehensive Health Manpower Training Act of 1971, which provides capitation support for medical students plus other special grants programs aimed at modifying the educational process. Appropriations thus far fall substantially short of authorization levels for these education programs. On the other hand, NIH research appropriations have increased significantly since 1970.

categorical objectives requires substantial expansion of basic biomedical knowledge and high scientific standards for work supported, resulted in an increasing commitment to the support of undifferentiated biomedical research. The device in common use was the investigator-initiated research grant, made on the basis of a peer-review process. This so-called "regular research grant" program has been, for the most part, the central component of the NIH development and has accounted for a major portion of the NIH expenditures for research purposes (Figure 3). Such investigations are more suited to satisfy the internal logic of science than the more artificial constraints of a categorical objective.

But, in actual practice, the effective decisions concerning NIH research-grant support are made at two levels. The judgment of scientific excellence is by a peer-review group that is concerned primarily with the scientific significance and excellence of a proposal. Judgments on the suitability of the program within the categorical purposes of an institute, and the priority determinations that will obtain in the distribution

TABLE I
DHEW Obligations to Schools of Medicine
Selected Fiscal Years
(Millions of Dollars)

	1960	1970	1972
TOTAL	$151.4	$781.6	$1,080.0
RESEARCH — Total	134.2	525.9	766.0
Conduct of research	92.7	360.1	591.0
Research training and fellowships	41.5	165.8	175.0
UNDERGRADUATE PROGRAMS — Total	—	71.9	143.0
Student assistance	—	15.7	23.0
Institutional support (capitation grants and special project grants)	—	56.2	120.0
CONSTRUCTION — Total	17.2	108.7	57.0
OTHER PROGRAMS	N.A.	75.1	114.0
Regional medical programs	⎫	45.3	80.0
Health services for children	⎬ N.A.	18.7	⎫ 34.0
Other	⎭	11.1	⎬

N.A. = Not Applicable
SOURCE: 1960, 1970 — National Institutes of Health.
      1972 — Federal Health Programs Special Analysis, Budget of U.S. Government, Fiscal Year 1973, Bureau of Health Manpower Education, NIH, and Association of American Medical Colleges.

AAMC-DOS — 1/28/72

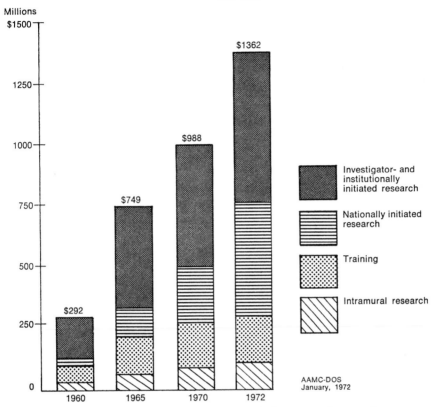

Millions

$1500

1250

1000

$1362

750

$988

$749

500

$292

250

0

Investigator- and
institutionally
initiated research

Nationally initiated
research

Training

Intramural research

AAMC-DOS
January, 1972

1960   1965   1970   1972

FIGURE 3. Distribution of NIH research funds by type of research support, 1960-1972.

of funds, are the responsibilities of advisory councils and the staff of the institute in its executive capacity.

In the past, the effectiveness of these mechanisms in achieving a set of categorical objectives was limited considerably by two phenomena. The part-time advisory councils and the full-time staff frequently were not inclined to interfere with the free dynamics of the scientific process; and interests vested in particular problems often were able to divert funds toward special purposes through the device of congressional earmarking in an institute's budget. At other times, when the executive function in the direction of programs was strongly exercised by an institute's staff, problems were generated with its various publics and disagreements of various intensities were engendered.

Underlying many of these confrontations is a matter of real import. The extramural mechanisms and administrative structure of the NIH tend to favor the support of research by project grants, the majority of which are investigator-initiated. With the possible exception of cancer, and despite the increasing amount of applied research that has been supported as opportunities developed, an explicit administrative framework for nationally initiated and directed research and development is probably less developed and less emphasized than is desirable, considering the state of the art within the biomedical sciences.

Further, the program activities concerned with the direct application of research findings through directed disease-control activities and other service types of activities — which had been part of the original responsibilities of the categorical institutes — were transferred to the then Bureau of State Services of the Public Health Service in the early 1960s as part of a reorganization of the service. These have not prospered well. The wisdom of the decisions that have produced this set of circumstances has been subjected to increasing questioning. As a consequence of these factors, when looking toward NIH from the outside and with a deep concern for clearcut and specific approaches to pressing needs in an important disease area — and an equal concern for the full use of the known, rather than a still-further pursuit of the unknown — much that the NIH is doing and, particularly, how it is being done may appear to some to be off-target and even irrelevant.

Such attitudes may not be warranted when there is less than a full understanding of the state of the art in a given area. But to say that such attitudes are unimportant is to make a serious strategic error in program management. Indeed, such a set of attitudes underlies the growing resurgence for a return to the broad categorical approach to related diseases, recombining research, training, application, and service, as exemplified by the enactment of the National Cancer Act of 1971 and the new Heart, Blood Vessel, and Lung legislation. On the other hand, in these various confrontations and frustrations of a well-meaning people, the forces at play must be recognized and, at the same time, a balance must be struck between a social need and the stage of development that has been reached in a specific area — a stage that might limit the means available for the search and application of new knowledge. The emotional bias for immediate action, however, will not be profitable if it violates the precise demands for coherence in the scientific enterprise.

Viewing this set of circumstances as unfortunate, and not wishing to make a set of general scientific judgments, is is reasonable to conclude that the pressure for further and more practical efforts, as defined in the new cancer legislation, results from more than simple disenchantment with the NIH and the methods used. A more fundamental motivation may well stem from the prolonged frustration, felt by so many concerned professionals, over our seeming inability to solve complex disease problems simply and, at the same time, to bring into being a rational and effective system of health services and medical care. To the extent that these views are correct, the faults stem from the nature of the problems under study and, until recently, from the rather fundamental deficiencies in the legislative authorities under which federal programs operated.

The scientific issues involved in these complex problems are substantially simpler than those with social dimensions. With all the new health legislation — Regional Medical Programs, Partnership for Health, Medicare, Medicaid, the medical programs of the Office of Economic Opportunity and of the Social and Rehabilitation Service of DHEW, and the Veterans Administration, and even the new health manpower and cancer legislation of 1972 and that proposed for other institutes — with all this, rational and reasonably costed health services continue to elude the American public. The essential decision-making in health continues to remain a private process, despite its increasing envelopment in public programs and its growing support from public funds. The question of how and by whom such a private process, if it is to remain private, is to be controlled in the public interest is the underlying, but unspoken, root issue in all the current national debates relating to health.

The avoidance of, or the inability to come to grips with, this basic issue has resulted in the concentration of national efforts around the essentially secondary and often peripheral activities just enumerated. This has often reflected the simplistic belief that a vigorous attack upon secondary problems will resolve the primary issue. Perhaps that will be the case, and certainly this approach has not been without its useful results. But it has also meant a substantial shift in what are perceived to be urgent priorities in the health area and in a greater emphasis on health-service needs and health-manpower problems. All of this has been at the expense of the prominent position once held by medical research in the federal health budget (Table II).

The End of the Period of Growth

This review of past events has now moved to what might be considered the end of an "Augustan Era" for biomedical science, circa 1967. The onset of the depression in support of science in general, as Dr. Haskins has termed it, has frequently been attributed to a combination of the progressive public disenchantment with science and technology, the apparent irrelevance of much of science to urgent social problems, and the adverse environmental consequences of some of its works. Then, too, it is not difficult to understand a negative public reaction to a vast activity, the growth and purposes of which are more the product of the long dominance of cold-war imperatives and the demands of an unpopular conflict in Vietnam than of a concern with pressing social problems and the conditions of life. These reactions may also have influenced the support of biomedical research in association with the administration's desire for a general retrenchment, but the immediate causes for the leveling of federal funding were different.

1. The programs of the NIH were the victims of their own success as represented by demands for an immediate and broad application of advances already made.

2. A reorganization of the Public Health Service brought a responsibility for health manpower into the NIH and placed the budgets for manpower and research in competition with each other for funds within a single agency.

3. Last, but not least, there was a sustained lack of leadership in medical affairs at DHEW and in matters relating to health.*

The rapid sequence and severe character of the curtailment in support funds generated widespread distress and disarray within the biomedical research community. Its maximum impact was felt during fiscal year 1970. A new director of the NIH had the difficult task of forestalling further erosion in the biomedical research-support base and, at the same time, responding in a responsible fashion to urgent demands for an increase in the production of physicians. The situation was further complicated by moderate budget cuts in training-grant programs, an administration measure taken to diminish demands for increases in research support. There was seemingly no recognition that training funds were essential to the continued functioning of the same medical-school departments that were being called upon for the education of even greater numbers of M.D. candidates.

Of the many reports that commented seriously upon these complex matters, three warrant specific notation: that of a Committee on Biomedical Research Policy of the Council of Academic Societies of the American Association of Medical Colleges (AAMC), chaired by Dr. Louis Welt[19] and entitled *A Policy for Biomedical Research*; an extended survey, *The Life Sciences*, conducted by a committee of the National

---

* Congressman John Fogarty died the night before the opening of the Ninetieth Congress, and his House appropriations subcommittee was yielded to interests less dedicated to medical research. Lister Hill was shortly to retire and, for the first seven to eight months of a new administration, there was no health leadership within the top departmental structure (DHEW).

TABLE II

National Health Expenditures, Total and Federal
Selected Fiscal Years
(Millions of Dollars)

	1955	1960	1965	1970	1973
NATIONAL HEALTH EXPENDITURES	$17,924	$26,367	$38,912	$67,240	N.A.
National expenditures for biomedical research	261	845	1,837	2,685	N.A.
Research as percent of national health expenditures	1.5	3.2	4.7	4.0	N.A.
FEDERAL HEALTH EXPENDITURES	1,948	3,508	5,161	18,066	25,527
Federal biomedical research expenditures	129	510	1,040	1,577	1,982
Research as percent of federal health expenditures	6.6	14.5	20.2	8.7	7.8

N.A. = Not Available
SOURCE: National Health Expenditures — Social Security Administration.
National Biomedical Research Expenditures — National Institutes of Health.
Federal Health Expenditures, Total and Research — 1955 — Social Security Administration, Other years — Federal Health Programs, Special Analyses Budgets of U.S. Government, Fiscal Years 1970, 1971, 1972, 1973.
AAMC-DOS — 1/28/72.

Academy of Sciences[20]; and the Carnegie Commission's report, *Higher Education and the Nation's Health.*[21]

These documents were not inconsiderable efforts. The Welt Committee report is a careful and thoughtful examination of both the problems and the promise of biomedical research. *The Life Sciences* is a landmark work of great value. The Carnegie report was most helpful in developing the terms for the new health-manpower legislation; its support of the need for science was more an article of faith than a well-articulated proposal. Each of these documents is an eloquent statement of the needs and oportunities in the biomedical sciences, but, in the aggregate, they were viewed as a sophisticated form of special pleading and had little immediate or obvious effect on research funding. Each report demonstrates quite clearly that there is no simple, much less absolute, rule that, of itself, can establish a proper level of federal funding for biomedical science. Alvin M. Weinberg seems most reasonable in his view that the decisions concerning the level and allocations of support for science, at least in the foreseeable future, will continue to be made in the political process within the context of the public purposes being sought.[22]

With this point we reach the current scene. The context of public purpose and public action, in which the further development of the biomedical sciences must be sought, clearly is being set by current legislation and appropriation enactments. These are the Comprehensive Health Manpower Act of 1971, the National Cancer Act of 1971, and the HEW Appropriation Acts for 1971, 1972 and 1973.*

This legislation, and the executive and legislative struggle from which they emerged, provide an insight into the likely direction of change and the kinds of influences that will operate within the biomedical science community. It is important to examine those actions that will have a particular influence on the federal support of biomedical science.

Manpower Legislation

The terms of manpower legislation reflect a significant departure from the previous Health Professions Educational Assistance legislation in three major ways.

1. Federal assistance will be through capitation grants.
2. The authorized levels of support represent a major increase over prior levels; the average is $2,875 per student.
3. The grant supports the "education" program of the institution rather than the "teaching" of earlier legislation.

This latter point is of special importance, because a provision of the new law requires the Secretary of HEW to carry out a study, through the National Academy of Sciences, of the annual per-student costs to schools in providing an educational program that leads to the doctoral degree in medicine and the other health professions.[23] Implicit in this charge is the task of defining the nature and content of the educational experience that qualifies an individual for the M.D. degree. Here, the medical educational community will be challenged to assert and defend that aggregate of research, teaching, and clinical activity that it believes is requisite to present-day medical education and that should be used as a basis of determining costs and, thus, the subsequent levels of federal funding for its educational programs. This study is fraught with problems relating to standards and quality, with implicit dangers for diver-

---

* Other actions of possibly equal importance are the proposed restructuring of the NIH, with the Cancer and the Heart and Lung Institutes achieving full Bureau status; broadening the authority of the National Heart and Lung Institute (s 3323), similar in many ways to the new Cancer Authority; and legislation expanding the Arthritis and Metabolic Disease Institute to encompass gastrointestinal diseases (PL 92-305).

sity, and with implications for major modifications in the funding structure of these institutions. However, it does offer the promise of a more rational structure for the support of medical education — one that can reverse the arbitrary distinctions and separations engendered by previous legislative approaches.

The Cancer Legislation

The Cancer Act and the struggle that preceded it over whether the cancer program would be separate from NIH are instructive. They clearly demonstrate the continued strength and the public attachment to the categorical approach that now has escalated with the initiation of "superprograms." In large part, this legislative drive was a direct reflection of the cumulative frustrations encountered in the long cancer effort. Those resulted from: the intractable nature of the scientific problems and a consequent slowness of progress; the lack of public perception of suitable emphasis upon directed research and the early application of the research findings; and the ponderousness of the bureaucratic processes.

With all knowledge obviously not put to general use in an effective manner, it is hard to argue that there does not continue to be a valid and important role for the categorical approach in health programs. Fortunately, though, the final legislation supported the view that substantial advantage would accrue through the continuation of a unified administrative framework for biomedical research.

In the debate that was resolved with the enactment of the new Cancer Authority, several important points were quite clear. First and all-important, regardless of what a program is in fact, support of a program of federal research derives in large part from a public perception of its direct, clearcut, and concentrated efforts on behalf of a specific problem. As a corollary, an administrative framework that does not provide a sufficiently substantial and direct engagement with such a specific problem is likely to engender public challenge from those most devoted to the solution of that problem, and these may be scientists or nonscientists. Both of the convictions carry with them the misleading quality of simplicity, which, when forcefully stated in relation to a given area of science or social need, tends to engender public acceptance.

These matters obviously were not handled adequately in the cancer field, for a challenge based on these simple convictions did derive from the activity of the Senate Panel of Cancer Consultants, and was strongly supported by testimony of its chairman, Benno C. Schmidt.[24] Without question, the solution sought by the Panel would have destroyed both the NIH and a coherent federal role in support of biomedical science.

Nonetheless, the legislative struggle itself emphasizes that the threat posed by the Senate-passed cancer legislation (S 1828) was substantial. It revealed the peril that present program arrangements at the NIH hold for a coherent, traditional approach to the support of biomedical science as such. Better arrangements surely must be devised for the very difficult task of providing for the scientific direction and management of high-quality, effective, problem-oriented research within the categorical programs, on the one hand, and effective and honest public-information programs on the other. This undoubtedly can be done in a fashion wherein social need does not simply override the limitations of scientific feasibility. But the purposes served by the research must be stated more clearly, and only then, perhaps, will stable public support of a rational nature be forthcoming readily.

The Decline of the Policy-Making Apparatus

Two other aspects of this struggle over the further program in cancer warrant separate comment.

First, the behavior of the administration relative to the cancer legislation was inconstant and inconsistent. Initially, the White House, in accordance with the prevailing view in the scientific community, assumed an opposition stance and serious efforts were made to rally active support for opposition to the legislation. The Association of American Medical Colleges opposed the bill in hearings before Senator Edward Kennedy, only to be confronted on a second occasion with a reversal of the administration's position and with Secretary Richardson's support of legislation that had been characterized previously by the executive branch as a threat to the continuation of an effective NIH. Throughout the struggle, the NIH was helpless in its own behalf and seemingly intellectually friendless within the executive branch of the government. It was only the courageous action of Congressman Paul Rogers (Fla.), supported by a massive response from the biomedical community, which thwarted what otherwise would have been a disaster for the biomedical sciences.

Second, this disarray in science policy-making within the executive branch, which was so clear in the cancer problem, seems to be part of an evident decline in the policy-forming role of the cabinet departments and the consolidation of the determining policy functions in the immediate White House apparatus.* The consequence, in association with

* Legislative proposals to establish a separate, independent Department of Health (s 3432, HR 14199) are a reflection of this concern in the Congress over health-policy making.

the executive branch's generally conservative position on budgets in the health field, has resulted in a shift of initiative to the Congress, a pattern reminiscent of the congressional leadership in health during the late 1950s and early 1960s. Germane to this situation is the resurgence of the role of the appropriations committees in advancing the levels of support for research in the research and related areas. In fiscal years 1971 and 1972, $400 million was added to the NIH research budget. For FY 1973, the increase voted in the Congress was $214 million over the President's budget.

Assuming that this resurgence of a dominance of congressional initiative is not a product of an election year, it has advantages and disadvantages. Clearly, the congressional process is much more responsive to public views. However, if it does not have suitable scientific staff and organization, its actions may lack coherence and may tend to reflect the conventional, rather than more innovative, concepts. But, in any case, such circumstances impose a grave responsibility on the nonfederal sector to create and utilize effective mechanisms capable of developing and providing advice on a national basis.

A NEW FRAMEWORK FOR SUPPORT OF THE BIOMEDICAL SCIENCES

An attempt has been made in this review to demonstrate that the program and support arrangements for the biomedical sciences within the NIH may well have satisfied the primary needs of research but that they became increasingly inadequate to satisfy the broader public purposes that involve these sciences and the broader and more complex academic functions of educational institutions that contain major science activities. In effect, with the simple support of research within an environment that perforce must have reasonable balance among research, teaching, and service (perhaps within the rubric of education), support of research alone tends to subvert the other functions if these, too, are not funded adequately. Importantly, though, biomedical research in the long run must not be limited or hampered by deficiencies such as characterize its present environment or those of the immediate past. For the biomedical sciences truly to flourish, these deficiencies must be removed, as must those that equally influence the biomedical science program within universities.

Sufficient information is now available to consider a new framework for the support of research that is both simple in conception, rational in nature, and possible of execution. It has a particular advantage — it would reflect visibly the three distinct public purposes that became obscured in the increasing flow of federal funds for the support of medical research. This support framework has three parts.

Research as an Essential Element of Education

The arbitrary distinction between "research" and "teaching" and between "research training" and "graduate education" that characterized past research-support policies have resulted, albeit unavoidably, in the financing within the context of research programs of some measure of what, in less prejudiced circumstances, must properly be termed and treated as "education." The growth in the amount and proportion of the salaries of tenured faculty members paid through research-project grants, previously noted, is a significant reflection of this circumstance.

It is generally agreed that contemporary medical education encompasses an integral mix of teaching, research, and patient-care activities, all three of which are essential to the qualification of an individual for a career of any sort in medicine. This means that there is a body of research activity that derives from and is requisite to the conduct of medical-education programs at the under-graduate and graduate level and should be dealt with as such in the pursuit of any public objectives relating to medical education. Thus, the allocation of public funds for the support of education of physicians to meet national needs incurs, ipso facto, the necessary and inescapable burden of supporting some measure of research activities, i.e., that body of research essential to the learning process and maintaining the competence of the faculty. Such research activity should be dealt with under the rubric of "education" rather than "research." Funds for such a purpose should be budgeted to provide for educational purposes, and the benefits that accrue to science should be considered secondarily. This distinction is essential if the public interest in both activities is to be served adequately and properly (see also John Millis[25]). This approach has implications for the broader federal role in education and science, where similar problems are receiving increasing comment.[26,27,28]

The basic problem, of course, is to establish the terms under which the amount and character of research activity to be so financed can be determined. This problem is the key challenge in the study of the cost of educational programs in the health professions that is to be undertaken by the National Academy of Sciences. The conclusions reached on this point in that study will be of profound importance for future public policy in the biomedical sciences.

To bring about such a policy approach within higher education and academic science will require a high order of bureaucratic statesmanship and, perhaps most importantly, great understanding of the fundamental issues at stake on the part of the academic and scientific communities.

The Support of Investigator-Initiated Research

The whole development of NIH programs, as noted earlier, has demonstrated the need to cultivate a considerable body of research activity in the broad context of the various disciplines within the biomedical sciences, rather than within the narrower and more specific objectives of the individual categorical programs. Here one is dealing with research activity emerging from the dynamics of the substance of science itself and represented, for the most part, by investigator-initiated proposals. The principal considerations that bear on policy and program development in this area of science center not on how much research is essential to education, but rather on the measure of support for investigator-initiated research proposals selected on the basis of their scientific merit and their significance for the meaningful advance of science and, thus, its long-run import for social purposes.

This body of research is roughly comparable with those activities encompassed within the "Regular Research Grant" programs of the NIH. Although each of the categorical institutes has a Regular Research Grant Program, such a "program" is, for the most part, the cumulative result of the central scientific review process and less the consequence of planned decision-making and selection on the part of the individual institutes. I have described how this pattern was built into NIH programs progressively as the necessary way to advance the base of fundamental science that is essential to progress in the categorical areas in the absence of and, perhaps more importantly, with the improbability of gaining support in more direct terms. Reports from appropriation committees regularly acknowledged and expressed support of this arrangement. These views, unfortunately, probably did not have broader congressional understanding and commitment.[29]

The body of scientific activity being dealt with in these indirect terms is now substantial, ranging up to $560 million in FY 1972, or roughly 40 per cent of the institute budgets. This program encompasses the research and scientific activity that is fundamental to all progress in medicine and health and to all social programs dependent upon biomedical science. In those terms, the support and advancement of this body of research activity should be administered as a primary policy and program entity within the overall structure of the NIH, above and beyond the support of educationally related research described above. Perhaps the greatest threat of the initial cancer legislation was that it would destroy what little coherence, albeit indirect, exists in the present NIH structure to deal with this body of scientific activity as a whole.

The importance of this fundamental area of science to broad public-policy objectives, both in science and broader social purposes, requires, I believe, a more forthright, visible, and responsive administrative framework. The development of such a structure would seem to be of vital interest to the scientific community involved. It would provide the opportunity to begin direct dialogue with executive and legislative decision-makers on the essentiality of this body of scientific activity and the needs for a more explicit and favorable support policy. Such an arrangement is becoming particularly urgent in the face of the increasing emphasis on applied research activity characteristic of present national science policies.

Under existing arrangements, support for this area of research is subject to increasing hazards, as a consequence of program actions in categorical areas. Thus, the addition of $100 million to the cancer program in the President's budget for FY 1972 was achieved largely through hard-to-perceive but real reductions in key elements of this regular grant program throughout the other institute budgets. The establishment of appropriation authorizations on a categorical institute basis, such as has been done for cancer and is proposed for heart, presents a further hazard for the stable and coherent support of this body of science.

Nationally Directed Problem-Oriented Research

The remaining area of public interest in biomedical research activity derives from nationally initiated and directed research programs aimed at expanding and concentrating purposeful scientific effort on selected problems in the achievement of a given national objective.

This area encompasses that additional volume and kind of research effort, above and beyond the research arising out of the first two areas of scientific activity noted above, that is considered necessary and desirable to achieve the earliest feasible attainment of the specific objectives sought. Here the initiative is of national origin, and the basic processes of program planning, design, selection, and assessment of results is nationally directed within a problem-oriented administrative framework. In general, such research requires substantial investments and must reflect a reasonable balance between scientific opportunity and feasibility, on the one hand, and the urgency and importance of the social problem to be solved, on the other. This, I think, is an essential concept underlying the categorical institutes. The obligation inherent in their role is the continuing analysis and synthesis of scientific findings that emerge from the full range of research activity as a basis for determining both the areas of ignorance and the areas of promise in relationship to the national objective sought. This synthesis should provide the basis for designing and directing specific exploratory and exploitive efforts, to which should be brought the most skillful scientific leadership. This approach also applies to broad areas of fundamental science, which would benefit by coherent and organized studies essential for ultimate progress in a number of disease problem areas. Good examples of the latter type of studies are the clarification of cell information systems at a molecular level and an elucidation of the fundamental biology and the disease significance of slow viruses.

The NIH does much of this kind of work at the present time. However, a more explicit organizational reflection of the work, undertaken together with a more effective public-information program, are essential to a better public perception of what is taking place.

SUMMARY COMMENT

The special case of the NIH and the university medical center and the support of biomedical research have been discussed in some depth. Some recommendations for the broad reorganization of the structure of support for these sciences through the NIH programs will, without doubt, be challenged vigorously. The details are subject to considerable variation. But the timing is critical and the substantive concepts seem to be valid. They offer a prospect for the rational approach to complex, but important, problems and are worth some risk.

If these recommendations were to be adopted, they would bring a new coherence to the NIH program and would permit the whole to constitute a more unified and mutually supportive structure. It would clarify the relationships among the public purposes now being sought in medical education, in the biomedical sciences, and these two as they relate to the solution of major health problems. They would not have too broad an impact on the program structure of the NIH, but they would influence the manner of its administration, with the elements of the program being utilized in a somewhat different manner.

Each of these three sets of programs can be budgeted for separately. Each would have quite different program objectives, as well as different terms and conditions covering the awards made. In such a view, the total research budget becomes a derivative of three considerations, or, alternatively and more desirable, two research items, with the educational-research component being budgeted simply as part of the educational cost.

In this approach, serious problems remain to be solved. The least of these relates to the determination of reasonable, aggregate figures for the budget. More important and more difficult would be an estimation of the continuously changing state of the art in each of the major categorical-program areas and the assessment of the benefits to be derived from any further increments in research efforts. But this is not a weakness of the proposal, because the same problems must be resolved within any modification aimed at improving the mechanisms for determining a reasonable level of support for research.

The three-way program grouping proposed would allow clear-cut policy decisions to be made about each area, based on full and direct knowledge of most of the factors involved. It would contribute in a substantial way toward the strengthening and stabilization of the pertinent academic institutions. Regularizing the research-support structure would reverse divisive influences upon institutions and would clarify and make possible better decisions concerning the scope and form of the academic involvement in research. This, in turn, would provide a greater measure of freedom and responsibility to institutions and a set of conditions in which the cultivation of stronger, movable, academic leadership could flourish.

To move in the proposed directions would require both bold and thoughtful action by the federal enterprise, by academic institutions, and by the scientific community. But even if the proposals are accepted as valid objectives, the prospect of change may be disturbing both to the administrators of federal programs and to the recipients of their support. On the other hand, if the decision is made to temporize with these matters and avoid or unduly delay a progressive process of correction, even greater hazards with their accompanying strains are possible, as the struggle surrounding the cancer legislation clearly revealed.

It is to be emphasized that although the discussions center around the relationships between NIH support and the university medical centers, it is appreciated that an increasing proportion of biomedical research funds are expended in other environments and that these are derived from both federal and nonfederal sources. However, the relationship between the NIH and the university medical centers will always be significant in advancing biomedical research and in applying new biomedical knowledge. Consequently, the problems generated within this relationship must be resolved as first priority. Given such a resolution, the problems in other areas are made more simple. It is for these reasons that such prominence has been given to the relationship in this chapter.

REFERENCES

1. Nixon, President Richard M. State of the Union Message, January, 1972. (White House press release, p. 33.)
2. Office of the White House Press Secretary, July 21, 1967 (press release).
3. National Cancer Institute Act. Public Law 244, 75th Congress, 1937.
4. Ewing, Oscar. The Nation's Health, A Report to the President. Prepared for the Federal Security Administration, Sept. 2, 1948.
5. Surgeon General's Committee on Medical School Grants and Finances. Financial Status and Needs of Medical Schools. Public Health Service Publication No. 54. U.S. Government Printing Office, Washington, D.C., 1951.
6. Health Professions Education Assistance Act. Public Law 129, 88th Congress, 1963.
7. Stewart, Irving. Organizing Scientific Research for War: The Administrative History of the Office of Scientific Research and Development. Little, Brown, Boston, 1948.
8. Shannon, James A. The advancement of medical research. A twenty year view of the role of the NIH. *Journal of Medical Education* 42 (No. 10):97-

108, 1967.

9. Rivlin, Alice M. The Role of the Federal Government in Financing Higher Education. The Brookings Institution, Washington, D.C., 1961, Chap. VII.

10. Digest of Opinions. Public Health Division Office of the Counsel, DHEW. Compiled April 1, 1965.

11. Issue Paper in the Training Programs of the National Institutes of Health, Part I, Table 3.17. Office of Program Planning and Evaluation, NIH, October, 1970, p. 44.

12. Health Research Facilities Construction Act. Public Law 835, 84th Congress, 1960.

13. The Advancement of Medical Research and Education. U.S. Government Printing Office, Washington, D.C., June, 1958.

14. General Research Support Amendments. Public Law 798, 86th Congress, 1960.

15. Kidd, Charles V. American Universities and Federal Research. Harvard University Press, Cambridge, 1959.

16. Comroe, Julius H., Jr. Research and Medical Education. (Report of the Teaching Institute of the Association of American Medical Colleges.) Evanston, Illinois, 1962.

17. U.S. Department of Health, Education and Welfare. Physicians for a Growing America. (A Report of the Surgeon General's Consultation Group on Medical Education.) Public Health Service Publication No. 709, Washington, D.C., 1959.

18. Ibid., p. 62.

19. Association of American Medical Colleges. A policy for biomedical research. (A report prepared by the Council of Academic Societies.) *Journal of Medical Education* 46(No. 8) (1971).

20. National Academy of Sciences. The Life Sciences. (Report of the Committee on Research in the Life Sciences of the Committee on Science and Public Policy.) Washington, D.C., 1970.

21. Carnegie Commission on Higher Education. Higher Education and the Nation's Health. McGraw-Hill, New York, 1970.

22. Weinberg, Alvin M. Correspondence on the economic benefit of basic research. *Minerva* 9(No. 2):294 (1971).

23. Comprehensive Health Manpower Training Act of 1971. Public Law 157, 92nd Congress, Sect. 205, 1971.

24. House Subcommittee on Public Health and Environment of the House Committee on Interstate and Foreign Commerce. Hearings on HR 8343, HR 10681, and on s 1828, amending the PHS Act to Provide for the Conquest of Cancer. 92nd Congress, 1st Sess., 1971, p. 265.

25. Millis, John S. A Rational Policy for Medical Education and Its Financing. The National Fund for Medical Education, New York, 1971, p. 115.

26. Bennett, Ivan L., Jr. Chapter VI, this volume.

27. Rosenblith, Walter. Chapter V, this volume.

28. Wilson, John T. A dilemma of American science and higher education policy: The support of individuals and fields versus the support of universities. *Minerva* 9(No. 2):196 (1971).

29. Senate Subcommittee on Labor, HEW Appropriations of the Senate Appropriations Committee. Report, Fiscal Year 1967.

X · *Industrial Research and Development*

PATRICK E. HAGGERTY

ONE OF THE GREAT VIRTUES of the American economic system has been its ability to change as the needs of American society have required. It is a system with a certain theoretical base, but primarily one which has evolved pragmatically in response to need and under the general premise that, wherever feasible, it is best to depend upon privately owned and privately managed enterprises to supply necessary goods and services. Inevitably, such a system is a complex one, dependent upon thousands and thousands of separate institutions: business and governmental, mostly nonhierarchial with respect to one another, relatively autonomous organizationally, and yet, in the overall sense, almost completely interdependent. Because it is such a system, how to generate effective public policy with respect to research and development for the industrial component of that system also is a complex and uncertain task. Because by public policy these days we generally mean some kind of government intervention, probably federal, it becomes even more difficult to be sure that such a centrally conceived and directed kind of intervention does not, with heavy-handed best intentions, injure as much as it aids.

There already is a great deal of federal intervention in the economy, much of it specifically relating to research and development. At the same time, we do seem to be in a period of transition which may call for more, or at least a different kind of, federal intervention. Authors of previous chapters in this book have referred more extensively to these problems, opportunities, and changes in our society that suggest the need for a different research-and-development emphasis, and I do not propose to repeat what they already have covered. However, the elements of the tran-

PATRICK E. HAGGERTY Chairman of the Board, Texas Instruments, Incorporated, Dallas, Texas

sition seem to include revising our value system, putting more emphasis on such aspects of the quality of life as the environment in which we live, facing the massive problems of our cities, and intensifying efforts to diminish discrimination, especially racial — all of this while we are at the same time experiencing some economic difficulties within our boundaries and a diminished capability to compete in a business sense outside of them.

This book relates to research and development in industry, so a few fundamental principles with respect to technologically based industry bear review.

Most important of all, a technologically based company *exists* to create, make, and market useful products and services to satisfy the needs of its customers throughout the world.

It does *not* exist to do research and development or to provide jobs for scientists and engineers, for skilled craftsmen, or for unskilled laborers. It does *not* exist to provide careers for its management. All of these, indeed, are useful contributions to society; for that reason, society frequently legislates with respect to them and, in the process — sometimes to its own detriment — acts as though one or the other of these were the prime business function. Further, it does *not* exist to provide a profit for its shareholders, although that may have been a primary motivation in the founding of the organization.

However, the *opportunity* to make a profit is a company's *incentive* to create, make, and market useful products and services. The profit it makes (if it makes one) is the only pay the company will receive for its services as an institution in providing such useful products and services. Everything else goes to its employees and suppliers — or the tax collectors! Furthermore, unless it is sufficiently effective to earn a satisfactory profit related both to sales volume and the assets required to do that volume, it will begin to falter in its primary objective: that of providing products and services to its customers throughout the world.

Thus, research and development in a technologically based company always must have as its objective either 1) improved or new products and services to satisfy the needs of its customers, 2) more effective operation to improve its profitability, or 3) some combination of both. Research and development which does not aid the attainment of such objectives is unsuccessful research and development, no matter how competent the professionals who conducted it, or how brilliant the results of the research and development itself.

R and D in industry can and often is aimed at simply increasing knowledge, but the increase in knowledge sought and attained must, in the long run, either improve the ability of the company to satisfy the needs of its customers, its own profitability, or both, or it should not have been conducted. If, for whatever reason, the company cannot take advantage of the consequences of the R and D, then that R and D should not have been pursued. For example, if all available financial resources of an organization are going to be strained to the utmost in order to pursue a line of business activity to which it already is committed and which is vital to its continued existence, then it is futile to pursue research and development in other fields, even though the results of the effort may be excellent in a technical sense.

Thus, any public policy with respect to industrial R and D must not be constructed simply to get industry to do more R and D. Instead, the public policy for industrial R and D must seek to improve the industrial objectives themselves and increase the probability of their being attained more effectively and more profitably.

As background, a review of the actual dollar levels of research and development activities in the United States will be useful. According to statistics provided by the National Science Foundation (Figure 1), total research and development in dollars of the year (current dollars, not deflated by any price index) has gone from less than $14 billion in 1960 to

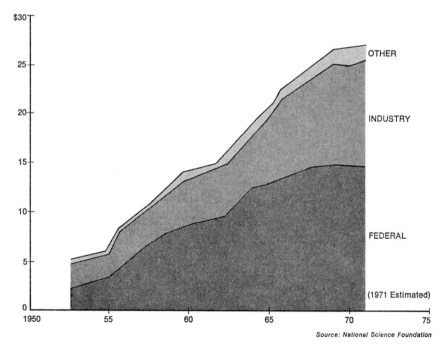

Source: National Science Foundation

FIGURE 1. Sources of funds for research and development in the United States in billions of current dollars.[1]

about twice that amount, or just under $27 billion, in 1971.* During this time, the federally supplied funds increased in dollars of the year from $8.7 billion in 1960 to $13 billion in 1965, but thereafter flattened out to about $15 billion.

The data on funds for the performance of research and development issued by the National Science Foundation are on a calendar-year basis and are the sum of monies reported spent or expended by hundreds of individual businesses, universities, and other organizations. According to the present 1971 estimate by NSF, $14.8 billion from the federal government will be used for research and development.

Looking to the future, some insight can be gained by studying the proposed new federal budget for fiscal year 1973. Budgeted expenditures for research and development in fiscal 1973 are about 4.5 per cent above fiscal 1972. I would not be surprised if the National Science Foundation ultimately reports a similar percentage increase in government funds used for research and development during calendar year 1972.

The situation has been different, however, with respect to dollars provided by industry itself. As federal dollars flattened out, industry dollars continued to increase, although at a slightly slower rate. So the increase in *total* R and D funds since 1966 has come primarily from the increase in funding provided by industry itself (Figure 2).

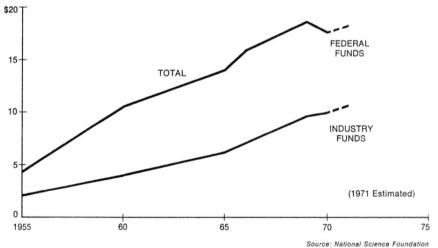

Source: National Science Foundation

FIGURE 2. Total research and development performed by industry. Figures are in billions of dollars.[3]

* The picture changes dramatically, however, when the current dollars are converted to constant 1958 dollars by means of the implicit price deflator,[2] which is the price index for gross national product, providing a ratio of GNP in current prices to GNP in constant prices. Then, the growth goes from $13.3 billion in 1960 to a peak of $20.5 billion in 1968, and drops to an estimated $18.9 billion in 1971. Thus, the real increase since 1960 was 42 per cent.

Total R and D performed by industry is the sum of two categories: R and D performed with funds provided by the federal government and R and D performed with funds provided by private industry. From 1960 to 1966, industry increased the portion of funds it provided from $4.4 billion to $7.2 billion. This presently is estimated by the National Science Foundation to have increased in 1971 to $10.5 billion. In 1960, out of the total United States R and D of less than $14 billion (Figure 1), industry performed $10.5 billion, as shown in Figure 2. Federal funds paid for $6.1 billion of industrial R and D, and industry paid for $4.4 billion.

The total R and D performed in industry grew from that $10.5 billion in 1960 to more than $18 billion in 1971. But since 1968, federal funds for industrial R and D have declined from $8.6 billion to an estimated $7.8 billion in 1971. The increase of $2.7 billion (17 per cent) in total industrial R and D since 1966 has come almost entirely from industry.

About 75 percent of the increase in industry funds used in industrial R and D is accounted for in Table I. [4, 5] Federal funds for industrial R and D were essentially flat from 1965 to 1970, whereas company funds for industrial R and D grew at an average annual rate of 9.3 per cent in that period. Overall, the decision to limit federal R and D funds for industry has resulted in a significant increase in company-funded R and D, which should be much more sharply focused on industry's own objectives and which should be affecting favorably industry's products and services and improving its ability to compete both here and abroad.

TABLE I

Average Percentage Increase in Company Funds for Research and Development Performed by Industry from 1965 through 1970

| Name of Industry | $ Millions | | Increase | Average % increase |
	1965	1970	1965-1970	per year
Chemical	1198	1622	35.4%	6.25
Machinery	860	1445	68.0%	10.90
Electrical equipment and communications	1206	2062	71.0%	11.30
Communications equipment and electronic components	677	1201	77.4%	12.10
Aircraft and missiles*	622	1107	78.0%	12.20
Motor vehicles and other transportation	898	1232	37.2%	6.50

* Although the aircraft and missiles industry showed an average increase per year over the five-year period, there was an actual decrease of 15 per cent in funding of R and D from 1969 to 1970.
Note that appreciable increases occurred in all of these categories.

Further, the rapid increase in research and development generated by federal funds in the years since 1953 very definitely stretched the resources of the entire nation and, as a consequence, produced sharp inflationary pressures. Similarly, the decrease in the rate of federal expenditure these last several years has tended to decrease the inflationary pressures. I strongly suspect that the combination of these two forces already has had a larger favorable impact on industrial R and D for industrial purposes than most of the much-discussed possibilities for federal intervention. This does not mean, however, that we should not seek to use effectively the presently under-used scientific and engineering potential of the United States, or that there are not other federal interventions which might produce a positive impact.

I am more confident of the ability of the federal government to take actions that will influence constructively both the economic atmosphere in which industry operates and the overall vitality of science and technology in the United States than I am of its ability to conduct or have conducted effective research and development in areas which are the prime responsibility of private industry. For example, the more effectively industry focuses its own R and D, the more certain is the need for a major effort in science and technology not coupled tightly to industry's immediate needs. Of course, we do have just such an effort, the major portion of which goes on in our universities and colleges under the reasonably descriptive title of Academic Science.

This effort has been the most rapidly growing component of the nation's research and development, more than tripling between 1960 and 1971 in dollars of the year (Figure 3). The total effort at universities and

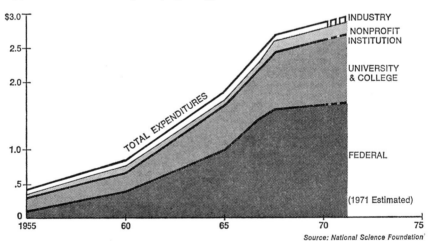

Source: National Science Foundation

FIGURE 3. Sources of funds for research and development in academic science, excluding capital expenditures, expressed in billions of dollars.[6]

colleges in 1960 was about $825 million. According to the National Science Foundation, the estimated level in 1971 was $2.9 billion with $1.7 billion coming from the federal government.

Most of the remaining funds have come from state and local governments, some from foundations, and some from industry. Indeed, industry's component has increased more than 50 per cent since 1965 — from $40 million to an estimated $62 million in 1971 — but that still is a very small percentage of the total support.

Unfortunately, although the dollar amount has increased since 1968, inflation in the intervening years means that, at best, the effort has been level. Because this does affect our overall vitality in science and technology and is an area in which federal support is essential, this leveling does disturb me. Admittedly, to a somewhat undetermined extent, the support through the years is associated not only with research but with training additional scientists, an appreciable percentage of whom, in turn, were required to expand the faculties of the universities and colleges to accommodate the rapid rate of growth occasioned by the rate at which federal support was increased. With that physical expansion curtailed, a relatively more modest annual increase in academic science support probably is appropriate. Consequently, my own recommendation for federal policy in this area would be a predictable and regular rate of increase, such as 5 to 6 per cent, for a number of years.

According to present estimates by the National Science Foundation, about $1.7 billion of federal funds was spent in calendar 1971 by universities and colleges for the performance of research and development. Federal obligations for academic science in fiscal year 1972 were $2 billion and President Nixon's proposed budget for fiscal year 1973 requests $2.25 billion, so it is probable that actual expenditures for academic science in calendar 1972 and calendar 1973 will increase 7 to 9 per cent per year when the difference between the calendar year and the fiscal year and the inevitable lag between obligations and actual expenditures are taken into consideration. While somewhat above my 5 to 6 per cent, these are reasonable increases and are not likely to strain our academic resources to the point of again causing inflationary pressures in view of the slack in these same resources that has been generated over the past few years.

At the same time, it is not clear that the overall accomplishments of academic science correspond to the enormous increase in support. I believe it is so important for a society such as that of the United States to conduct the most profound and most competent program in science of which it is capable that the President of the United States should request a really intensive and extensive evaluation of our overall national efforts in academic science.

I would suggest that the evaluation be a joint responsibility of the President's Science Adviser and the director of the Office of Management and Budget, to insure that it be a completely dispassionate evaluation and better to avoid the appearance or actuality of advocacy. Surely, our experiences in developing our present academic science efforts over the past quarter-century have enough coherence to allow evaluation. I am not suggesting in any sense that I would expect such an evaluation to enumerate a multitude of scientific discoveries that have produced corresponding revolutions in one aspect or another of our way of life. Nevertheless, the change in our scale of effort has been profound, and surely we can document in a meaningful fashion the significant consequences of that change in effort.

As one such example, the Nobel prizes awarded in physics, chemistry, physiology, and medicine, may be considered one measure of the scientific activities and discoveries of a nation. Figure 4 plots the percentage of the total Nobel prizes awarded in these fields to citizens of the United States for important discoveries. In the pre-World War II period, from 1901 through 1940, only about 10 per cent of the awards were made to our citizens each year. There was a striking change in the postwar years. From 1950 through 1969, citizens of the United States were awarded 40 to 50 per cent of the prizes. In the most recent four or five of these years, our scientists claimed 65 to 70 per cent of the prizes annually. This sharp

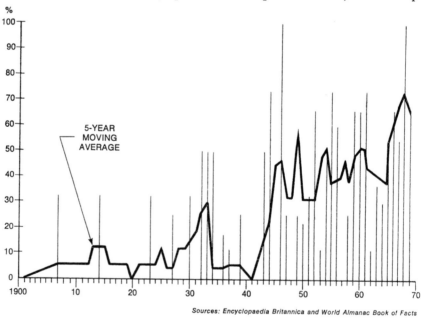

Sources: Encyclopaedia Britannica and World Almanac Book of Facts

FIGURE 4. Percentage of total Nobel prizes in science awarded to citizens of the United States.

increase in the percentage of Nobel prizes won by our citizens since World War II correlates well with the increase in federal support for academic science in this same period.

What we need is a really comprehensive, overall survey that penetrates and illuminates the extraordinarily diffuse structure of academic science — with its hundreds of institutions, multiple thousands of programs, and tens of thousands of individual investigators — with sufficient coherence to permit conclusions to be drawn both as to the effectiveness of the program as presently structured and how we can make it better. Over and over again the advocates of science assume that the negative effects of inflation cannot be overcome by improved productivity and, hence, that the funds made available for academic science must be increased annually by an amount sufficient to overcome the inflation and to add additional real growth. This is a common attitude in the entire sector of our society that can be described under the general category of services, and it is an extremely destructive one. (I shall have more to say about it later in connection with education and the services area generally.) I recognize that it is extraordinarily difficult to associate the concept of productivity with an effort so unpredictable as to its consequences as academic science. Yet, I think it is imperative that we make a really serious effort to improve the overall effectiveness of the total program. Even though no matrix of tangible measures of accomplishment can be developed, I am convinced that, with the benefit of such an extensive survey, those who are qualified professionally could determine subjectively courses of action that would improve markedly the conduct of our efforts. Unless the evaluation is really comprehensive, however, there is no point in making it.

After all, since 1954 our total expenditures for academic science have been more than $25 billion, of which the federal government has provided more than $14 billion. Surely, it would make sense to spend $5 million or even $25 million in a really extensive examination of that massive effort, with the specific objective of gaining a really improved effectiveness in academic science from an overall program planned to grow steadily and at a moderate rate from this point forward.

Another aspect of our program in academic science bothers me. The coupling between academic science and industry does not exist on a broad enough scale. I believe that the nation, the universities, and industry all would gain if a broad-scale, not-too-tight coupling existed between industry and the universities and covered one-quarter to one-third of total R and D of the universities. If a coupling of that scale could be generated gradually over the next five to ten years, I am convinced that it could vitalize the applicable sectors of both the universities and industry.

I suggest this could be accomplished best by giving a tax credit. There has been a considerable amount of discussion about granting tax credits to industry for research and development work, stimulated partly by unemployment among scientists and engineers and partly because, as a nation, we seem to do best economically, in international competition and in generating domestic employment, in products and services that involve high technology.

A general tax credit for research and development poses some real problems of identification, in addition to the difficulty of designing a tax-credit mechanism that would avoid paying for research and development work that would get done anyway. However, a tax credit for research and development sponsored by private industry at colleges and universities would be relatively free of most of these problems. If the tax credit were approximately 25 per cent, it would provide a large stimulation for industry to conduct sizable research and development at our colleges and universities and insure that the R and D was coupled effectively, because the sponsoring company still would be paying for approximately 30 per cent of the R and D after offsetting the expense of the R and D itself through the federal income taxes it pays.

To me, the most important aspect of this approach would be the broadened coupling it would begin to forge among a variety of companies and the universities and the colleges of the nation. Undoubtedly, its impact would be to increase the total research and development at universities and colleges and to substitute some privately supported effort for the about $1.7 billion worth of academic science presently being paid for by the federal government. I would think it important that not too many restrictions be placed on the arrangements between industry and the universities and colleges, that they be allowed to arrive at whatever type of mutual agreement seems best to each, and certainly that not all of sponsored R and D be in the public domain. Of course, many institutions, including some of the best in the country, are unwilling to do proprietary work. On the other hand, some universities presently are willing to conduct proprietary research, and I see no objection to letting the usual market mechanisms operate and allowing companies and universities to work out whatever arrangements are satisfactory to both.

Over a decade, this kind of cooperative effort might have the same significance for the generation of products and services in the commercial and industrial areas as the cooperative effort of government, industry, and universities had for the military during and after World War II.

I have commented that the high quality of the industrial research-and-development staff or the brilliance of their results is of little consequence unless the company can apply the necessary resources to convert that effort into useful products and services or to improve profitability.

I have suggested also that American industry was finding itself less able to compete at home and abroad than it did a decade ago. As previously outlined, industry has increased its self-financed R and D significantly (about 60 per cent) in the last half-dozen years. Whereas further increases in industrially aimed R and D, whether financed by the federal government or by industry, are desirable, what we need even more are actions aimed at increasing the general vitality and competitiveness of industry.

We are all aware that our unemployment rate is higher than we would like; it reached a peak of 6.1 per cent in 1971 and still stood at 5.7 per cent in February 1972. Not as many are aware that our total civilian employment has continued to increase at a very steady rate throughout this entire period, growing from about 71.1 million in 1965 to more than 79 million in 1971, and this in spite of the fact that since 1968, more than a million and a quarter jobs have been eliminated in the defense and space areas alone (Figure 5). In addition, about a half-million mili-

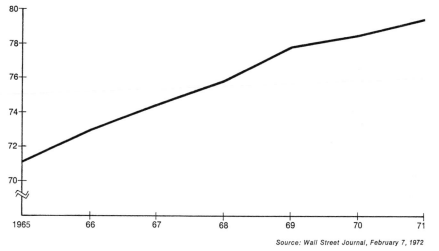

Source: Wall Street Journal, February 7, 1972

FIGURE 5. Total civilian employment figures, 1965 to 1971, in millions.

tary personnel released in the last few years are adding to the need for new jobs.

However, concealed within these overall numbers are some sharply differing trends. For example, let's examine three principal components of total civilian employment (Figure 6). Note that trade employment has grown from just over 13 million in 1966 to 15.5 million in February 1972. Services have grown from 9.5 million in 1966 to more than 12 million in February 1972. However, manufacturing, which employed 19.2 million in 1966 and reached a peak of 20.2 million in 1969, had a total employment in February 1972 of 18.6 million.

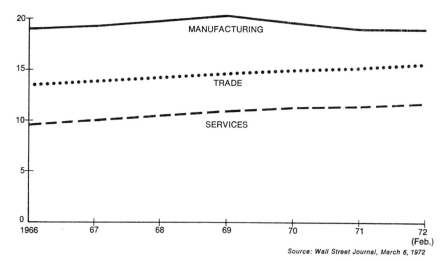

Source: Wall Street Journal, March 6, 1972

FIGURE 6.   Employment, in millions, of civilians in manufacturing, trade, and services.

Why is this so? Partly, it is because productivity increases per person in manufacturing have allowed somewhat larger real volumes to be turned out without corresponding increases in people employed.

Another important reason is that imports of manufactured products into the United States have grown steadily at a very high rate, from $5.3 billion in 1958 to $30.5 billion in 1971. Note in Figure 7 how much more rapid the rate of increase has been since the middle 1960s than it was in the first half of that decade. Our gross national product has grown 134

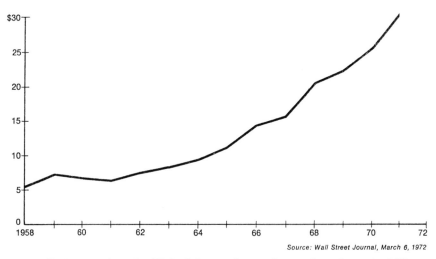

Source: Wall Street Journal, March 6, 1972

FIGURE 7. Imports into the United States of manufactured products, in billions of dollars.

per cent since 1958, but the par value of imported manufactured products increased 473 per cent in that same span of time.

Why? Primarily, it is because in the United States the dollar value of payrolls is going up much more rapidly than the output of work; and even though increasing productivity per person in industry has allowed the number of people on the payrolls to be decreased markedly, the dollar values of these same payrolls still have gone up at an excessive rate (Figure 8).

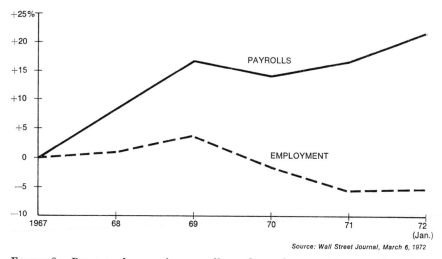

Source: Wall Street Journal, March 6, 1972

FIGURE 8. Percent changes in payrolls and employment in manufacturing, using 1967 as the base year.

As compared to about five years ago, in 1967, and though physical output is up, increasing productivity has allowed the manufacturing industry to decrease its total employment by about 6 per cent. But the dollar payrolls for those 6 per cent fewer people are up almost 22 per cent. It is not an isolated or short-term phenomenon that employment in trade and services has continued to grow although manufacturing employment actually is lower now than it was in 1967.

There probably is no clearer way to trace the development of the United States from an agricultural to an industrial society and the continuing shift to what some are now terming a "postindustrial society" than to examine the changes in how our people are employed (Figure 9).

As recently as 1890, four out of every 10 workers were engaged in agriculture, forestry, or fisheries. By 1930 that percentage had been halved, and in 1970 only 4 per cent of our workers produced relatively even more food and forest products.

Twenty-eight per cent of our workers were in industry in 1890, and that percentage grew slowly, reaching 34 per cent in 1950. Since then,

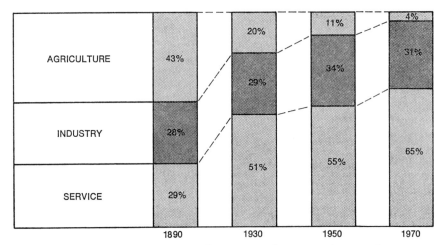

FIGURE 9.   Relative employment in the economy by economic sector.[7]

however, in spite of the increasing quantity and variety of industrial goods we produce, the percentage of our total workers in industry declined to 31 per cent in 1970.

The really striking shift is in the category known as "service," which includes transportation, communications, utilities, wholesale and retail trade, government, and education, in addition to other services. In 1890 only 20 per cent of our workers were engaged in service areas. By 1950 this percentage had nearly doubled, and in 1970 almost two out of three of our workers were so engaged.

The implications of these shifts are profound. They have come about because the ever-increasing productivity per person, especially in agriculture and industry, has allowed us to turn our efforts to providing services, particularly in education and government.

Productivity per person engaged in agriculture no doubt will go on increasing at 4 to 6 per cent per year, and in a few decades perhaps 2 per cent of our working population will produce all of the agricultural products we need. However, even though agriculture goes on increasing in productivity per person, it can no longer have a very large impact on improving the standard of living of our society or, to look at it another way, to free workers now engaged in producing food for work in government, education, or health care.

Increasing productivity per person in industry, too, will mean that we require relatively fewer workers to produce the ever-increasing quantity of material goods we use to live. It is highly probable that by the year 2000 only 25 per cent of our total workers will be needed in agriculture and industry to produce all of the food and goods we need, and three out of four of all who work will be in services.

Increasing productivity per person, of course, is just another way of saying that output per hour worked per man has gone up. Indeed, in the private sector of our economy, our society now produces about six times as much in each man-hour worked as it did in 1890, and from this increase in output per man-hour we have attained our real improvement in standard of living. This consistent ability to improve our output per man-hour is probably the most significant material accomplishment of contemporary industrial society.

At Texas Instruments, for example, we know very well that if wages and salaries go up 5 per cent, either our prices must go up or our costs must go down accordingly. Because competition limits our prices, we spend a very large proportion of our total professional effort in improving our effectiveness — in management systems, in new products, in new processes for manufacture, in marketing, in more effective tools and machines and layouts, and in training people. In product lines, which encompass about half our total volume, we have faced price cuts approximating 15 per cent per year for more than a decade. Yet, with wages and salaries increasing at least 3 to 5 per cent per year, we have managed not only to survive but to grow and to profit.

Profits before taxes at Texas Instruments have been running at about 8 per cent. Of that amount, a little less than half is paid out in the form of income taxes. About one-quarter of the 4 per cent-plus that remains goes to our stockholders in the form of dividends, and they, in turn, pay out from one-quarter to one-half or more to governments in the form of income taxes. The percentage that remains, recently 3 per cent — but sometimes more, sometimes less (and it really needs to be 5 per cent or better) — is what has produced most of the necessary funds that have allowed us to grow to 400 times the size we were in 1946. Thus, it would have taken only a relatively small decrease in our effectiveness through the years to put us in a loss instead of a profit position. This would have stopped our growth promptly and, if continued over a few years, would have been cured either through a change in management or through the death of the organization. Thus, we have no alternative to improving our productivity. It is built into our culture.

But this ability to improve productivity per person at a high rate is not automatic, and it is not universal throughout all the endeavors of our society. There is a good reason to feel, for example, that productivity per person in such services as government, health care, and education has decreased over the past decade or two.

Let's examine education specifically (Figure 10). Since 1930, our population has grown from 123 million to 205 million — about 60 per cent. During that same span of time, our school enrollment doubled — from

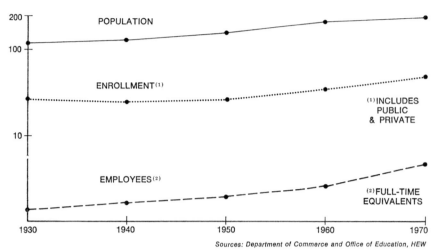

Sources: Department of Commerce and Office of Education, HEW

FIGURE 10. Population, school enrollment, and education employees, expressed in millions of persons.

29.7 million to 59.2 million. But the number of full-time equivalent men and women employed in education grew more than four times, from 1.3 million in 1930 to 5.4 million in 1970. Thus, in the last 40 years, the number of full-time employees in education has grown twice as fast as the number of students and more than three times as fast as the population.

Expressed in 1970 dollars, between 1930 and 1970 our total expenditures for education for all levels have grown more than nine times, from $7.5 billion to $70.3 billion (Figure 11). Or, what is much more mean-

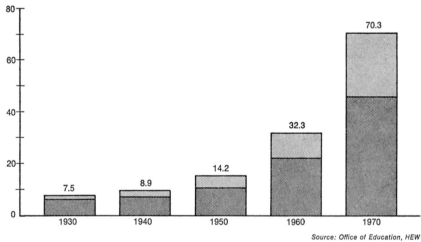

Source: Office of Education, HEW

FIGURE 11. Growth of expenditures, in billions of 1970 dollars, for education between 1930 and 1970. Dark shading, elementary and secondary schools; light shading, higher education.

ingful — again in constant 1970 dollars (that is, the base is 1970) — our expenditures per student have grown nearly five times, from $253 per student in 1930 to $1,188 per student in 1970; and the biggest increases have come since 1950. We now spend nearly three times as much per student in constant dollars as we did in 1950 (Figure 12).

These comparisons are not completely fair, because the number of students in higher education, where the costs per student are obviously much higher, has increased more rapidly than in elementary and secondary schools. Still, as Figure 12 shows, costs for elementary and second-

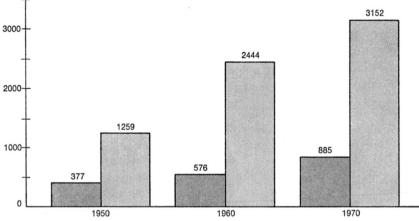

Source: Office of Education, HEW

FIGURE 12. Education cost per student, in constant 1970 dollars. Dark shading, elementary and secondary schools; light shading, higher education.

ary education have grown since 1950 from $377 to $885 per student — or more than 2 1/3 times — while the costs of higher education increased somewhat more rapidly, from $1,259 per student to $3,152 — or 2 1/2 times.

As to the nature of the forces generating these disparities, let me quote from *The Economics of the Major Private Universities,* a paper by Dr. William G. Bowen, President of Princeton University, that was published by the Carnegie Commission on Higher Education:

Let us imagine an economy divided into two sectors, one in which productivity is rising and another in which it is constant, the first producing automobiles, and the second, "education" (defined as some amalgam of students and knowledge). Let us suppose that in automobile production output per man-hour increases at an annual rate of 4 percent, compared with a zero rate of increase in the education industry. Now, let us assume that money wages in the automobile industry go up at the same rate as productivity in that industry. This means that each year the typical auto worker's wage goes up by 4 percent, but since his output increases by exactly the same percentage, the labor cost of manufacturing a car will be unchanged. This process can continue indefinitely, with auto workers earning more and more each year, with costs per car remaining stationary, and with no rise in automobile prices necessary to maintain company profits.

But what about the education industry? How it fares in this imaginary economy depends on what assumption is made about the relationship between increases in faculty salaries (treated, for the sake of simplicity, as an index of all salaries in the education industry) and the increases in the wages of auto workers. Over the long run, it is probably most reasonable to assume that faculty salaries increase at approximately the same rate as wages in other sectors. (Between 1948 and 1966, professional salaries have increased slightly faster than earnings of production workers in manufacturing — 4.8 percent per year for the former and 4.2 percent for the latter. However, if we take either 1929 or 1939 as our base year, we find that faculty salaries have increased somewhat less rapidly than earnings in manufacturing. It was during the World War II period that the relative income position of faculty members deteriorated so markedly.)

If the salary of the typical faculty member does increase at an annual rate of 4 percent, so that his living standard improves along with the living standard of the auto worker, but if output per man-hour in the education industry remains constant, it follows that the labor cost per unit of educational output must also rise 4 percent per year. *And there is nothing in the nature of the situation to prevent educational cost per unit of product from rising indefinitely at a compound rate of this sort.*

The particular assumptions included in this analysis are, of course, merely illustrative, and the numerical results can be changed by assuming a different rate of productivity increase and a different rate of increase of money wages in the non-educational sector, by assuming that faculty salaries increase at a somewhat different rate from money wages in general (either faster or slower), and by allowing for some increase in productivity in the field of education. But modifications of this kind will not alter the fundamental point of the argument, which is that *in every industry in which increases in productivity come more slowly than in the economy as a whole, cost per unit of product must be expected to increase relative to costs in general.* Any product of this kind — whether it be a haircut, a custom-prepared meal, a performance of a symphony concert, or the education of a graduate student — is bound to become ever more expensive relative to other things.[8]

The pressures Dr. Bowen outlines would apply if the ratio of students per employee in the education industry were constant. In fact, the ratio has been decreasing, and we have been using more employees in the education industry to produce the same number of students, so a double compounding has been taking place.

Now let me suggest a conclusion that is a sort of mirror image of Dr. Bowen's. He pointed out that if the automobile workers' productivity and wages both go up 4 per cent in a year, no change in price is necessary to preserve a company's profitability. Some of the data in the graphs

I have presented on manufacturing demonstrate, however, that payrolls rose more rapidly than output. Dr. Bowen is right in that, if the auto workers' wages and productivity both go up 4 per cent, there is no need to increase automobile prices, but that in itself is not sufficient to stop inflation. If enough workers in society have low annual productivity increases, then wage increases in those industries in which the productivity increases are high must be held sufficiently below their annual productivity increases to absorb the higher relative costs in those areas of work in which annual productivity increases are low.

This really is not feasible, now that we have more than half of our work force engaged in areas that have not learned how to use technology, capital, and management to increase productivity per person on a regular basis. As a consequence, the auto worker and the steel worker, among others, are asking for wage increases large enough not only to reward them for their own productivity gains but also to cover the increasing costs of the services they are buying. Dr. Bowen is right in that wages and salaries in the low-productivity increase areas will tend to rise at the same rate as they do in the high-productivity increase areas. That is exactly what is happening in education, and the rate of increase in pay per person in government and in health services is at least as high. When workers in these areas represented a minority of our total work force, then, in a sense, the workers in the high-productivity increase areas could carry wage increases in the rest of society on their shoulders or, to the extent that they did not, the rate of inflation would be modest. But these sectors no longer require only a minor part of our work force.

The Department of Labor has projected the probable changes in total employment by industry through 1980 (Figure 13). On the basis of that projection, I have grouped manufacturing, agriculture, mining, and transportation, comunications, and public utilities together as having a high potential for continuing high annual rates of growth. Construction, the personal-service industries, trade, finance, insurance, real estate, health services, education, and government are grouped in a second category as having a lesser potential for reaching or sustaining high average annual rates of growth in productivity. The division is arbitrary and is based on the record and apparent susceptibility to continued high rates of increases in productivity through the application of technology and capital investment.

Note that of a total increase of 24 million in total employment, 21 million are in the category that seems to have a lesser potential for reaching and sustaining high average annual rates of increase in productivity per worker. Further, the percentage of total employment in this category is projected to increase from 62.3 per cent in 1965 to 68.8 per cent in

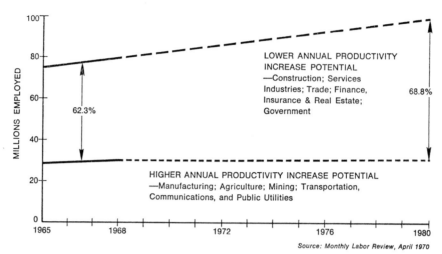

Source: Monthly Labor Review, April 1970

FIGURE 13. Productivity increase potential in sectors of employment in the United States.[9]

1980. Thus, we soon will have more than two out of three workers in those employment sectors where, in general, we either have not learned how to apply capital and technology effectively to increase productivity or where the organizational structure itself, as in education and government, simply is not oriented to increasing productivity per person.

Thus, I suggest that effective federal intervention in these areas could have a much larger impact on the general industrial sector than any intervention in it directly. In this sense, the administration's efforts to stem inflation are of prime importance. Further, research and development efforts aimed at more effective organizational structures, better understanding, and markedly improved productivities per person in these areas, especially in state and local government, in health services, and in education, would have bigger payoffs than in industry.

To pursue this point, let me return to a discussion of education, where improvements in effectiveness would be of significance to industry, not just because of decreased costs resulting in decreased pressure for wage increases and lower taxes, but also because the graduates of an improved educational system would make larger contributions to industry itself.

It has been pretty much doctrine that all that was necessary to solve the problems of the education industry was sufficient money. It would seem to me that the events of the past 20 years should have dispelled that illusion completely. After all, spending that is approaching three times as much per student (in constant dollars) does not seem to have improved the effectiveness of the system or the quality of the end product appreciably.

More money will help, but not much if the record of the past 20 years means anything! Remember Dr. Bowen's observations. If the productivity in the rest of the economy is increasing and that in education is not, then it will take a considerable amount of money per year merely to keep the pay scales of those in the education industry comparable to those in the rest of society, even though nothing more is being produced for the additional funds.

Four vital points must be made:

1. Any questions raised with respect to decreasing productivity per person within education itself are not about the advantages of education for all but only about the institutions and the procedures — with how and what and when we have chosen to provide the education. Education for all to the maximum of capability and desire is a proper objective in that higher standard of living (expressed in the broadest terms) we seek for the United States.

2. A portion of the increasing productivity per person in the private sector is attributed to the constantly increasing educational level of our total population. Thus, to the extent that the additional costs go to training a larger percentage of the population to a higher level of education, the education industry is entitled to a share in the productivity gains made by the private sector.

3. The problems within the educational system that have produced the constantly decreasing productivity are at least as much the fault of society itself as they are of the education industry. After all, we outsiders make up most of the population, and we elect the school boards and set the general standards and specifications of the system within which the teachers operate. It is that same greater society which is responsible for the turmoil, the problems of race and discrimination, the imposed solutions such as busing, three-month summer vacations, and a variety of other limitations, strictures, or frictions that both create the system within which education operates and interfere with its operating effectively.

4. This unhappy state of affairs is not because the professionals in the education industry are less able or more venal than the rest of us. On the contrary, I suspect that the average professional in education works as hard, is at least as well trained and, if anything, more dedicated, than those of us who operate in the areas where productivity has been improving.

Nevertheless, there is a striking difference between the educational system and private enterprise. The difference is in the different cultures of which each is a part. The kinds of products and services we produce and sell in industry lend themselves to measurement and to pricing, and the system requires that we improve productivity or die. As a consequence, every product or service decision involves a dichotomy — the nature, the quality, the specifications of the product or service itself, and always its cost. When the market decides what combination of quality or product or service and cost it prefers, as often as not the decision is in favor of a little less product or service for quite a lot less cost. On the other hand, all of us also come from or still are a part of a school culture that equates a reduced adult-to-student ratio in the school system as the primary route to improved education. Indeed, within the present system, it is difficult to conclude otherwise.

Yet, there can be no escape from the constantly escalating costs if the only solution is the expenditure of more man-hours of adult instructional and administrative time per student hour. Somehow, our goals must change in order to find ways that maintain the quality of education with fewer adult hours per student hour.

Most of the discussion thus far has been discouraging. Indeed, Dr. Bowen, in the remainder of the paper previously mentioned, substantially concludes that educational costs will go on increasing relative to the rest of society, simply because productivity can't be improved at an adequate rate.

Frankly, I cannot agree with that conclusion. It is inconceivable to me that, if we really want to, if we apply the multitude of talents we possess as a society, and if all who are in the profession of education apply their enormous skills enthusiastically, we cannot get 2 to 5 per cent more work done each year than we did the year before. That is all it takes: 3 per cent more productivity per person per year would keep up with the rest of society; 5 per cent more productivity per person per year would generate a lead over the remainder of society and produce some surplus funds, which, in turn, could be used to improve the quality of education itself without increasing real costs.

Before anything else, we need to ask ourselves if the kind of education we are providing now is right for all of the more than 14-million teenagers who presently are in high school.

According to the United States Office of Education, well over 60 per cent of this year's high-school graduates will enter college. In another ten years, the figure probably will be 70 per cent. Now we have eight million in colleges and universities; assuming present trends, in another ten years we'll have 12 million. Is the only route to a college-level education to continue to coop up 12 million of our young people in the classrooms and the relatively artificial atmosphere of school for so much of their lives? Mightn't it be wiser if, beginning at 15 or 16, those who wished could go to work for four to six hours a day and attend classes via television in classrooms at their work, alone or with small groups of fellow workers for two hours or more a day?

In the north-Texas region we have a closed-circuit TV network with talk-back capabilities that couples nine universities and colleges and 46 classrooms in seven industrial organizations in a complex of nine locations around Dallas, Fort Worth, and Sherman. The Association for Graduate Education and Research of North Texas (TAGER) TV network opened in September 1967 and presently is in its fifth year of operation. This spring a total of 70 graduate and undergraduate courses in business, engineering, science, and mathematics are being offered to a course enrollment of approximately 2,000. At Texas Instruments alone, we have 243 persons enrolled in programs, most of them working toward master's degrees. This is out of a total Texas Instruments professional population in the Dallas area of about 4,500, of whom about 1,200 already have been awarded a master's or a doctoral degree. The program is an overwhelming success, yet we have not designed an educational system based on TV. We really just have augmented the present educational system geographically. Although individual organizations exert some influence on the graduate-level subject matter, in general, the schools are establishing the curricula and the industrial organizations are furnishing the classrooms, the students, and most of the funds.

Further, for all my emphasis on the necessity for considering cost, and although costs were considered in establishing the network, it was not designed with specific and reduced costs per student hour in mind. Actually, the cost per student instructional hour is about comparable with normal university costs. However, the convenience of the classroom locations and the scheduling of classes throughout the working day and evening insure that many more professional people in the participating companies go on to postgraduate degrees and that the cost to the companies in lost working hours is markedly reduced.

The opportunities for really significant improvement in course applicability and quality are enormous, and the potential for producing this kind of improved educational opportunity at a striking decrease in costs is large. The system as presently constituted never has been designed or operated to achieve the really low cost per student instructional hour of which it is capable. Thus, because we really just have augmented the present system, rather than designed a new system of education, using these new tools and concepts, we still are not producing anything like the results which are potential. I am convinced that the development of a true television-based educational system for the kind of education that the people at such companies as Texas Instruments both desire and need, all the way from high school through the Ph.D. and beyond into continuing adult education, can produce both a quality of education and a productivity per educator far above that accepted as the norm in the high school or university and, further, that the system can be self-supporting.

I suggest that we need a radical revision in the institutional approaches we use to provide broader education to massive groups of people. I believe that our limited experience in Dallas in substituting TV in plants and offices for classrooms in universities indicates that, for most students, required in-school classroom attendance could be terminated after the tenth year. Thereafter, the broader education requirement for these students would be fulfilled in close connection with their jobs and at their place of work through highly flexible programs that use TV cassettes as well as TV classrooms operated as adjuncts to live classrooms. Such programs should be as open-ended as possible, so that one could continue working through any requisite number of years to attain various diploma levels from high school up. Quite properly, the course content should be set to augment the career being pursued and with the collaboration of the organization at which the individual is working, but the diplomas still would be granted by the appropriate degree-granting institutions, such as the Dallas Independent School District for the high school diploma or our regional universities for the baccalaureate and advanced degrees.

Because the individuals concerned would be working in institutions, both business and nonbusiness, and because anyone who wanted to do so could proceed as far, regarding a diploma, as his competence and desire led him, it would remove a large part of the status-based social compulsion to complete high school and then college in order to "belong," to be "eligible" for a suitable career. Actually, most vocational courses appropriate to the work done probably could be given more effectively and in a more applicable and timely fashion this way than the present system allows. This is at least as true for college-level vocational training, such as cost accounting or tax law, as it is for study we customarily think of as being at the trade-school level, such as machine shopwork or office procedures.

One thing that definitely bothers me is that, even in industry, the road to anywhere near the top from the shop is becoming more and more difficult to traverse. The present mechanisms insure that such a large percentage of those likely to succeed in management will have gone to college that, in general, enough college graduates will be put in the very lowest kinds of supervisory positions to acquire experience, and some of them will proceed from there to the top. If the kind of open-ended educational process described could be established, presumably a fairly sizable number with adequate ability would start in shop jobs while comparatively young. They would acquire their college educations or equivalents along the way via a combination of experience and the organized, but nonresidential, kinds of programs suggested, and once again there truly could be people who progress from the shop to the top — and be much better prepared, in addition.

On the basis of our training experience at Texas Instruments, there simply is no doubt that a carefully prepared instructional program on TV cassettes, plus the requisite supplementary written materials for reference and testing, plus occasional tutorial help, is superior to conventional classroom teaching for much subject matter. It does have to be well done and the student must want to learn, but those are requisites for any successful program of education.

A completely new system of career education, designed and supervised both by professionals in education and by those who employ the students and graduates of the new educational system, based on a combination of such carefully prepared TV cassette programs plus TV classrooms operated in conjunction with live classrooms, would allow good teachers to reach many more students than they now do and break the present self-defeating emphasis on decreasing teacher-student ratios.

Indeed, as we all know, adequate preparation for a career in today's complex society is a process that needs to continue throughout one's working life. There is no conceivable way in which packing all formal education into one's early life, terminating it with a diploma, whatever the level, in the 'teens or early twenties, and then going to work, can be the best way of career preparation and development. Surely, the completely new educational system described, in which many fellow workers of varied ages and experience are continuing their formal education in such a visible, convenient, part-of-the-working-environment way, would induce a similar interest in a larger proportion of all of us who work. A properly structured curriculum would insure that, in addition to career-oriented studies, a suitable proportion of cultural and social courses also would be available. Surely, this kind of educational system would enhance not only the productivity of the educational system itself but that of the entire society, as well as enriching the individual.

I have suggested to Superintendent Nolan Estes of the Dallas Independent School District that he lead the preparation of a proposal either to the federal Office of Education or to the National Science Foundation to conduct an experimental career-education program in which most formal classroom attendance would be concluded after the tenth grade. At the same time, the proposal would include working out an open-ended, cooperative program with industry, banks, retail stores, hospitals and a variety of other nonbusiness institutions that would allow students thereafter to continue in an organized, but highly flexible, program that would lead, first, toward a high-school diploma and then toward the bachelor's degree and postgraduate levels for those who so desire.

I am confident that, whatever the complexity, so long as the system is designed to predetermined student-instructional-hour costs and is based on an adequate and improving level of productivity per instructional and overhead person involved, the end result will be a lower cost per student instructional hour and a superior education, and we will have less difficulty financing it than we do our present system. The consequences of this kind of experimental educational program, if successful, would have far more positive results for industry than would many, if not most, of the kinds of federal intervention in industrial R and D that have been suggested by many people.

Now, I do believe that federal R and D efforts in educational and other public areas would be more productive than would federally supported activity in areas which are the primary responsibility of the private sector. However, it is probable that the federal government should get involved more deliberately and deeply in private sector R and D under certain conditions. For example:

1. When the results of R and D are likely to have major beneficial effects on the welfare of a large segment of the population (e.g., agriculture in the past and, perhaps, housing in the future) and when one of the following additional conditions holds true:

   a. The industry is made up of so many small organizations that no one of them is large enough to be able to finance a meaningful feasibility demonstration.

   b. The risks of failure, the length of the effort, and the total size of the investment, combined with the relatively small fraction of the resulting economic value that might accrue to the developer, contribute to the discouragement of private investment (e.g., nuclear reactors, highspeed transportation).

   c. Social returns appear to be so high that acceleration is required.

2. When there is a set of phenomena newly discovered or not yet sufficiently explored (e.g., high-energy lasers), for which basic research investigation appears likely to lead to new insights of significant importance to the government or to the possibility of creating a wholly new industry.

3. When a great variety of payoffs is expected, but R and D is not profitable to individual firms because of the narrowness of their product interest relative to the range of R and D application (e.g., social research on cities).

4. When the generation of the requirements themselves requires substantial investment in R and D. This is particularly true of completely

new technologies, the applications of which are not easily foreseen (e.g., nuclear energy, space, high-power lasers).

Wherever there is federal involvement in private-sector R and D, adequate mechanisms should be developed for the full and extensive exploitation of the fruits of R and D. For example, built into the mechanisms for federal support of research and development should be the means for expeditious and timely transfer of the effort, as well as the funding responsibilities, when it becomes appropriate, to mission-oriented agencies, state governments, and private companies.

Finally, I believe that the overall research and development effort of the United States is far too important for us to continue as we are without any kind of central mechanism for evaluating the general effectiveness of that total effort.

I suggest that this central mechanism could be best obtained by strengthening, but especially by changing its orientation to perform this function, the present science and technology advisory mechanism of the President (including the Science Adviser, the Office of Science and Technology, the President's Science Advisory Committee, and the Federal Council of Science and Technology). Such a strengthened Presidential science and technology advisory mechanism should:

1. Assess for and make recommendations to the President with respect to the general health and vitality of science and technology in the United States.

2. As to its major function, join with the Office of Management and Budget to evaluate for and make recommendations to the President with respect to federally supported R and D, particularly:

   a. the adequacy and appropriateness of research and development programs for achieving the objectives stated by the federal agencies involved and the coupling of these programs to the other activities of these agencies; and

   b. the general adequacy of the organizational structures of the respective agencies for initiating, supervising (and conducting, where appropriate) such research and development.

I began this discussion with the conclusion that the American economic system, because of its pragmatic nature and its great complexity, made the generation of effective public policy with respect to research and development for the industrial component of that system a complex and uncertain task. Probably I have unintentionally proved my point with the complexity and uncertainty of some of my recommendations. They are by no means all-inclusive, but complex and uncertain as they may be, if all could be accomplished, the impact on our American economic system would be significant.

REFERENCES

1. National Patterns of R&D Resources: Funds & Manpower in the United States, 1953-71. National Science Foundation (NSF 70-46). Table B-5, p. 36. (Figures for 1969, 1970, and 1971 updated by Mr. John Chirichiello of NSF, 3/29/72.) Statistical Abstract of the U.S., 1960. Table 706, p. 538.
2. Economic Report of the President. Council of Economic Advisers, January, 1972. Table B-3, p. 198.
3. NSF 70-46, *op. cit.* Table B-1, pp. 28-29 (updated as indicated in Reference 1).
4. Research and Development in Industry 1969, Funds 1969, Scientists & Engineers 1970. National Science Foundation (NSF 71-18). Table B-8, p. 36 (for 1965 through 1969 figures).
5. Industrial R&D spending, 1970. *In* Science Resource Studies Highlights. National Science Foundation (NSF 71-39), December 10, 1971, p. 4.
6. NSF 70-46, *op. cit.* Table B-1, pp. 28-29 (updated as indicated in Reference 1).
7. Economic Growth in the United States. Committee for Economic Development, New York, October 1969, p. 33.
8. Bowen, William G. The Economics of the Major Private Universities. Carnegie Commission, Berkeley, 1968, pp. 14-16.
9. The U.S. economy in 1980: A preview of BLS projections. *Monthly Labor Review*, 93 (No. 4): 15 (April, 1970) (Department of Labor, Bureau of Labor Statistics.)

SUPPORT OF SCIENCE

XI · *Federal Science and its Prospects*

EDWARD E. DAVID, Jr.

POLICY, AND PARTICULARLY SCIENCE POLICY, is a nebulous and diffuse subject. Under the rubric of science policy, I have been asked questions on such diverse topics as oil import quotas and overhead charges in the Defense Department. However, we can get a grip on the subject of science policy without wandering too far afield.

Ordinarily, we think of policy as a portfolio of principles that guide decision-making and the administration of programs — in the science area, research and development programs. Ideally, such a set of guiding principles is general enough to provide flexibility, yet definitive enough to provide an effective framework for the operation of a large and diffuse enterprise. In any case, the announcement of a policy is not enough; it must be applied. Thus, in policy-making we must consider both the formulation of policies and their application in decision-making.

This chapter discusses both of these aspects of federal policy as they apply to science and technology in the United States. Setting policy for the enterprise is an awesome task because of its size and diversity. This coming fiscal year, beginning in July, the federal government expects to obligate some $17.8 billion for research and development activities. A crude estimate of private spending adds another $10 to $12 billion, making the total size of the enterprise $30 billion in round numbers. Such a number is difficult to fathom; however, it represents about 2.8 per cent of the gross national product and about 12 per cent of the federal budget.

An enterprise of this size is necessarily carried out by a highly diffuse infrastructure. Decision-making is decentralized and occurs at every level, from the laboratory bench to the President's office. It is clear that no small set of policies will govern all of the details of the enterprise. The

EDWARD E. DAVID, JR. Former President's Science Adviser, The White House, Washington, D.C. *Present address*: Executive Vice President, Gould, Inc., Chicago, Ill.

best that can be expected of science policy is the setting of general directions and goals. Most importantly, policy made and enunciated by the federal government sets the climate for science and technology, which is probably the most effective change agent in our society as a whole.

With this overview and the limitations it projects, let us look first at some issues related to national programs that have required a policy base for decision. We can start with national security.[1] The B-1 is a new manned aircraft that the Air Force is developing for a strategic role in the 1980s to replace the B-52. The TRIDENT submarine and missile is a new undersea weapon system to provide modern capability to our undersea missile forces. And we are engaged in efforts to make our land-based forces both more effective and more survivable. These efforts[2] are part of the policy of maintaining our strategic deterrent posture through an effective mix of offensive forces — land-based missiles, sea-based missiles, and manned bombers. The thought here is that a sufficient, mixed force of this kind provides, through its resistance to technological surprise in three diverse areas, a much more survivable deterrent force than can any one element alone. Thus, defense R and D and its directions are strongly influenced by national security policy.

In the space field, the shuttle is another case in point. The shuttle is a new space-transportation system designed to replace expendable rockets with a reusable vehicle for launching payloads. Here the policy base is that the nation should continue to explore space and to utilize it for applications such as communications, navigation, weather prediction, and earth-resources assessments.

In medicine, the newest development has been the large cancer effort, which was determined to be desirable because of the very special dread with which this disease is regarded by the general public and also because the field was considered to be ripe for exploitation at this time.[3] Another concern in the medical area is health-care delivery systems. Here the policy level is tied up with the family health insurance plan proposed by the administration. It is clear that when such a plan is adopted, the supply of health care in the country will have to be expanded considerably.

In energy, the federal government is funding a rapidly increasing program of research, development, and demonstration.[4] The President, in his energy message to Congress on June 4, 1971, announced a commitment to demonstrate the liquid-metal, fast-breeder reactor by 1980 and to develop certain conventional energy technologies on a priority basis (specifically, coal gasification and sulphur oxide suppression systems, both pointed at generating "clean energy from dirty fuels"). The policy decisions were made in the context of increasing energy demand, limited domestic supplies, and increasing environmental concern. The broader policy question that underlies this decision and many other decisions on technical programs involves the whole issue of population and economic growth. The general subject has recently been the subject of extensive public discussion that followed the report by Meadows and others for the Club of Rome.[5] The point of all these examples, again, is that decisions on technical programs are influenced heavily by policies that go far beyond technical considerations or are completely atechnical. This is true, too, of policies that endeavor to set the priorities between fields. If, for example, we consider the question of domestic versus military and space R and D, we see immediately that the relative emphasis between them will be set by nontechnological pressures.

The kinds of decisions I have been discussing concern national programs and issues. As we look at the more detailed level, we see that some policies do indeed hinge primarily on scientific and technological judgments. As an example, the discussion of the relative emphases that should be placed on basic and applied research hinges upon judgments as to the relative effectiveness of contrasting techniques for creating the new, the innovative, and the useful.

All of these examples, however, point to the fact that science policy as we defined it earlier is an integral part of national policy. It is not a subject isolated unto itself. There was a time in the past when science policy could be largely detached from national policy. I am thinking of the era when Vannevar Bush wrote his famous document, *Science, The Endless Frontier*.[6] In that day when the scientific and technological enterprise was only an embryo of what we see now, the policies that governed it were not closely coupled to national policy except in the military sphere. Over the years, the situation has changed and one of the first national programs that we saw was Apollo, stimulated by Soviet space achievements.[7] Here science was to be used in a civilian pursuit for the nation's purposes; namely, to demonstrate our technological prowess and to put us into a world leadership position. We now see similar motivations in many other areas, some of which I have already named.

This coalescence of science and national purposes makes it all the more essential that we examine the processes whereby science policy is set. How is balance achieved between what is desirable in terms of the goals of society and what is possible in terms of science and technology? It is certainly clear that policy cannot be set entirely from the side of need. Technical substance also must be considered. The drain on resources — human, physical, and economic — must also be considered. In other words, policy-setting requires a deep study of technical matters coupled with concern about how those matters interact with economic, social, and political considerations. At the White House level, this is accomplished through a coalition of organizations. The Office of Science and Technology provides the technical inputs, the Office of Management and Budget provides economic judgment, along with the Council of Economic Advisers, and the Domestic Council, which is chaired by the President and contains his representatives from all of the Cabinet-level departments, provides the viewpoint of needs and that of the political process. For example, these executive offices, along with the heads of the cognizant operating agencies, have been working on the energy problem through the Domestic Council's Energy Subcommittee. This group provides the forum for conducting high-level studies and setting energy policies for the country, including energy R and D priorities.

During the past year, this mechanism has undertaken an extensive look at science and technology in the context of national policies. Out of this have come a number of suggestions, which I will discuss in detail later. However, the first-order signals from this effort have been three Presidential statements. The first of these was a substantial section of the President's State of the Union message in which he expressed his concept of science and technology as a resource for accomplishing national goals.

The second document was the President's budget message, which contained significant new R and D thrusts.

Finally, in March 1972, President Nixon sent to the Congress the first message on science and technology. This message was policy-oriented and provides the basis for much of what I will talk about in terms of specific policy directions.

Science policy is thus set through the joint efforts of a number of organizations at the White House and the departmental levels of government, only some of which are primarily oriented toward science and technology. The policies appear in Presidential messages to Congress and in his budget documents and legislative programs. Thus, although the President makes his own decisions on policy, the staff work that precedes his decisions is based upon an evaluation of many differing viewpoints.

The second aspect of policy, mentioned earlier, is the process by which decisions are made pursuant to announced policies. This process is one of developing the various options that can give vent to the policy. For example, the policy of this administration with respect to the space program is to sustain it at approximately its present level, while at the same time developing space applications and continuing space science. Within this policy, how were decisions on the space shuttle decided upon? In June, 1971, NASA proposed a space shuttle that would consist of a fly-back booster carrying a second-stage, winged orbiter that would also fly back from low earth orbit and land much like an airplane. This program was projected to be an expensive one, in the order of $10 to $15 billion total development cost. No other options had been developed at that point. A study group was convened under the Office of Science and Technology to examine other possibilities for future manned space flight and low-cost space transportation. The group was given the policy outline within which the shuttle program should fit; namely, a continuation of space activities at about today's level but not closing off future possibilites for space exploration, space science, and applications. NASA cooperated closely in this effort and by Fall, 1971, a large number of alternatives had been developed. Out of this, the President selected the current space-shuttle configuration. The overall cost will be less than half of that originally projected and the configuration now consists of a fly-back orbiter with parachute-dropped boosters that are recoverable. The final choice between liquid- and solid-propelled boosters was made on the basis of an economic analysis, which showed clearly that the solid boosters would provide a funding profile and capabilities much more in keeping with the spirit of our space policy. This plan was approved by Congress in its consideration of NASA's fiscal 1973 budget.

This process of developing options and evaluating them is the one through which policy can be exercised in a rational way. It does not involve a great deal of advocacy on the part of the individuals or agencies. It does involve careful analysis of costs, impacts, and capabilities in the policy framework. Once this is done the political process takes over.

Now what has come out in terms of policy from our efforts during 1971, and what policies do we see governing the R and D enterprise in the future? First of all, we see a substantial build-up on the domestic side of the federal budget as is shown on the next page. Military spending for R and D has been more or less level over the past 10 years, but has begun to rise recently. Space spending reached a peak in the middle 1960s and has declined since to a value that is now leveling off. At the same time, the domestic programs have grown until now they represent an expenditure of $5.4 billion each year. This means that efforts in many domestic areas have reached a critical mass in which we can see coherent programs emerging and, of course, the policies to guide them. Let me mention a few.

First, in space, as I have said, our policy is one of sustaining the present level of effort and pointing it toward the creation of new space transportation systems that will open many doors for future exploitation. We intend to capitalize particularly on the capability of earth satellites for communication, navigation, weather forecasting, and earth-resources monitoring.

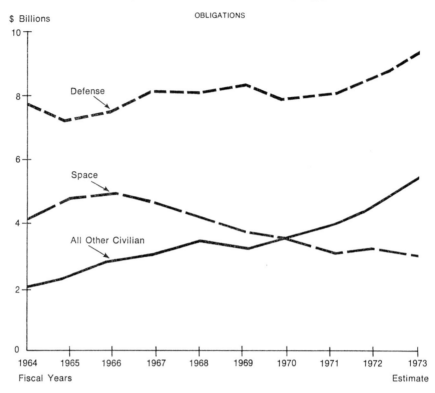

OBLIGATIONS

$ Billions

Defense

Space

All Other Civilian

1964 1965 1966 1967 1968 1969 1970 1971 1972 1973

Fiscal Years   Estimate

The President's energy message in 1971 set a clear direction for energy research and development policy. It recognized the need for adequate supplies of clean energy to meet the nation's growing requirements, together with the role new technology could play in meeting this need. Three technologies were selected for priority development: the liquid-metal, fast-breeder reactor; pipeline gas from coal; and sulphur oxide control systems. Each depends on our domestic energy resources, coal and uranium, and is to be developed in partnership with industry. Although the basic policy was not to restrict the growth of energy usage, the message indicated the need for technology and action to make more effective use of the energy we now use. Improved efficiency in both the production and consumption of energy was stressed.

In health, again the policies are set forth in the Presidential health messages, one delivered on February 18, 1971, and one on March 2, 1972. Here the emphasis is on the balance between supply and demand for health services. It is clear that increasing demand is not being matched by increasing supply. There are several approaches to this problem.

First of all, biomedical research provides techniques for reducing the onset of diseases and simplifying treatment. The prime examples here, of course, are polio and tuberculosis. The drain of these diseases on the health-care system has been virtually eliminated through advances in biomedical research. Research is also being pursued in the health-care delivery systems. The Health Maintenance Organization pioneered by Kaiser Industries is becoming a prototype for the expansion of health care in many parts of the country. New technologies incorporated in such centers can increase the effectiveness and efficiency of health care significantly. For example, the use of modern technology for emergency treatment can save many lives annually, and an active program of developing systems for this purpose is being undertaken.

There has been no Presidential message as yet on transportation, so there has been no overall policy guidance from the top. However, studies are proceeding and it is very clear that new technologies on the horizon can invigorate urban and interurban transportation in the country. It appears, for example, that the combination of new quiet aircraft engines and more complex air traffic-control systems can increase the traffic-handling capacity of airports and, at the same time, reduce exposure of the population to noise and air pollution caused by aircraft engines. New aircraft types combined with these features can give us effective corridor and feeder lines of transportation in many areas of the country not now served. New high-speed ground vehicles are promising for such heavily traveled corridors as the Boston-New York-Washington complex. Many cities are considering restricting the use of automobiles because of both pollution and congestion. New personal transportation systems that can effectively replace automobile travel in such urban areas are becoming technologically feasible and promise to provide an extremely attractive option.

Issues in the area of pollution policy are difficult to deal with because of the emotional overtones that accompany them.[8] The President's annual environmental message to Congress provides a good backdrop under which R and D can operate. For example, the President has said that we should do the research necessary to put science behind our regulatory decisions, not only with respect to pollution but also with respect to drugs and food. Once we have adequate scientific back-up, optimum strategies can be developed for maximizing the benefits and minimizing the costs to society.

Policies governing the support of science and technology should be concerned not only with specific applications, but also with basic research, upon which future technological development will depend. When a critical piece of scientific knowledge is identified or a demand for it materializes, it is gratifying to find that it is in stock. Let me give you some examples that have to do with life and death or crippling disease.

The Salk and Sabin polio vaccines were made possible because of J. F. Enders' basic finding that viruses could be grown in vitro in monkey kidney cultures; hemophiliacs are indebted to Dr. Judith Pool, whose basic research led to the development of a simple method for precipitating the antihemophiliac factor from frozen plasma; and tuberculosis, once a scourge, has been tamed, thanks to Selman Waksman's discovery of streptomycin.

These examples illustrate the importance of basic research, which the President has directed all agencies of the federal government to support. Thus, even though the National Science Foundation will continue to be the balance wheel for basic research, the mission-oriented agencies will also be supporting this vital activity as a matter of policy.[9]

One of the most influential aspects of basic science is that, through technology, it creates entirely new worlds that actually change the fiber of society and individual's perception of the world.* Another equally important result is cultural. Research into the origins of our universe and the life in it is changing man's view of himself and his place in the cosmos. Both the pragmatic and the cultural influences are determinants of policy for science.

On a different policy level, the domestic thrust in R and D calls for new directions. In the past, a preponderance of our R and D has been carried out by the military and space agencies. Domestic agencies such as Interior, Housing and Urban Development, Transportation, and even elements of Health, Education, and Welfare currently do not have the background and culture to undertake large R and D ventures. This means that we must utilize our present resources in the high-technology agencies to aid efforts by the domestic agencies. For example, we expect NASA to give substantial assistance to the Department of Transportation in its new efforts on advanced urban transportation systems. The Atomic Energy Commission and, in some cases, Defense laboratories and procurement organizations will play a role in initiating and supporting new domestic R and D efforts.

In the past, the federal government has sponsored R and D principally to satisfy its own needs, so it has little experience in meeting the demands of the public market place. It is a new experience for many of the high-technology agencies of the federal government to do R and D leading to commercial products. We do have some experience with this

* Marshall McLuhan.

situation in the AEC civilian power-reactor programs, in which government-financed research and development for military and civilian applications has led to the evolution of the civilian nuclear-power industry.

Clearly, some forms of industrial/federal cost-sharing must be found so that the public investment can be protected and at the same time industries can find the incentives and proprietary interests worth the risks of financing product development. This is not a trivial problem, because the typical cost of research for a product is about 10 per cent of the overall development cost, and those costs are about 10 per cent of the tooling, marketing, and service investments required by commercial companies. The roles of the federal government and industry are going to be significantly different in domestic R and D than they have been in space and military, where the federal government set the requirements, contracted for R and D and production, and consumed the product.

As domestic purposes permeate research, new relationships between industries and universities are also going to be required. One way of putting this is that fine research which could lead to a vital product can remain unfulfilled unless adequate relationships do exist. In a similar vein, we know that much research that is done in universities and by the federal government is relevant to the problems of local governments. Here, again, we must begin to encourage the flow of new ideas and new technology from its sources into the places where the problems are to be solved. All of this requires innovation on a large scale, and the federal government began investigating these matters, beginning in July 1972, with the fiscal 1973 budget. Forty million dollars has been earmarked as a beginning for this program.

We are seeing, too, the emergence of a new level of international cooperation in science and technology. It has long been recognized that the international camaraderie of scientists and engineers has provided an important base for mutual understanding and respect in the world. Now that is being augmented by joint attempts to solve the problems shared between nations.

The United States and Canada, for example, recently signed an agreement to cooperate on the cleanup of the Great Lakes.[10] Recently, cooperative agreements in health,[11] the environment,[12] and science and technology[13] were signed with the Soviet Union during President Nixon's visit to Moscow. These examples illustrate that science and technology are being focused not only on national purposes but on international ones as well.

These are some of the policy directions that we have charted for science and technology in the 1970s. We have developed them over the past year or two and they were outlined in the Presidential message on science and technology, which he sent to the Congress on March 16, 1972. That message is the beginning of a coherent science policy for the United States. We will see the proposals in that message developing over this decade and the next. A new focus will be on domestic problems that affect the well-being of our society. I foresee the coming years as a period of great challenge and promise for American science and technology.

REFERENCES

1. Nixon, Richard M. United States Foreign Policy for the 1970s. President's Message to Congress, Feb. 9, 1972.
2. Laird, Melvin R. National Security Strategy of Realistic Deterrence. Statement of Secretary of Defense before the Senate Armed Services Committee, Feb. 15, 1972.
3. Report of the National Panel of Consultants on the Conquest of Cancer, Report 91-1402. U.S. Government Printing Office, Washington, D.C., 1970.
4. Federal Energy R and D funding. Press Release, Office of Science and Technology, May 25, 1972.
5. Meadows, Donella H. and Dennis L., Jorgen Randers, and William W. Behrens III. The Limits to Growth. Universe Books, New York, 1972.
6. Bush, Vannevar. Science, The Endless Frontier. (A Report to the President on a Program for Post-War Scientific Research.) National Science Foundation, July, 1945.
7. Logsdon, John. The Decision To Go To The Moon, Project Apollo and The National Interest. MIT Press, Cambridge, Mass., 1970.
8. Office of Science and Technology. Cumulative Regulatory Effects on the Cost of Automobile Transportation. U.S. Government Printing Office, Washington, D.C., 1972.
9. A Framework for Government Research and Development. A Memorandum by the Government presented to Parliament, November, 1971. Her Majesty's Stationery Office, London. (An interesting analysis of the current British debate on the role of basic research.)
10. Agreement between Canada and the United States of America on Great Lakes Water Quality. Signed by President Nixon and Prime Minister Trudeau on April 15, 1972, in Ottawa.
11. Agreement between the Government of the United States of America and the Government of the USSR on Cooperation in the Field of Medical Science and Public Health. Signed by Secretary of State Rogers and Minister of Health Petrovsky in Moscow on May 23, 1972.
12. Agreement on Cooperation in the Field of Environmental Protection between the Government of the United States of America and the Government of the USSR. Signed by President Nixon and President Podgorny in Moscow on May 23, 1972.
13. Agreement between the Government of the United States of America and the Government of the USSR on Cooperation in the Fields of Science and Technology. Signed by Secretary William Rogers and Chairman V. A. Kirillin of the USSR State Committee for Science and Technology in Moscow on May 24, 1972.

XII · *The Role of*
Graduate Education

GERARD PIEL

IN THIS VOLUME ON SCIENCE AND PUBLIC POLICY there has been relatively little mention of the university. Perhaps the things that ought to be said under this heading have gone, so far, without saying. Nonetheless, I believe it useful to declare that science — pure science: rational and verifiable inquiry into nature and into the nature of man himself — belongs in the university. This is necessarily so, because no other institution in our society is chartered to promote such an inquiry in the absolute freedom that is its very life. Our actual universities do not always provide the environment of freedom in which science lives. Other institutions, notably certain government agencies and a few industrial laboratories, have sponsored significant work in science. Admittedly I am speaking of the *idea* of the university, in the words of Alexander Heard, as the seat "of inquiry and ultimately inquiry about anything."

It follows from my main point that if we would foster science we must take measures to cherish and perfect our universities. This statement has more than piety in it; it gives us an operational approach to policy for the public support of science. As we are so often assured, the nation cannot enjoy the fruits of applied research without basic research. Other approaches to the definition and distinction of pure and applied science lead into aimless refinement and dispute about the taxonomy of science, in the happy phrase of Victor Rothschild. They provide no handle for policy to allocate the human and material resources to the one or the other kind of research. To recognize that science will thrive as we make our universities thrive clears the ground for policy in another significant way. It decouples pure science from applied and disengages the justification of science from the threadbare and so often corrupting arguments

GERARD PIEL Publisher, *Scientific American*, New York, N.Y.

in favor of its utility. Science in the university can be seen more plainly for what it truly is: an enterprise we carry on for its own sake, as an end in itself, as the supreme expression of our humanity and of our success in the attempt at civilization.

The neglect of the university by my colleagues in this volume provides most of the occasions for my dissent from what they have had to say. There has run through the arguments of some of them the sound of propitiation to forgetful gods that is to be heard in the ritual of a cargo cult. If only the correct prayers are said, the right promises made, those DC-4's will come winging over the horizon again, bearing project grants! That is the futility of the cargo cult; it looks to the past and not the future. In fact, as I shall show, the arrangements under which the federal government has assumed the primary patronage of science over the past 25 years have been damaging to our universities and so, inevitably, to our society as well.

Nonetheless, we have heard here, again, cogent arguments for the project grant. It has been described as an instrument for effecting public policy in much the same terms as in the succession of reports from the National Academy of Sciences in the middle and late 1960s. Those described "support by research project grants and by fixed-price contracts (not too unlike grants)" as the keystone of "the permanent interrelated system" that links the federal government and the science establishment. Significantly, those National Academy reports had little to say about our universities. That was, of course, because they issued from the "invisible colleges" that manned the panels of the granting agencies.

In keeping with the renewed commitment to project support, there has been parallel argument for continuation of the plurality of federal granting agencies. No embarrassment is found in the fact that 85 per cent of the funds still issue from mission-oriented agencies and nearly half from the military and paramilitary agencies. As the late Lloyd Berkner said, instead of one National Science Foundation, the nation has seven or eight. This penchant for plurality stems from the familiar fear of "government control" and wariness of "politics" found so often among the citizens of our democracy.

Such attitudes comport with the national ethos of free enterprise. Americans like to rely upon what they think of as the "natural" and "self-regulating" play of the market as against the deliberate framing of public policy. In Patrick E. Haggerty's well-chosen words (Chapter X) ". . . by public policy these days we generally mean some kind of government intervention, probably federal. . . ." But the unseen hand of the market has not protected science, as Robert Morison observed, from "the invisible hands of the Office of Management and Budget" (Chapter

IV). If I am not mistaken, the symposium on which this book is based was called to consider public policy for science precisely because the strategy of "no policy" has failed.

That strategy or nonstrategy did, of course, work for a time. It worked with enormous success. The achievements of American science under this kind of public sponsorship have been celebrated sufficiently to require no prolongation of the celebration by me. As Mr. Haggerty pointed out, the rate of bestowal of Nobel prizes on United States scientists correlates well with the generosity of federal funding. The percentage of prizes brought home to this country rose from the average of 10 per cent, established in the pre-World War II period, to 60 or 70 per cent in the most recent four or five years. The luster of these statistics is somewhat dulled, however, by an observation of Lord Rothschild; he was able recently to cheer his countrymen with this rhetorical question: "Have we not got 4.6 Nobel Prize-winners per ten million of our people, in comparison with America's 3.3?"

The enormous success of American science still does not suffice to establish the prevailing arrangement for its public support as the ideal or ultimate. Nor can those arrangements be evaluated without due regard for their effect upon the universities engaged in them. Even now, with the flow of funds throttled down, the federal outlay for science must be reckoned with as a federal subsidy not alone for science but for our great universities, as well. It amounts to more than 10 per cent of the total national expenditure for all higher education and makes up from one-third (Harvard) to three-quarters (Massachusetts Institute of Technology and California Institute of Technology) of the total budgets of our 100 largest and most distinguished universities. Such radical revision in the relations of these institutions to the federal government deserves deep and thoughtful study and reflection that it has not yet had. In this attempt at an overview, I can do little more than echo the disquiet of others and express my own misgivings.

Despite the success of science, the great universities of America stand lower today in popular esteem than they did at the end of World War II and the beginning of their "federal period." It was not to be thought, in fact, that institutions dedicated to such high purpose could ever find their way into such low standing. A tide of anti-intellectualism and disillusionment with science runs strong among the people, especially within the university communities. A profound disruption of the faculty community — by the overwhelming external support for the sciences as opposed to the arts and, within the science faculties, by the competition for loyalty as between the invisible college and the university — was exposed in the instant collapse of the grandest institutions before the challenge of the student rebellion. Speaking of the rebellious students, Milton Katz has concluded: "In most cases, such students question not the inherent values of the humane tradition, but their viability and practical meaning in a world which these students tend to regard as dominated by big bureaucracies and impersonal technologies."

As other contributors to this book have observed, science and the great universities are identified in the public mind with the overhanging, unthinkable catastrophe of World War III and the actual, intolerable war in Indochina. In the view of millions of disadvantaged and alienated citizens, the adventure in space represents a no less callous misappropriation of resources.

The commitment to the exotic technologies involved in the revolution of warfare has weakened, apparently, the nation's command of domestic industrial technologies. In this volume, Mr. Haggerty and Professor Morison have remarked on the consequent reduction of the competitive strength of American industry, even in its home markets.

In Washington, science and the universities face what is, perhaps, their most humiliating loss of status. It is not only that federal funding has stopped increasing and has been seriously discounted by inflation. It is also that neither science nor higher education has a claim on the national treasury in its own right.

The funding of university science came by overflow from R and D expenditures for other purposes — for weaponry, for space, for health. Science prospered as those expenditures increased though the 1950s into the 1960s. Such funding financed the great work done in that period; it also brought work into university laboratories that did not belong there. But now that expenditures for weapons, space, and health have stopped growing or have declined, university science — especially in our great universities — is in crisis. Federal patronage, supplied from ulterior motives, stopped from equally irrelevant motives. After 25 years and $15 billion in federal funding, science and higher education have no claim in their own right, as I have said, on the national treasury. Parenthetically, I deplore the fact that the decline in funding from the mission-oriented agencies should now, under the RANN rubric, burden the limited resources of the National Science Foundation, the agency created to support pure science, with the support of applied research projects.

All of this goes to confirm my own misgivings about the performance by our universities in this period of their constitutional function in American society. In *The Higher Learning in America,* Thorstein Veblen defined the university as "ideally and in popular apprehension . . . a corporation for the cultivation of the community's highest ideals and aspirations." Speaking further to the *idea* of the university, Alexander

Heard said: "A university, to fulfill itself as a university, will seek to make it possible to examine the assumptions, the conventions, the taboos of the time, and the structure of knowledge and belief that rests upon them." In finding their way into service as contractors for the federal government — as "instruments of national purpose," in the exultant phrase of one university president — our universities have jeopardized their role as centers for the independent criticism of public policy and the formulation of human purpose.

I suppose the commitment to the space adventure supplies the most immediate example of what I have in mind. There came from the universities no real consideration of the advisability of this enterprise and no vision of alternative goals to which such extravagant outlay of human and material resources might have been committed. Space, as a paramilitary exercise, helped to offset the decline in direct military outlays for research in the universities.

At this juncture, looking toward a more hopeful future, it may be useful to recall how our universities got into their present insecure and unsatisfactory, as well as demeaning, relationship to the federal government. According to J. B. Conant, who found an occasion to go into the story not long ago, "the close connection between university research and the armed forces was in a sense an accident." He recalled that Vannevar Bush had been appointed by Franklin D. Roosevelt in 1945 to draw the "blueprint for the federal subsidy of scientific investigation in the postwar world." Dr. Bush recommended "the establishment of an entirely civilian agency"; his report, *Science, the Endless Frontier,* "contained no indication that the Navy, the Army, or the Air Force would be involved in the furthering of scientific research by the Federal Government." When, in 1947, legislation for a National Science Foundation on the Bush design arrived on the desk of Harry S. Truman, however, it was promptly vetoed for the reason that "The administrative arrangements were unsatisfactory to the most influential of Truman's advisers." Three more years had to pass before a satisfactory bill got through the two houses of Congress. This time, the President signed, but, says Mr. Conant, "it was too late. The armed forces had taken over."

The armed forces did indeed take over; military and paramilitary agencies provided as much as 65 per cent of the federal funds for university science when these funds were at their peak. Even now, the National Science Foundation holds a junior interest in that enterprise. I think it took more than the Truman veto, however to bring ths situation about. The President found in the Bush design for a National Science Foundation features that reflected, in his opinion, "a distinct lack of faith in democratic processes." The Bush bill sought, in fact, to insulate science and the universities from politics. It called for a National Science Foundation under a board of part-time directors — to be appointed by the President, to be sure, but for staggered terms that would place the appointment of a majority beyond the reach of a President's term in office. This board was to appoint the management of the Foundation.

I add this footnote to Mr. Conant's concise history because I think it illuminates the strategy of university administrators and scientists since then. Their skittishness about engaging in democratic processes has been expressed in their preference for the closed politics of their relations with the executive branch and its plurality of mission-oriented granting agencies, including the military; their contentment with an undernourished National Science Foundation, and their satisfaction in the policy of no public policy for science.

The record shows it was politicians, not scientists or university presidents, who first raised the alarm about the impact of federal patronage of science on the universities. Until the Congress invited them to come testify, the entrepreneurs of university science had kept a cautious distance from the legislative branch, where politics is necessarily open. To this day, science has no spokesman on the floor of either house and no committee formally charged with its overseeing, except a subcomittee of the House committee that is more interested in the big money that goes into "astronautics."

What we know today about the federal funding of science we owe to a succession of hearings in the House of Representatives, beginning early in the 1960s, that was organized by Carl Elliott of Alabama, Henry Reuss of Wisconsin, and Emilio Q. Daddario of Connecticut. The National Science Foundation was supposed to generate such information; the best it had to offer was estimates, predicated upon uncertain taxonomic criteria, of the relative flows to pure and applied research. It was the House hearings that developed the complete matrix of the source and application of funds. They revealed for the first time the entangling alliance of the universities with the military. This exposed, in turn, the correlation between the concentration of university research funds and the geographic distribution of military procurement contracts; the resultant slighting of the important graduate schools of the Big 10 and the private universities of the Midwest; the consequent distortion of emphasis by fields of inquiry; and the de-emphasis of education, even graduate education, in some of the most handsomely subsidized institutions. To these proceedings, witnesses from the universities contributed little more than testimony to their satisfaction with the now-established arrangements. The suggestion that other arrangements might be considered brought from these witnesses alarmed protest.

The record nevertheless established the need for a policy for support of higher education, if not of science. To the credit of Lyndon B. Johnson and his science advisers, it can be said that they made the first attempt to adumbrate such a policy. In an executive order issued in September 1965, the President declared the plain fact that "research and education [are] inseparable" and that "Federal expenditures have a major effect on the development of our higher education system." Department and agency heads were accordingly enjoined "to insure that our programs for Federal support of research in colleges and universities contribute more to the long-run strengthening of the universities and colleges . . . [and] to find excellence and build it up wherever it is found so that creative centers of excellence may grow in every part of the nation."

If the need for public policy in the support of the higher learning in America were still in doubt in 1965, there can be no mistake about that proposition in 1972. Our great private universities, almost without exception, are operating on capital-eroding deficits; some face actual insolvency. In state, as well as private, universities the admission and enrollment of graduate students has been ruthlessly curtailed. The argument that the country is oversupplied with Ph.D.'s must be recognized as a specious and discreditable rationalization for the shrinkage of federal support. That some thousands of our ablest young people should now be cheated of the opportunity for fulfillment of their promise in consequence of the reduction of military outlays for university science is as plainly immoral as the notion that their education should ever have been funded from such sources.

The crisis of our universities is ethical, in other words, as well as economic. Perhaps, for our pragmatic culture, the dollars can serve as a measure of the void in ethics. According to the Carnegie Commission on Higher Education, the university system stands in need of a $13-billion federal subvention by 1976. This is on the order of 80 per cent of the country's present expenditure on higher education.

The United States is the only industrial country that has not committed resources from its national treasury to the support of science and higher education. Our democracy is the only one that expects each university tub to stand on its own bottom and invites its graduate students to pay their tuition from the family bank account. Every other industrial country makes significant annual appropriation to its universities and has devised one sort of institution or another to administer it. As we consider now the making of our commitment, we have many precedents to choose from.

Such precedents may guide us in the task of institution-building that we must face at last. The hazards in this undertaking must not be underestimated. There is sound common sense in the identification of public policy with governmental intervention. Public support of autonomous institutions implies an uncrackable paradox. Yet our experience proves that the underlying issues must be faced and dealt with in the open. The longer we attempted to avoid them, the more dangerously unmanageable they became.

A useful lesson in institutional design is offered by the troubled launching of our National Science Foundation. The defect in the Bush bill lay in its attempt to draw the line of autonomy across the link between the federal government and its granting agency. That surgical incision must be drawn not there but between whatever federal agency we create and the autonomous universities. The National Foundation for Higher Education, let us call it, must be explicitly chartered for its mission and made publicly accountable to the President and the Congress for its performance. That mission is to see that the universities have enough resources to promote their excellence and to secure their autonomy.

This much is easy to declare. To carry the analysis and design closer to any conceivable implementation calls for the wisdom and devotion of every citizen who cares. University administrators and professors of the present generation have a special obligation to join in the task. They are the trustees of the integrity and autonomy of their institutions, which are otherwise weakened so ominously. It is necessary to think past the proposal from the Carnegie Commission on Higher Education, for example, that federal subsidy should take principally the form of scholarships. That is another subterfuge for no policy. The more simple-minded the formula and the more ironclad its administration, it is true, the fewer are the strings tied to the money. Yet no formula that involves human behavior can be expected to work automatically. Policy will make itself if it is not made by conscious and, we may hope, rational design.

The operation of the University Grants Committee in the United Kingdom commends itself for study at this juncture. This agency allocates its funds in accordance with a sufficiently simple formula: it makes institutional grants on a straight capitation basis, so much per student. In blandly British style, however, it employs the formula to enlist the universities in the design of the evolving national policy for higher education. Its so-called recurrent (capitation) grants are offered by the quinquennium. This induces each university to come forward with a five-year plan. Those plans provide the basis for the nonrecurrent grants to capital projects. Toward planning at all institutions, the u.g.c. offers cues that embody its own estimate of the demands to be laid upon the universities by the society around them.

The school year 1971-1972 started one of the quinquennial planning cycles, and the u.g.c. "Preliminary Memorandum of General Guidance" is instructive. As a "working hypothesis" it sets out a "suggested capacity" of 320,000 students for 1976-1977, an expansion of 30 per cent over the 1971-1972 year, split 45 per cent to 55 per cent between "arts-based" and "science-based" students. Forecasting "strong pressure to reduce unit costs," it counsels certain economies of scale. The average size of arts and social-studies departments "should not be below about 100 full-time equivalent students"; whereas science and technology departments "should not average less than about 120 to 150." In this connection, it advises that "larger departments have the great academic advantage of making it easier for staff to preserve time for their research."

With cost pressures still in mind, the document proffers the hint that the "enlargement of existing departments in those universities which currently have them is more economical than the creation of new departments and new institutes." By way of indicating the range of opportunity in this direction, the document goes on to observe that demand for graduates in "the less common languages" is likely to be small. On the other hand, the Committee urges "universities . . . engaged in management education [to] submit plans for expansion"; that priority be given "for increasing the flow of Mathematics, Science (particularly Physics) and French teachers to schools"; that "instruction in mathematics and computing is desirable for as many students as possible"; and that high priority be given to developments in educational technology.

My purpose in this recital is to show that even a simple-minded formula can serve as a vehicle for sensible policy-making, principally by encouraging competition among securely independent institutions. Conversely, I want to show that policy need not trench upon autonomy. I do not deceive myself with the idea that the u.g.c. model so appropriate to a homogeneous society, which has a generous regard for its elite and does not yet send as much as 10 per cent of its young people to college, can be translated to our diverse and often divided American culture, which now attempts to extend the opportunity of higher education to half of the rising generation. The essence of the u.g.c. model deserving of serious consideration here is that it does work to secure the autonomy of the British universities against the stresses exerted upon them by public funds from other quarters, especially by scholarships and fellowships and by project grants.

A commitment to the primary support of universities by institutional grants does not, therefore, exclude the public funding of scholarships and fellowships. It is time our country dismantled the economic hurdles that discriminate against talent from low-income families and relieved those families of the humiliation of the means test.

Nor does institutional granting exclude project funding. The instruments of Big Science call for capital inputs in big lumps, and sound precedents have been established in the funding and management of our national laboratories. Project funding — even from mission-oriented granting agencies, under invisible-college administration — is equally appropriate for little science and for research in the arts and humanities, providing the recipient professor is secure in his own estate in his own university.

The great healing promise of institutional support for American universities lies in the provision of economic incentive for their reconstruction as communities. Such incentive can be amplified by federal grants that match institution-building funds from other sources, from state, municipal, and private funds. It is significant that the University of California — need I say, a state institution — stood third last year in the list of universities receiving private benefactions.

The leadership in the setting of rational federal policy for the support of higher education ought to come from the great privately endowed universities of the Northeast. These institutions have provided the model that secures the independence of our state universities. They can no longer pretend that they are not federal universities. Harvard, with its princely endowment, ought to recall that, as recently as a century ago, it was a college of the Commonwealth, supported by annual appropriations from the General Court of Massachusetts.

In placing — even burying — the support of science in the larger context of support for higher education, I have sought to reinforce by a clearly visible institutional identity the difference in our motives for sustaining pure, as distinguished from applied, science. This proposition collides at 90 degrees broadside with the model advanced at the begining of this book by Sir Harold Himsworth. By extrapolation from his own Medical Research Council, he proposes that the support of basic research be tied to technology in each autonomous "province of learning"; that such grandly defined end-needs as "health," "energy," "materials," and so on determine the allocation of resources to the learning that answers to each. I could observe that British scientists, never so generously supported as our own, would seem to be acquiring American habits, just at the moment when we have learned that basic research cannot be supported safely in return for services rendered to mission-oriented agencies. I could add that Sir Harold has to contend at home with Lord Rothschild's proposal that the autonomous Research Councils be, in effect, dismantled and their applied research enterprises made to answer to Her Majesty's various Ministers — in Rothschild's words: "to democratic society itself and its elected representatives." But I have my own grounds for dissent from the Himsworth model.

I have the same dissent from the science policy that Edward David discerns in the present practices of our federal granting agencies. This country, Dr. David says, is learning to allocate its support for science in accordance with its commitment to a range of National Objectives. As in the Himsworth model, the end-need for a technology sets the subsidy for the support of pure science; the province of learning that embraces the technology and science in each case does not find autonomy, however, in the David model. Against both models, I urge disengagement of the support of pure science from the financing of applied research. I would let expenditures for higher education set the general level of primary funding for university science. This implies further that the making of policy for pure science — the choosing of objectives and the setting of priorities — be returned from Washington to the universities. My inexplicit premise is innocent enough. In the words of Warren Weaver, it reads: "The most imaginative and powerful movements in the history of science have arisen not from plan, not from compulsion, but from the spontaneous enthusiasm and curiosity of capable individuals who had the freedom to think about the things they considered interesting." To Dr. David I commend the autonomy of our universities as an urgent National Objective.

Science belongs in the university because science is integral to the mission of the university in our civilization. It is the line of inquiry that invariably makes a difference. With gathering, accumulative force, science has changed the condition of man over the past four centuries. No less than the arts and humanities, science is concerned with value, purpose, and goals. Its work must be carried on, therefore, in the presence of and in interaction with the other disciplines in the only setting where this is possible, the university.

We are assured we live in a postindustrial world. In that case, we live no less in a strange new posteconomic world. The familiar criteria of economics, with their misplaced concreteness cast in numbers, hold less and less relevance for a society two-thirds of whose members are employed in trade and services. When our fellow citizens reckon with these numbers, they are all too often inclined to overlook the fact that the fastest-growing sector of employment in the American economy is Government. Add to direct government employment the employment directly generated by government expenditures in the private sector; to these add the millions living on social security and public welfare, and you find that more than half the American population gets its wherewithal by political decision taken for public purposes. The gross national product provides a relatively empty measure of the size and content of this economy. That is why we hear increasing mention of the Quality of Life — one of the numerous clichés floated into popular discourse by that professor of posteconomics, J. K. Galbraith. Under this heading, people are seeking to objectify such noneconomic values as justice, equity, the livability of city and country, the joy and purpose of life itself. To the universities our society turns, figuratively and actually in the enrollment of nearly half of its children, for articulation of the consensus on these aims and values. The disciplines of science, which have brought such change in the human condition, must be securely lodged in the university to play their part in man's quest for his identity.

CONTRIBUTORS

IVAN L. BENNETT, JR.
Director and Dean
New York University Medical Center
550 First Avenue
New York, New York 10016

DR. IVAN L. BENNETT, JR., received his M.D. degree at Emory University. After various teaching and hospital positions, he became Deputy Director and Acting Director of the Office of Science and Technology, Executive Office of the President. In 1969 he was appointed Vice President for Health Affairs, New York University, and Director of the University's Medical Center. In 1970 he became Dean, N.Y.U. School of Medicine and Professor of Medicine in the University.

He has served as adviser, consultant, or committee member for many government organizations, including the armed forces, the Department of Health, Education, and Welfare, the National Research Council, NASA, and several of the National Institutes of Health. In addition, Dr. Bennett has been active on committees concerned with medical affairs in other countries, including India, Iran, Egypt, and Japan. He has held numerous lectureships at universities in this country and has served on the editorial boards of several medical journals. He received the Francis Gilman Blake Award from Yale in 1954; the Gordon Wilson Medal, 1958; and the Arun Bannerjee Medal from Calcutta University in 1963.

HARVEY BROOKS
Dean, Division of Engineering and Applied Physics
Harvard University
Cambridge, Massachusetts 02138

DR. HARVEY BROOKS was born in Cleveland, Ohio, in 1915. He received his Ph.D. in Physics from Harvard in 1940. During World War II he was a staff member of the Harvard Underwater Sound Laboratory. After four years at the General Electric Company's Knolls Atomic Power Laboratory, he returned to Harvard in 1950 as Gordon McKay Professor of Applied Physics and became Dean of the Division of Engineering and Applied Physics in 1957. Since 1961, he has been a member of Harvard's Faculty of Public Administration, and since 1967 has served as Chairman of the Faculty Committee for the Harvard Program on Technology and Society.

Brooks has served on the Advisory Committee on Reactor Safeguards, the President's Science Advisory Committee, the National Science Board, and the Naval Research Advisory Committee. He also chaired the Committee on Science and Public Policy of the National Academy of Sciences and served as Chairman of the National Research Council's Committee on Undersea Warfare.

He is a member of the National Academy of Sciences, the National Academy of Engineering, and the American Philosophical Society, and is currently President of the American Academy of Arts and Sciences.

He was awarded the Ernest Orlando Lawrence Award of the U.S. Atomic Energy Commission in 1960. In 1956 he founded a new international journal, *Physics and Chemistry of Solids*, and has served as its editor-in-chief ever since.

EDWARD E. DAVID, JR.
Executive Vice President for
   Research, Development, and Planning
Gould, Inc.
8550 West Bryn Mawr Avenue
Chicago, Illinois 60631

DR. DAVID, who, from September 1970 through December 1972 was Science Adviser to the President and Director, Office of Science and Technology, was born in Wilmington, North Carolina, in 1925. He received the S.M. and Sc.D. degrees from M.I.T. Prior to his Washington assignment, Dr. David was Executive Director, Research, Communication Principles Division of Bell Telephone Laboratories.

The author of many technical articles on communication theory, speech hearing, speech recognition and processing, vocoders, and computing, Dr. David is co-author of two books: *Man's World of Sound* and *Waves and the Ear*.

Before joining the government, Dr. David was also Professor of Electrical Engineering at Stevens Institute of Technology and a member of the Board of Directors of the Summit, New Jersey, Speech School.

He is a member of the National Academy of Sciences and the National Academy of Engineering; a Fellow of the American Academy of Arts and Sciences, the Acoustical Society of America, the AAAS, and the Institute of Electrical and Electronics Engineers; and a member of several engineering societies and associations.

He has received honorary doctoral degrees from Stevens Institute of Technology, the Polytechnic Institute of Brooklyn, Michigan State University, and Carnegie-Mellon University.

PATRICK E. HAGGERTY
Chairman of the Board
Texas Instruments, Inc.
P.O. Box 5474
Dallas, Texas 75222

PATRICK E. HAGGERTY was born on March 17, 1914, in Harvey, North Dakota. He is a graduate of Marquette University. In November, 1945, he jointed Geophysical Service, Inc., the company which evolved into Texas Instruments, Inc. In 1951 he was elected Executive Vice President and Director of Texas Instruments and, in 1958, President, in which position he served until year-end 1966. At that time he was elected Chairman of the Board of Directors, the capacity in which he continues to serve.

Mr. Haggerty now serves on the President's Science Advisory Committee, the Business Council, the National Academy of Engineering, the American Red Cross Members and Funds Committee (National Fund Co-chairman, 1972-73), the Board of Governors of the U.S. Postal Service, the International Advisory Committee of Chase Manhattan Bank, the Board of Trustees and Executive Committee of the University of Dallas, and the Board of Trustees of The Rockefeller University.

His contributions have been recognized by honorary degrees from Marquette University, St. Mary's University, Polytechnic Institute of Brooklyn, University of Dallas, North Dakota State University, Catholic University, and Rensselaer Polytechnic Institute.

Other recognition includes the Distinguished Service Award, University of Wisconsin, 1964; Distinguished Alumnus Award, Marquette University, 1966; Medal of Honor, Electronic Industries Association, 1967; Founders Award, Institute of Electrical and Electronics Engineers, 1968; Medalist, Industrial Research Institute, 1969; Eminent Membership, Eta Kappa Nu, 1969; Medalist, John Fritz Society, 1971; and Alumnus of the Year, Marquette University, 1972.

CARYL P. HASKINS
Suite 600
2100 M Street, N.W.
Washington, D.C. 20037

CARYL P. HASKINS retired from the Presidency of the Carnegie Institution in 1971, having served since 1956. A graduate of Yale University and a Harvard Ph.D. in physiology and genetics in 1935, he served as a staff member of the General Electric Company, and was the co-founder of Haskins Laboratories, a nonprofit institution devoted to training and research in biophysics and linguistics, now centered in New Haven. During World War II, he served as Senior Liaison Officer of the Office of Scientific Research and Development and as Deputy Executive Officer of the National Defense Research Committee. From 1955 to 1958, he served as a member of the Scientific Advisory Committee of the President and, subsequently, as a consultant to that body. He served on the founding board of the Joint U.S.-Japan Science Advisory Committee, and as a member of a special advisory committee to the Director of the National Institutes of Health. He was also a member of the National Advisory Committee on Libraries from 1966 to 1967, and has at various times served as a consultant to the Department of Defense, the State Department, and the Atomic Energy Commission. He has had a lifelong interest in subjects of science and public policy.

HAROLD HIMSWORTH
13 Hamilton Terrace
London N.W. 8
England

SIR HAROLD HIMSWORTH, who was born in 1905, has been a research worker, a physician, and an administrator in England during his career. From 1939 to 1949 he was Professor of Medicine at the University of London. He was Secretary, and later Deputy Chairman, of the British Medical Research

Council from 1949 to 1968. He was a member of the Advisory Council on Scientific Policy from 1949 to 1963 and Assessor on that Council from 1963 to 1968. He served on the Advisory Committee on Medical Research, World Health Organization, from 1959 to 1963.

Sir Harold was elected a Fellow of the Royal Society in 1955 for research he carried out on diabetes mellitus and disease of the liver. He was Lowell Lecturer in Boston in 1947, and his other honors include: Honorary Foreign Member, the American Academy of Arts and Sciences and the American Philosophical Society; and recipient of the Medal of New York University.

He is the author of *The Development and Organization of Scientific Knowledge*, which was published in 1970 by Heinemann, London.

WILLIAM D. McELROY
Chancellor
University of California at San Diego
La Jolla, California 92037

DR. WILLIAM DAVID McELROY was born in Texas in 1917 and received his education at Reed College, Stanford, and Princeton Universities. From 1952 to 1957, he was Chairman of the AIBS Microbiology Advisory Committee, Office of Naval Research. He was a member of the President's Science Advisory Committee from 1962 to 1967, and is on the Board of Directors of Planned Parenthood Association of Maryland and the National Institutes of Health. In 1969 he became Director of the National Science Foundation, a position he held until 1972, when he was appointed Chancellor of the University of California at San Diego.

Dr. McElroy is a member of the Society of Biological Chemists (President, 1963-1964), the American Academy of Arts and Sciences, American Institute of Biological Sciences (President, 1968), the National Academy of Sciences, and many other scientific organizations.

His honors include an honorary D. Sc. from the University of Buffalo; the Barnett Cohen Award, American Society of Bacteriology; the Rumford Prize, American Academy of Arts and Sciences.

He was Executive Editor of *Archives of Biochemistry and Biophysics* from 1958 to 1959, and is Editor of *Biochemical and Biophysical Research Communications*. He has published widely in books and journals.

ROBERT S. MORISON
Program on Science, Technology, and Society
632 Clark Hall
Cornell University
Ithaca, New York 14850

DR. ROBERT SWAIN MORISON was born in Milwaukee, Wisconsin, in 1906. In 1930 he was graduated from Harvard University with a B.A. in biochemical sciences, and received his M.D. from Harvard Medical School in 1935. He was with the Rockefeller Foundation until 1964, when he became Director, Division of Biological Sciences, Cornell University. He is now the Richard J. Schwartz Professor of Science and Society in the Program on Science, Technology, and Society at Cornell.

Dr. Morison has served or is serving as a member of the boards of many organizations and institutions, including: Association for the Aid of Crippled Children; Bennington College; Environmental Studies Board of the National Academy of Science-National Academy of Engineering; Grass Foundation; Institute for Society, Ethics and the Life Sciences; National Science Board, National Science Foundation; Reed College; Russell Sage Foundation; and Woods Hole Oceanographic Institute.

In 1972 he was Vice President of the American Academy of Arts and Sciences. He is a member of various medical societies and is on the Overseers' Committee to Visit Biology and Related Research Facilities, Harvard, and the Overseers' Committee to Visit Harvard Medical School and School of Dental Medicine.

Dr. Morison was honored at the Centennial of Loyola University, 1970, with the degree of Doctor of Science, *honoris causa.* He is the author of many scientific papers and journal articles, and is the author of *Scientist,* published by the Macmillan Company in 1964.

JOSEPH S. MURTAUGH
Director
Department of Planning and Policy Development
Association of American Medical Colleges
One Dupont Circle, N.W.
Washington, D.C. 20036

JOSEPH S. MURTAUGH, now Director of the Department of Planning and Policy Development of the Association of American Medical Colleges, has had a long and distinguished career in program and policy development relating to health and medical research.

A graduate of the College of St. Thomas, St. Paul, Minnesota, Mr. Murtaugh entered federal service in 1935 as a Junior Statistician in the Works Progress Administration. Subsequently he served as Chief of the Operating States Program of the National Youth Administration. During World War II, he served in the Office of the Surgeon General of the Army, developing data on the utilization of Army medical facilities in the Zone of the Interior. After a brief postwar service in the United Nations Relief and Rehabilitation Administration, Mr. Murtaugh joined the Public Health Service in 1947 as Director of Statistical Analysis and Special Studies in the Bureau of Medical Services. He was later appointed Assistant Executive Officer of the Bureau and received an outstanding performance citation for his role in the transfer of the Indian Health Program from the Department of the Interior to the Public Health Service. Early in 1956, Mr. Murtaugh was appointed to the staff of the Office of the Director of the National Institutes of Health, initially as Assistant Chief of the Office of Research Planning. In 1961, he was appointed Director of Program Planning at NIH, in which post he served until his retirement from federal service in 1968.

During his twelve years at NIH, Mr. Murtaugh was involved in all of the major administrative and policy developments associated with the emergence of NIH as the nation's, if not the world's greatest medical research institution. For his service at NIH, Mr. Murtaugh was awarded both the Superior Service and Distinguished Services awards of the Department of Health, Education, and Welfare. Upon retirement from the federal government, Mr. Murtaugh was appointed Executive Secretary of the Board on Medicine of the National Academy of Sciences and participated in resolving the issues surrounding the creation of the Institute of Medicine, now the principal instrument of the NAS dealing with medical- and health-related policy matters.

GERARD PIEL
Publisher
Scientific American
415 Madison Avenue
New York, New York 10017

GERARD PIEL was born in Woodmere, Long Island, in 1915 and was educated at Harvard College, where he received his A.B. *magna cum laude* in 1937. After serving as science editor of *Life* magazine from 1939 until 1945, he became assistant to the president of the Henry Kaiser Company and associated companies, and worked in that capacity in 1945 and 1946. In 1948, in association with two colleagues, he launched the new *Scientific American*. Mr. Piel holds the honorary degrees of Sc.D., Litt. D., L.H.D., and L.L.D., and is also a member or fellow of the American Philosophical Society, the American Academy of Arts and Sciences, and the Institute of Medicine of the National Academy of Sciences. He serves as a Trustee of Radcliffe College, Phillips Academy, The American Museum of Natural History, the Mayo Foundation, and, a former Overseer of Harvard College, as a member of various visiting committees of the Overseers.

He was awarded the UNESCO Kalinga Prize in 1962, the George K. Polk Award in 1964, the Bradford Washburn Award in 1966, and the Arches of Science Award in 1969. Mr. Piel lives in New York, is married to a successful attorney, and has two children.

HENRY W. RIECKEN
Professor of Behavioral Sciences
School of Medicine
University of Pennsylvania Medical Center
36th Street and Hamilton Walk
Philadelphia, Pennsylvania 19104

DR. HENRY W. RIECKEN, Professor of Behavioral Sciences at the University of Pennsylvania School of Medicine, received his Ph.D. from Harvard University. He is former Director, Division of Social Sciences, and Associate Director (Education) of the National Science Foundation. From 1971-1972 he was a Fellow, Center for Advanced Study in the Behavioral Sciences. He is currently a member of various boards and committees, including the Association for Aid to Crippled Children; the National Institutes of Health Advisory Committee on International Research (International Centers Committee); Institute of Medicine, National Academy of Sciences; Visiting Committee to the Department of Social Relations, Harvard University; Visiting Committee to the Department of Psychology, Princeton University; Yale University Council Committee on the Graduate School; and Visiting Committee to the Division of Social Sciences, University of Chicago.

He is a Fellow of the American Psychological Association, the American Academy of Arts and Sciences, and the American Sociological Association, and is a member of the Board of Trustees of the American Psychological Foundation. He has published extensively on various aspects of social psychology.

WALTER A. ROSENBLITH
Provost
Massachusetts Institute of Technology
Cambridge, Massachusetts 02139

DR. WALTER A. ROSENBLITH was born in Vienna, Austria. After a brief period as a research engineer in France, he taught at the University of California at Los Angeles and the South Dakota School of Mines and Technology. He joined the faculty of the Massachusetts Institute of Technology in 1951, became Associate Provost in 1969, and Provost in 1971.

He has served or is serving on many committees and boards, some of which are the NAS-NRC Committee on Computers in Science, Education, and Research; the President's Science Advisory Committee (Life Sciences Panel) and Consultant, Office of Science and Technology; Chairman of the HUD-OST Summer Study on Science and Urban Development; the President's Committee on Urban Housing; the Advisory Committee to the Director of the NIH; the NAS Board on Medicine; and the NAS Institute of Medicine.

He is a Fellow and a member of the Executive Board of the American Academy of Arts and Sciences and a Fellow of the AAAS. Internationally, he serves on the Executive Committee of the International Brain Research Organization of UNESCO, and is a former president of the Commission on Biophysics of Communication and Control Processes, International Union for Pure and Applied Biophysics.

Dr. Rosenblith is presently on the editorial boards of *Daedalus, Kybernetic,* and *Experimental Brain Research.*

JAMES A. SHANNON
Professor and Special Assistant to the President
The Rockefeller University
66th Street and York Avenue
New York, New York 10021

DR. JAMES A. SHANNON was Director of the National Institutes of Health for thirteen years. Before becoming Director, he held the post of Associate Director and was responsible for the Institutes' direct research program. Prior to 1952 he was Associate Director in charge of research of the National Heart Institute of NIH.

A graduate of the College of the Holy Cross, Worcester, Massachusetts, Dr. Shannon received his medical degree from New York University in 1929 and his Ph.D. in Physiology from the same university in 1935. Following his internship at Bellevue Hospital in New York, he was a member of the Department of Physiology at New York University College of Medicine (1931-1941) and

Associate Professor of Medicine and Director of the Research Service (Third Medical Division), Goldwater Memorial Hospital (1940-1946).

From 1946 to 1949 Dr. Shannon was Director of the Squibb Institute for Medical Research and a special consultant to the Surgeon General, U.S. Public Health Service. He entered the Public Health Service as a commissioned officer in 1949. He is now a Professor of the Biomedical Sciences, The Rockefeller University.

Dr. Shannon's initial research was in the fields of renal physiology and electrolyte metabolism. During the war he had a prominent role in the successful malaria research activity, in recognition of which he received the Presidential Medal for Merit, at that time the highest award for civilian service to government.

Among the many awards Dr. Shannon has received are the Rockefeller Public Service Award in 1964 and the Presidential Distinguished Federal Civilian Service Award in 1966. Dr. Shannon also received the National Academy of Science's Public Welfare Medal in 1962. These were in recognition of exceptional imagination, courage, and high ability in carrying out the mission of the federal establishment in the biomedical sciences.

INDEX

Note: Numbers in italics refer to pages on which tables and figures appear

A

academic employment
  in 1960s 111
academic freedom
  federal policy and 97
academic institutions
  teaching-research dichotomy in 166ff.
academic reseach (see also applied
    research; basic research; doctoral
    degrees; universities; etc.)
  decline in support for 110
  federal support of 195
  nonbiomedical, increases in 109
  political concerns and 93
Advanced Research Projects Agency
  civilian management of 109
academic science viii (see also doctoral
    degrees; higher education;
    research; universities; etc.)
  accomplishments of 195
  activities included in 89
  agency inconsistencies and 100 ff.
  basic research and 89 ff.
  categorical research and 171-175
  defined 89
  evolution of 196-197
  expenditures for 197
  federal organization and 101ff.
  federal support and 89ff., 168ff.
  funds for 99, 194ff., 194, 229
  goals of 101
  industry and 197ff.
  needs and problems of 99-103
  NSF and 95
  policy and structure for 100
  recommendations for 98
aerospace industry
  shrinkage of 110
Aigrain, Pierre 62
American Association of Medical
    Colleges
  report on biomedical research 176
American Cancer Society

career-investigator awards of 127
antipoverty programs
  controversial aspects of 137
applied research (see also industrial
    research; research; research
    and development; etc.)
  basic research and 227
  cost of 58
  defined 89
  executive supervision of 58
  leads and 59
  needs and 58, 59
  priorities in 59
appropriation committees
  resurgence in research funding 181
Ashby, Sir Eric 1, 12
assistance to developing nations
  graduate training and 70
Association of American Medical
    Colleges
  opposition to cancer legislation 180
Association of American Universities
    99
Atomic Energy Commission viii, 91,
    105
  decline in support of 56-57
  natural-science research and 109
  origin of 115
  science activities in 53
automobile
  social and economic effects of 137

B

Bacon, Francis 35
Bane Committee 169-170
Barbarossa 71
basic research (see also applied
    research; research; research
    and technology; etc.)
  applied research and 227
  "dangerous knowledge" and 50
  defined 89
  executive supervision of 59

freedom for 5
higher education and 10-11
national science policies and 223ff.
NSF allocations for 63
public education about 88
society and 50
support of 50, 138
technology and 22
universities and 118
video-tape recorder and 22
basic research, industrial
federal support for 214
Bayne-Jones Report 165
Behavioral and Social Sciences Survey 154
behavioral sciences 136ff. (*see also* social and behavioral sciences)
applied for social reform 138
Bell Laboratories 61
Bennett, Ivan L., Jr., 87-104
biography of 239
beri-beri
and discovery of vitamins 37-38
Berkner, Lloyd 228
biological science
and social sciences 139-140
biomedical research (*see also* biomedical sciences)
and development 158
funding for 157 ff., *158, 177*
increase in medical schools 109
reasons for federal funding drop 176ff.
reports on 176, 177
biomedical sciences 157-187 (*see also* biomedical research)
federal support of 157ff.
public policy objectives and 183ff.
reorganization of support for 181-186
Bologna
law school in 32
Bowen, William G. 205-207, 209
Boyle, Robert 20
Braun, Werner von 61
Brooks, Harvey 105-134
biography of 239-240
Brooks Report 76fn.
Bryce, James 42
Bureau of Standards 60
Bureau of State Services
of Public Health Service 174
Bush, Vannevar 21, 53, 59, 106, 219, 231

C

Cancer Authority
effect of public on 179-181
cancer legislation 161, 178-180
as categorical approach 39ff., 179
national policy for 218
career-education
program for 213ff.
Carnegie Commission on Higher Education 124, 205, 233, 234
report on biomedical research 177
Carnegie Institution, The
as research university 17
Carnot, Sadi 52
categorical research
academic science and 171-175
cathedral schools
and medicine 32
Caty, Gilbert 76
Center for Advanced Study in the Behavioral Sciences
RANN grant to 138
central research organizations
and social organization 43
chemistry xii
doctoral degrees in 15
practical discoveries in 22
Clemenceau 47
Club of Rome 219
Commission on the Social Sciences 154
Committee on Science and Public Policy 64, 121, 123
Comprehensive Health Manpower Act 178
Conant, James B. 106, 231-232
consortia
as "bridging institutions" 82
Conquest of Cancer 88
Copernicus 12
cost sharing
industrial-federal 225
Council of Advisers in Education and Science
recommendation for 102ff.
Council of Economic Advisers
policy inputs from 220
Cronbach, L. J. 146

D

Daddario, Emilio 56, 232
Daddario Subcommittee 13
David, Edward E., Jr. 217-226, 237

emphasis on xi, xii
social concepts and 6, 20
student decreases in 77-78
engineers
agency decision-making and 59ff.
future shortages of 16
surplus of 15
Enlightenment, the
secular base of universities and 68
environment
President's messages on 223
enzymes
in industrial use 24
evolution
adaptive 80ff.
Ewing, Oscar 161
Executive Office
organization of for science and
education 102ff., 217-225

F

federal administration
of academic science 101ff.
federal agencies
and academic research support 95ff.
Federal Council of Science and
Technology 58
Federal Security Agency 161
federal support of science 10-11,
176ff., *176*
drop in vii, x, xi, xiv, 13, 176ff.
general research support grants 126
granting agencies, plurality of 228
in universities xiv, 14, 72-73, 90ff.,
229, 233
problems of 230
prospects for 217-226
research training grants under 126
university administration and 96ff.,
229ff.
Flexner, Abraham 52, 57
Fogerty, John A. 61, 163
Folsom, Marion 163
Food and Drug Administration
and contraceptive research 23
foundations
organization of 34
private research and 34
France
science support in 62
Frank, Philipp 79
Franklin, Benjamin 68

G

Galbraith, J. K., 238
Galileo 20
game theory
population studies and 22
Gates, Frederick T. 52
General Medical Service
biological research and 109
General Research Grant Support
163, 165
Gilliland, E. R. 70, 76
goals
changing patterns of 14
choice of 10
national defense and 53
scientific 5-6
social purpose and 3
government (*see also* federal support
of science)
funding changes by 59
research support and 14
social change and 6
graduate education (*see also* doctoral
degrees; higher education)
cost of 90ff., 204ff., *204, 205*
expansion of 164ff.
federal support for xiv, 14-15,
72-73, 90ff., 229, 233
in science, recommendations for 98
OST and 102ff.
Ph.D. overproduction and 15
role of 227-238
source of funds for *92*
support methods for 87-104, 125-130
graduate students
and job opportunities 110-111, 120
granting mechanisms
multiplicity of 125ff.
Groves, Gen. Leslie R. 61

H

Haggerty, Patrick E. 189-216, 228-230
biography of 240-241
Haskins, Caryl P. 1-18, 159, 175
biography of 241
health
national concern for 163ff.
President's message on 222-223
total federal expenditures for *177*
health care
as a "public good" 25
"bridging institutions" and 81
cost of 175, *177*

Kapista, P. 44, 61
Katz, Milton 230
Kennedy, Edward 180
Kennedy, President J. F. 71, 76, 180
Kidd, C. V. 99
Knipling, E. F. 60
knowledge
    complex structure of 79
    expert, growth of 33
    provinces of 38ff.
    specialized 39
"knowledge industries" 81
Kranzberg, Melvin 20-21
Kristol, Irving 2

L

Life Sciences, The 176, 177
Linnaeus 48
Lipset, S. M. 123
Locke, John 28
Lofland, John 151
Los Alamos Meson Facility 121

Mc

McElroy, William D. 19-29
    biography of 242
McLuhan, Marshall 224fn.

M

management
    graduate training and 71
Manhattan Project 21, 78
manpower legislation
    in health and medicine 178-179
manufactured products
    imports of 200ff., *200*
mass production
    debilitating effects of 26
Mathematica, Inc. 147
mathematics 70-71, 105-134
Maxwell, Clerk 52
Medicaid legislation 170
medical care
    financing of 170
    problems of 174-175
medical advancement
    graduate training and 70
medical education
    federal support of 161-162, 164, 169
    research as part of 182
medical facilities
    construction of 165
Medical Research Council 236

medical schools
    DHEW funding for *172*
    multiple-source funding and 169ff.
    teaching hospitals and 81
Medicare legislation 170
medicine
    national policy for 218
Midwest Universities Research Assn.
    119
military security
    graduate training and 70
military services
    and research and development 106
mission agencies (*see also* applied
        research; basic research)
    academic financing and 101ff.
    basic research and 224
    new support systems and 128
M.I.T. Radiation Laboratory 78
Mitre Corporation 13
Morison, Robert S. 47-66, 228, 230
    biography of 242-243
Morrill Act 69
Moynihan, Daniel 2
Murtaugh, Joseph S. 157-187
    biography of 243

N

Napoleon
    French education under 68
NASA 105, 115
    decline in support of 56-57
    federal investment in 27, 91
    grant methods of 102
    natural-science research and 109
    origin of 115
    research efforts of 57
    space shuttle and 220-221
    success of 60
    support of physical sciences 112
National Academy of Sciences 105
    centenary of 71
    Committee on Science and Public
        Policy 64
    nuclear-structure physics and 120
    public-policy reports of 228
    report, *The Life Sciences* 176-177
    social scientists in 141
    Westheimer Committee of 21
National Accelerator Laboratory 121
National Advisory Committee for
        Aeronautics (NACA) 105
National Aeronautics and Space

economic inputs from 220
Office of Naval Research
    military research and 109
    natural-science research and 109
    relevant research under 57
Office of Science and Technology
        62-63, 109
    new programs of 58
    strengthening of 102ff.
    technical inputs from 220
    technology assessments for 13
Office of Scientific Personnel 90
Office of Scientific Research and
        Development (see OSRD)
Oppenheimer, J. Robert 61
    on basic research 69
optical technology
    physical sciences and 117
Organisation for Economic Co-
        operation and Development
        25, 76
organization
    growth of 33
    national research 34-35
OSRD
    as civilian agency 50
    contract distribution of 162
    university support by 162
overspecialization 113-115
OXR 109

P

Pascal, Blaise 20
Perkins, James 75
Permanent Science Advisory Board 109
physical sciences 70-71, 105-134
    emphasis on xi, xii
    energy supply and 116
    equipment for 112
    information technology and 116
    optical technology and 117
    science policy for 105-134
    social sciences and 139-140
    student decreases in 77-78
    unity of 113
physician education
    and funding constraints 167ff.
physics
    doctoral degrees in 15
    solid state 7, 22
Piaget, Jean 79
Piel, Gerard 227-238
    biography of 244

Pippard, A. B. 7, 18
Policy for Biomedical Research, A 176
policy-making
    decline in apparatus 180-181
poliomyelitis
    attack on 50
politics
    and science policy 57ff.
pollution 1, 2, 25, 223
Pool, Judith 224
population
    problem 25
    U.S. 204
postdoctoral education
    need for 16
President's Science Advisory
        Committee 109
    NIH grant program and 125
    social scientists on 141
Price, Don K. 14-15
priorities
    changing patterns of 14
    in applied research 59
    national 2, 3, 47ff.
    research 109-110
    scientists' 6
    selection by leads 52ff.
    selection by needs 52ff.
privacy
    right to 135
problem-oriented research
        (see also applied research)
    nationally directed 184
productivity
    education and 203ff.
    growth rate of in Europe 26
    growth rate of in Japan 26
    growth rate of in U.S. 26
    increase potential 207ff., 208
    per person in industry 201ff., 208
professions
    application of knowledge in 43
    goals of 41ff.
    mission-oriented knowledge in 41
project funding 236ff.
    NIH and 173-174
    problems of 165
provinces of knowledge 38ff.
    mission-oriented 41
    public policy and 43
    research organizations and 41ff.
public health
    national concern for 161, 163ff.

public information
  graduate training and 70
public policy
  biomedical sciences and 182ff.
  development in re science 43
  industry and 189
  National Academy of Sciences and 228
  provinces of knowledge and 43
  science and 42
  toward industrial R and D 191

R

R and D (*see* research and development)
RANN 55, 88, 230
  origin of 61
  plans for 13
  projects of 23-24
  refuse-disposal study 24
  social studies and 138
Recent Social Trends 142
recreation, public
  as a "public good" 25
Regular Research Grant program of NIH 183
reproduction, physiology 22-23
research
  as element of education 182
  critical size in 118-122
  environmental 64
  federal support of xv, 10ff., 54ff., 97ff., 157ff., 162, 233
  funds for 118-122
  institutional support for 165ff.
  investigator-initiated 182ff.
  national needs and 47ff.
  support of in U.S. 87-104, *173*, 180ff.
  U.S. vs. world 130-132
research and development vii, x, xi, xiv (*see also* research and development, industrial)
  academic, federal support of 194ff., *194*
  administration of 47
  applied 63
  basic 63-64
  biomedical, support for *158*
  budget allocation for 64
  domestic vs. military and space 219, 224
  evaluation of, by industry 13

federal support of 12, 54ff., 110, 214ff., 217ff., 220
federal support of in universities 93ff., *94*
federal support for social benefits 214
future national commitments for 221
increase in 192ff.
individual agencies and 62
national budgeting for 63
national, conduct of 218ff., *222*
NSF data on 192ff.
political responsibility for 57ff.
sources of funds for *191*
technological innovation and 27
social problems and 82, 214ff.
total U.S. investment in 27, *158*
university research and 93ff.
research and development, industrial
  increase in 192ff., *193*
  investment in 26, 27
  public policy for 191
  tax credit for 198
  total 192ff., *192*
  universities and 194ff.
  with federal funds 193ff.
  with private funds 193ff.
research, applied (*see* applied research)
Research Applied to National Needs (*see* RANN)
research, basic (*see* basic research)
research organizations
  centralized 34-35
  in Europe 76
  provinces of knowledge and 41ff.
  public needs and 41, 43
  purpose-oriented 44ff.
research scientists
  national need for 164ff.
research-training grants 126
  as funds for institutions 165
research universities 17, 76
Reuss, Henry 232
Rice Research Institute 53
Richardson, Elliot L. 180
Riecken, Henry W. 135-155
  biography of 244-245
Rivlin, Alice 142, 149
Rockefeller Foundation, The 52-53
Rockefeller University, The xv
  as research university 17
Rogers, Paul 180
Rogers, William Barton

and M.I.T. 69
Roosevelt, President Franklin D. 231
Rosenblith, Walter A. 67-85
 biography of 245
Rothschild, Victor 227, 229, 237

S

safety, public
 as a "public good" 25
Salerno
 medical school in 32
Schilling, Warner 106
Schmidt, Benno C. 179
Schools of Applied Behavioral
  Sciences 154-155
science (see also academic science;
   applied research; basic research;
   science and technology; etc.)
 American attitude toward 159, 229
 basic research and education in
   10-11
 environmental effects of 138
 federal 217-226
 federal support of 10ff., 230ff.
 French support of 62
 future of 3
 goals and priorities for 4, 47-66, 219
 "good," definition of 20
 growth in financing of 5, 230ff.
 interpretation of 17
 justification for 138
 military and 60
 public attitude toward 5, 13, 28,
   73ff., 88ff., 159, 229
 public control of 4
 public support of 10, 13, 20
 social goals in 4, 10
 structure of 11-12
 technology, the university, and 67ff.
 utility of 19ff.
Science Adviser, President's 58, 61
science and engineering
 cooperation between 78-79
 graduate training and 70
science and society ix-xi, 1-18
 administration for xi
 education for 17-18
 interfaces of 25
 scientists' focus on 6
science and technology (see also
   applied research; basic research;
   science; technology)
 advisory mechanisms for 215

complex interactions of 20, 21
economic well-being and 26
federal agency needs for 97
federal support of xv
graduate training and 70
increase in universities 78
international 225
impact of 82
national policy and 220
priorities for 21, 25
resistance to 80-81
social goals and 6
societal reaction to ix, 1, 135
support for 54ff.
universities and 83
science, applied 4-6, 47ff. (see also
   applied research; basic research)
 basic and 37
 challenges to 8-9
 misconceptions about 9-10
 needs, in changing social structure 7
 organizations and 34
 research organizations for 36
 social problems and 9
science, basic 4, 5, 47ff. (see also
   applied research; basic research)
 applied and 37
 fields of 8
 misconceptions about 9-10
 needs, in changing social structure 7
 priorities in 11
 public interest and 8
 technology and 20
science
 peer system in 123ff.
science budget cuts
 reasons for 54ff.
science faculty
 loss of market for 110
science information
 interpretation of 8
science policy
 centralized management and 115
 in the United States 217ff.
 military and 105ff.
 national 107-108, 220
 overspecialization and 113-115
 political aspects of 57ff.
 unresolved issues of 113-132
 World War II effect on 105-106
science, progress of
 as news 88
science support
 drop in 53ff.

science system
  self-regulation in 122-125
Science, the Endless Frontier 21, 53,
    106-111, 219, 231
scientific development
  organization for 42
scientific knowledge
  government need for 35
  growth of 31-45
  need to synthesize 40
  organization and growth of 31-66
  public policy and 42-43
  synthesis of information and 44
scientific organizations
  specialized 32ff.
scientific research (*see also* applied
    research; basic research; etc.)
  applied 34
  cost of 35
  public attitudes toward 34, 77
scientific societies
  development of 32, 68ff.
  promotion of knowledge and 41
scientists
  agency decision-making and 59ff.
  applied-research organizations and
    44
  articulation of research goals and
    88-89
  career motivations and 49
  curiosity and 48
  employment among 75
  future shortages of 16
  imposed organization systems and 45
  methodology of 48
  morale of 110
  motivation of 48-49
  pragmatic concerns of 51
  priority determinations and 49
  shortages in 69-70
  society and 49
  surplus of 15
Servan-Schrieber, Jean-Jacques 3,
    13, 18, 28, 113
Shannon, James A. vii-xvii, 61,
    87-89, 163, 169
  biography of 245-246
Shaw, George Bernard 2
Simon, Herbert 144
social and behavioral sciences
  applied 139
  cautionary note to 141-142
  related to biological and physical

sciences 139-140
  federal funding for 138-139, *139*
  new demands and 140
  U.S. as leader in 139
social change
  social science and 135-155
social experimentation
  dangers of 146ff.
  ethics of 152ff.
  New Jersey study and 147
  psychological effects of 151ff.
social indicators
  national system of 144ff.
  need for 142ff.
social needs
  science and 20
  universities and 83
social opinionating
  vs. social science 141
social problems
  unchanging aspects of 142-143
  university relations to 79ff.
social reform
  National Institute of Mental Health
    and 138
  social sciences and 137ff.
social research
  and legal concerns 150
Social Security Act
  health amendments to 161
social sciences
  applied for social reforms 138
  Daddario proposal for 11
  employment in 140
  graduate enrollment in 140
  natural sciences and 101
  social change and 136ff.
  social opinionating vs. 141
  social reform and 137ff.
social scientists
  code for 151ff.
  legal protection of 151-152
society
  and support of science 10
sociomedical pathologies
  alcoholism 25
  drug addiction 25
  environmental problems 25
space program 218
  and overspecialization 114
  decisions on 220-221
  graduate training and 70
  national policy for 218ff.
  psychological effect of 12-13

and NIH 185
University of Wisconsin
   Institute for Research on Poverty
      147
university science (*see also* universities,
      federal support of)
   federal funding of 227ff.
urban blight 1, 2, 9, 25
Urban Institute
   model for change in income use 145
U.S. Public Health Service
   NIH and 57
   science activities in 53
U.S.S.R.
   science and technology in viii, ix
   financing science in 5
utility of science 19-29
   definition of 19
   "quality of life" and 29
   societal problems and 26

V

Veblen, Thorstein 230
veneral disease program 161

virus research 50, 224
vitamins
   and beri-beri 37

W

Waksman, Selman 224
war on poverty
   congressional reaction to 149ff.
Watt, James 20
Watts, Isaac 52
Weaver, Warren 237
Webb, James 61
Weinberg, Alvin M. 81, 177
Weiss, Paul A. 75, 124
Welt, Louis 176-177
welfare system
   and employable poor 147
Whitehead, Alfred North 5
Wilson, John T. 125
Wolfle, Dael 99
World Wars I and II
   and defense funding 106ff.

Z

Ziman, J. M. 124